The Art and Science
of Intelligence Analysi

The Art and Science of Intelligence Analysis

Julian Richards

OXFORD
UNIVERSITY PRESS

OXFORD
UNIVERSITY PRESS

Great Clarendon Street, Oxford OX2 6DP

Oxford University Press is a department of the University of Oxford.
It furthers the University's objective of excellence in research, scholarship,
and education by publishing worldwide in

Oxford New York

Auckland Cape Town Dar es Salaam Hong Kong Karachi
Kuala Lumpur Madrid Melbourne Mexico City Nairobi
New Delhi Shanghai Taipei Toronto

With offices in

Argentina Austria Brazil Chile Czech Republic France Greece
Guatemala Hungary Italy Japan Poland Portugal Singapore
South Korea Switzerland Thailand Turkey Ukraine Vietnam

Oxford is a registered trade mark of Oxford University Press
in the UK and in certain other countries

Published in the United States
by Oxford University Press Inc., New York

British Library Cataloguing in Publication Data

Data available

Library of Congress Cataloging-in-Publication Data

Richards, Julian (Julian James)
    The art and science of intelligence analysis / Julian Richards.
        p. cm.
    Includes bibliographical references and index.
    ISBN 978-0-19-957845-0 (pbk.)
        1. Intelligence service—Methodology. 2. Intelligence service—United States. I. Title.
JF1525. I6R515 2010
    327.1273—dc22

                                                                2010013598

Typeset by MPS Limited, A Macmillan Company
Printed in the UK by the MPG Books Group, Bodmin and King's Lynn

ISBN 978-0-19-957845-0

Preface

Writing this amidst the celebrations for the twentieth anniversary of the Berlin Wall coming down, I am reminded how much the world has changed since that incredible night on the interface between East and West. As the protestors took their axes to the wall, and the East German guards stood aside, it all suddenly became clear to everyone there and everyone watching that the world was about to change comprehensively and irrevocably.

For those involved in intelligence analysis, the events of 1989 were a surprise, but the events that quickly followed were even more so. Within a couple of years, parts of Europe were suddenly thrown into ethnic and nationalist turmoil, forcing history books to be dusted off and place-names that had not been considered for decades to be relearnt. Language requirements across a range of sectors suddenly altered in difficult ways. The new security and intelligence challenges were complex and multi-faceted, involving not massive standing armies, but small, ethnic militias, and conflicts where the differences between soldier and civilian were suddenly much less clear.

Although it was not very obvious at the time, we now know that many of the key figures in Al Qaeda were cutting their physical and ideological teeth in the conflicts that raged in and around Bosnia and its Muslim community. By the turn of the twenty-first century, Al Qaeda was ready to make itself known on the international stage in dramatic style, with the attacks in New York and Washington DC.

Many commentators have said, not unsurprisingly, that everything changed on that fateful morning in September 2001. It is perhaps more accurate to observe, with the benefit of hindsight, that 9/11 and Al Qaeda merely punctuated a shift in global security which had been underway for some years, and which accelerated with the fall of the Berlin Wall. The shift was part of what has been called globalization. From a security perspective, as Peter Gill has observed,[1] the process of globalization has seen a collapsing and intermingling of three critical dimensions in the security picture: first, the difference between local and international, between home and abroad, has blurred considerably, as the residents of New York found to their horror on 11 September 2001. Secondly, the difference between military, civilian, and criminal has also become less clear in many circumstances, as those battling the Taliban in Afghanistan found. Finally, the intelligence sector has broadened, whereby it is now no

---

[1] P Gill, 'Not just joining the dots but crossing the borders and bridging the voids: constructing security networks after 11 September 2001' (2006) 16 *Policing and Society* 27, 30.

longer just about state agencies and capabilities, but also sometimes about the corporate and 'communitarian' sectors.

The conclusions of the post-9/11 enquiry in the US, and of a number of enquiries into 'intelligence failures' before and after these events, were that something was amiss in the way that the intelligence community gathered its data, analyzed it, and disseminated it up to the policy-makers. In many cases the failings were seen to be organizational, such as barriers to sharing information between agencies, but there were also question marks over the process of analysis itself— the very tradecraft of intelligence.

The Butler enquiry in the UK in 2004 noted that intelligence analysis needed to be 'professionalised'. Further, Lord Butler noted that this needed to happen collaboratively across the range of intelligence personnel: from the law enforcement officer looking at tactical intelligence, to the state intelligence agency analyst looking at longer term, strategic assessments. All are engaged in analysis, and their trade can be broken down into a number of generic skills and techniques.

This book deconstructs the profession of intelligence analysis in the contemporary, globalized world, and asks: Is it an art, a science, or both? The answer to this question is critical in allowing us to understand how to make the improvements that countless enquiries have suggested the intelligence sector needs to make.

In producing this book, a number of acknowledgements are in order. First, I would like to thank Lucy Alexander at Oxford University Press for being persistently good humoured, and patient. My good friend and colleague at the University of Buckingham, Professor Anthony Glees, also deserves my thanks for providing endless inspiration and encouragement throughout the process. The rest of the team at the university have also been a great help, by providing a fantastic environment in which to work.

My parents deserve special thanks for supporting and encouraging me all the way, and generally making sure I did not get into trouble! For proof-reading duties, and comprehensive but very constructive pedantry, my father deserves enormous thanks. Finally, my family have been an enormous help, as ever, by being patient and allowing me to lock myself in the study for hours on end, when, arguably, I should have been spending more time with them. All have played essential parts in delivering this book.

Julian Richards
November 2009

Contents

Part Two Art and Science in Intelligence Analysis

PART ONE

The Intelligence Process in the Modern World

1

Definitions: What is Intelligence and Intelligence Analysis?

A definitive concept of intelligence has proved somewhat elusive for many years. Something called intelligence is gathered and used in a variety of sectors in our society, from state intelligence agencies to the police, and also commercial organizations, financial traders, and even sports teams.[1] Twenty years ago, Walter Laqueur observed that 'all attempts to develop ambitious theories of intelligence have failed'.[2] Ongoing debates have revolved around what makes intelligence different from 'information' or 'data'. In different cultures and languages the concept is rendered in different ways. Many cultures do not make the distinction; as Andrew, Aldrich, and Wark point out, in French the word for intelligence (*renseignement*) is the same as for 'research', while Chinese languages make no distinction between information and intelligence.[3] In German, the word (*Nachrichten*) is synonymous with 'news' or 'information'. The nature of intelligence agencies also varies between countries and sectors in terms of what they do, and the limits of their activities, as we will explore. As Laqueur noted, intelligence generally refers both 'to an organisation collecting information and . . . to the information that has been gathered'.[4]

The question could reasonably be asked: why bother to develop a theory of intelligence? Peter Gill posed this very question at a major symposium organized by the Office of the Director of National Intelligence (ODNI) and RAND Corporation in the US in 2005.[5] On the one hand, academics and theorists can

---

[1] See, eg the case of spying between rugby teams during the 2003 Rugby World Cup: P Gill and M Phythian, *Intelligence in an Insecure World* (Cambridge: Polity, 2006) p 1.

[2] W Laqueur, *A World of Secrets: The Uses and Limits of Intelligence* (New York: Basic Books, 1985) p 8.

[3] C Andrew, RJ Aldrich, and WK Wark, *Secret Intelligence: A Reader* (Oxford: Routledge, 2009) p 1.

[4] Laqueur, *A World of Secrets*, n 2 above, p 12.

[5] P Gill, in GF Treverton et al, *Toward a Theory of Intelligence: Workshop Report*, Conference Proceedings (Arlington VA: RAND, 2006) p 4.

think about and try to develop theories of intelligence, but practitioners have to get on and do it; often without time to consider its philosophical underpinnings. The answer is that intelligence is more than just a theoretical construct—it is also a practical activity with very real consequences. In addition to complex theories of how information is received and processed to produce assessments, intelligence contains within it real-world organizational, resource, and policy questions concerning how the intelligence function is structured and operates to maximum effect. This includes questions both for agencies conducting intelligence gathering themselves, and for the overall structure of government and policy within which such agencies operate. The questions include those of technical tradecraft and capability, resources and priorities, skills and techniques deployed by the workforce, and—increasingly—ethical and legal issues surrounding the appropriate role of intelligence within a liberal democracy in the twenty-first century. It is around these practical issues that this book aims to generate discussion and understanding.

The ODNI conference in 2005 concluded with the thought that, while it remains difficult for disparate observers and practitioners of intelligence to agree on whether and how intelligence needs to be developed and reformed, and that some observers 'questioned the utility of exploring theories of intelligence', there was a feeling among many present that 'it is possible to establish causal relationships between intelligence and certain outcomes, and . . . exploring these relationships was essential to improving intelligence'.[6] It is the case, therefore, that intelligence is actually a process with several stages, ending with an 'outcome'. To examine ideas and methods for improving intelligence, it is necessary to begin with some definitions of what the intelligence process entails, and where it starts and finishes.

In this chapter we will examine the nature and scope of intelligence as it applies to contemporary security challenges. The aim is to work through the various debates and definitions in providing a workable conceptual model of the scope and boundaries of intelligence. We will use, as a framework and starting point for this model, a version of the much used and abused 'intelligence cycle'. It should be said straight away that to use this as a framework carries risks, as the somewhat linear nature of the intelligence cycle, as it is often presented, is not necessarily an apt model for the way in which intelligence organizations and structures operate in day-to-day twenty-first century reality. However, it can be argued that the elements of the cycle provide useful touch-points for understanding the various elements and processes that combine to form the process of intelligence.

Much of what has been written and studied in the academic field of intelligence relates to state intelligence agencies, and to strategic security targets. In this chapter, and throughout the book, parallels and connections will be drawn between the intelligence-gathering process in the state security arena, and that

---

[6] Treverton et al, n 5 above, p 30.

in the law enforcement arena. This is for two reasons. First, the manner in which security threats have evolved and developed since the end of the Cold War has increasingly blurred the dividing line between national security, and law enforcement concerns. De Lint noted in 2006 that 'liberal democracies across the world are ramping up intelligence budgets [and] dismantling the "wall" between criminal and national security information'.[7] Organizationally, this has meant that intelligence actors in both arenas have inevitably come closer together and started to work in tandem. This has not been a process without issues and problems, certainly, and we will explore these in depth throughout the book. But there is an increasing need for practitioners to ply their trade in coordination with one another across the intelligence sectors. As Marilyn Peterson recently noted in a study for the US Department of Justice: 'A critical lesson from the tragedy of September 11, 2001 is that intelligence is everyone's job'.[8]

Second, I would also argue that there are many points of convergence in the basic essence of intelligence analysis in terms of a skill and a tradecraft, whether the intelligence problem in question is a pattern of burglaries, a terrorist threat, or the issue of whether a nation is developing nuclear weapons. Of course, there are important differences between tactical, operational, and strategic analysis, and these will be explored in depth, but the basic elements of cognitive process and techniques for improving analytical performance show some important similarities across all of the intelligence communities. This is a positive point, because it offers opportunities for training and exercising at scale across intelligence sectors.

To begin the analysis, it is worth reviewing the historical development of the intelligence-gathering function.

A Brief History of Intelligence

It is difficult to examine intelligence academically without making reference to the great Chinese military strategist, Sun Tzu. One of many quotations attributed to Sun Tzu's classic document, *The Art of War*, is the observation that 'the reason the enlightened prince and the wise general conquer the enemy wherever they move and their achievements surpass those of ordinary men is foreknowledge'.[9] Many have understood this to mean that a concept of gathering intelligence on the enemy's movements and intentions has been central to the essence of effective military strategy for many centuries. In the modern world, the enemy is signified by any threat to national security, whether it is a military threat, or that from terrorists or organized criminals.

---

[7] W de Lint, 'Editorial: Intelligence in Policing and Security: Reflections on Scholarship' (2006) 16 *Policing and Society* 1.

[8] M Peterson, *Intelligence-Led Policing: The New Intelligence Architecture* (NCJ 210681, US Department of Justice, Bureau of Justice Assistance, 2005) p 1.

[9] Sun Tzu, *The Art of War*, trans by Samuel Griffith (Oxford: Clarendon Press, 1963) xiii(3), p 144.

The intelligence function in history was often seen as fundamentally central to statecraft.[10] Elizabethan England had a strong sense of the importance of 'intelligencers' to its activities.[11] Mattingly noted that the shape and structure of the diplomatic system which emerged in Europe in the sixteenth and seventeenth centuries was essentially built around the state's need for information on foreign countries.[12] Organized intelligence capabilities in Europe emerged after the Renaissance with the modern nation-state, and were inextricably linked to national security in the sense of military intelligence, counter-espionage, and counter-sabotage.

Within states, questions of national security have also meant identifying and countering internal subversive threats. In Britain, the gathering Irish rebellion against colonial rule through the nineteenth century saw the formation of the first Special Branch unit in 1883 (initially called the Special Irish Branch) under the Metropolitan Police. The unit was tasked with gathering intelligence on the activities of the Irish Republican Brotherhood in subversive and 'terrorist' activities within the UK. In Russia, similar problems of populist, anarchist rebellion against the Tsarist regime through the second half of the nineteenth century led to the formation of a state police force, the Okhrana (established in 1881), which operated both within Russia and abroad, gathering intelligence and carrying out covert operations against perceived enemies of the state. The Okhrana was a forerunner to the much-feared Cheka, and later to the KGB intelligence agency. In these developments we can see very early examples of state security—and intelligence—overlapping with issues of strategic national security, long before any notion of globalization.

The end of the Cold War provided an enormous boost to economic and technological developments already well in train. Economic and social connectivities between all regions of the world accelerated, aided by technological advancements in communications. For many this process represented tremendous opportunity. It has also given a boost to a number of new security threats which capitalize on the breaking down of borders, such as international organized crime and terrorism.

Within the academic field of Security Studies, the orthodox paradigm prior to the latter part of the Cold War was one in which security and intelligence were seen primarily as factors of war and international relations. The increasing globalization of the economy brought with it new dynamics and balances of power, which in turn funnelled into a much wider pool of security threats. Academic views of security moved from 'neo-realist' views of the world, which saw that security could be affected by economic and societal factors as much as by military ones, to a generally more 'pluralist' view which came to encompass a considerable range of issues affecting security balances, from resource issues to health, crime, and the environment. Crucially, it was increasingly seen that

---

[10] J Keegan, *The Mask of Command* (London: Penguin, 1987) p 325.

[11] M Herman, *Intelligence Power in Peace and War* (Cambridge: Cambridge University Press, 2008) p 9.   [12] G Mattingly, *Renaissance Diplomacy* (London: Cape, 1955) pp 242–4.

security threats—and responses to them—did not necessarily conform to state boundaries, but to regions or international groupings.

We can see this development reflected in the way that new global security threats are articulated. Tony Blair said, for example, a few days after the 9/11 terrorist attacks in the US:

> Whatever the technical or legal issues about a declaration of war, the fact is we are at war with terrorism. What happened on Tuesday was an attack not just on the United States, but an attack on the civilised world.[13]

The threat of terrorism was seen not as a specific military threat to one nation, but a much wider conflagration transcending national borders. Many said at the time, and have done so since, that the Al Qaeda-sponsored attacks in New York and Washington on 11 September 2001 were a 'turning point' in global security; a watershed after which the world's view of security would never be the same. In many ways the events of 9/11 were seminal in terms of the security response, but in other ways they were simply an expression of a shift in the security paradigm that had been underway for some time. In the above statement, Tony Blair was perhaps unconsciously recognizing that, like globalization generally, security issues transcended borders at the beginning of the twenty-first century, both in terms of the threat they posed, and the networked nature of the required response. Many, including the former US Vice President Dick Cheney, echoed Huntington's theory of a new 'clash of civilizations'[14] by suggesting that it was not a traditional war at all, but rather a 'battle of ideas'.[15]

The contemporary terrorist threat is central to our analysis throughout this book. Particularly in Western Europe, the fact that many young people are identifying with transnational group and community identities above local or national identity, and that some are becoming drawn to the violent message of revolution espoused by the likes of Al Qaeda, means that intelligence responses to the threat have to cross borders and be similarly undiscriminating as to what is 'domestic' and what is 'foreign'. Now, developments in the Taliban-held areas of northern and western Pakistan become directly relevant to communities in Bradford, Baltimore, or Brussels. Modern communications techniques and their fundamental mobility further underline the importance of this approach. Organizationally, this poses considerable challenges to the way in which intelligence structures in the West have been established and are evolving.

In addition, developments in the field of terrorism mean that the police officer working with local communities domestically increasingly needs to have a connection with intelligence analysts looking at the strategic international picture, and both need—ideally—to be exchanging intelligence to ensure identification and penetration of the terrorist networks.

---

13 *The Independent*, 16 September 2001.

14 SP Huntington, 'The Clash of Civilizations?' (1993) 72/3 *Foreign Affairs* 22.

15 <http://www.aipac.org/Publications/SpeechesByPolicymakers/Cheney-PC-2007.pdf>, accessed 24 January 2010.

Intelligence structures in the West and in many other parts of the world have had to reassess what are their key intelligence priorities. By 1994, three quarters of the resource of the UK's domestic intelligence agency, MI5 (the Security Service) was devoted to countering terrorism, whether concerning Northern Ireland or 'international'.[16] The same year, the placing of the Intelligence Services Act on the statute books in the UK revealed that the Secret Intelligence Service (SIS, or MI6) and Government Communications Headquarters (GCHQ) were working on the prevention and detection of serious crime, and in the interests of the UK's 'economic wellbeing', in addition to questions of national security. In the former, they worked with the newly established National Criminal Intelligence Service (NCIS), whose purpose was to gather and coordinate intelligence gathered by the police and HM Customs and Excise on major criminal activity impacting the UK. A year later, MI5 announced that it was joining the party and expanding its remit to assistance with the detection of serious crime.[17] Aside from reflecting that the intelligence machinery, in the UK at least, was turning its attention to new and essentially 'societal' issues rather than the traditional targets of state espionage, the move also showed how the act of intelligence-gathering as practised in intelligence agencies and in law enforcement agencies was starting to converge.[18]

In the policing realm, intelligence has held a variable role over history. Models of policing have, for many years, been an increasingly managerialist issue about how best to drive down the crime statistics in the face of considerable public interest in issues of law and order, and the subsequent degree of political capital invested in the whole question of policing. Maguire described developments in both 'intelligence-led policing' and multi-agency 'community' oriented policing in the post-Cold War era as

> part of a huge multi-institutional project to assess and manage risk, itself a response to the powerful feelings of fear and insecurity which are endemic to the fragmented communities of late modernity.[19]

Intelligence-led policing as a defined model was pioneered by Kent Constabulary in the UK in the mid-1990s. It emerged in a climate of increasing budgetary pressure on policing generally, and was built around the theory that more efficient targeting of crime in key sectors (such as burglary and vehicle theft) could be achieved by a more effective use of intelligence to establish the primary causes of the crime. It subsequently proved to have a substantial impact on crime statistics in these sectors, and the principles were followed by many constabularies and services within and beyond the UK subsequently.

---

[16] S Rimington, *Security and Democracy: Is there a Conflict?*, Richard Dimbleby Lecture (London: BBC Educational Developments, 1994) pp 7–8.

[17] <http://www.mi5.gov.uk/output/serious-crime.html>, accessed 30 December 2009.

[18] Herman, *Intelligence Power in Peace and War*, n 11 above, p 350.

[19] M Maguire, 'Policing by Risks and Targets: Some Dimensions and Implications of Intelligence-Led Crime Control' (2000) 9 *Policing and Society* 315.

At a similar time, the New York Police Department was developing a managerial and business process called *Compstat*, which included a combination of a greater emphasis on generating crime intelligence, with a more effective process of sharing and using that intelligence within the police function. Again, the dramatic impact on crime statistics in the city that resulted attracted the attention of police services and analysts alike.[20] In both cases, one of the key drivers was an improvement in information technology which allowed for more innovative and effective handling and dissemination of large amounts of data.

The organizational aspects of both approaches have evolved in the UK into the National Intelligence Model (NIM), launched by NCIS in 2000 and made mandatory across all police forces in England and Wales by 2004. While the NIM addresses the question of intelligence products and outcomes, it is primarily a 'business model' which is as much concerned about processes of management and organization within the police service. The NIM, therefore, underlines the notion that intelligence is both a piece of information, and an overarching process that governs how that information is generated, managed, and disseminated. It is to this process that we now turn.

Conceptualizing the Intelligence Process

To understand what intelligence is, and where its boundaries are situated, the Intelligence Cycle provides a useful conceptual framework for understanding the different elements that combine to make the essence of intelligence.

Figure 1.1 represents a version of the Intelligence Cycle. In this instance, the cycle is slightly condensed from its usual presentation, in that some of the elements of the cycle (eg collection and processing of information) are combined.

It is worth reiterating straight away that the notion of a linear sequence of steps in the intelligence process is a dangerous one and should be viewed with great care. Hulnick describes the cycle as 'not a very good description of the ways in which the intelligence process works',[21] identifying that it is almost invariably the case that interactions between each stage of the process are never as clean and transactional as the cycle tends to suggest, and business will tend to leap back and forth across the cycle. Perhaps more importantly, the linear 'production line' process implied by the cycle may be exactly not the way in which the intelligence sector needs to approach the networked and rapidly changing international security threats of today. This is the key argument of Clark's 'Target-Centric Analysis' model,[22] to which we will return in detail later. For now, however, it is worth expanding on the elements of the cycle.

---

[20] WF Walsh and GF Vito, 'The Meaning of Compstat: Analysis and Response' (2004) 20 *Journal of Contemporary Criminal Justice* 51, 58.

[21] AS Hulnick, 'What's Wrong with the Intelligence Cycle' (2006) 21 *Intelligence and National Security* 959.

[22] RM Clark, *Intelligence Analysis: A Target-Centric Approach* (Washington DC: CQ Press, 2007).

Figure 1.1 The Intelligence Cycle

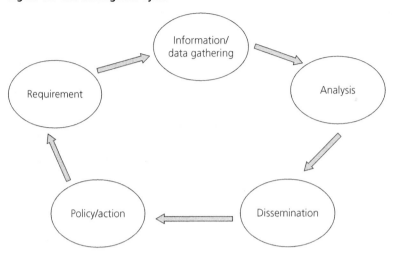

The cycle, in orthodox analysis, begins in the top left of the diagram with the **Requirement**. This is a particular intelligence question that has either been posed of the intelligence-analysis function by the 'customer', or has emerged as a strategic requirement within the agency in question. In a strategic security context, this could be an analysis of whether a particular country is close to establishing a nuclear capability, for example. In a policing context, this could be a question such as how to reduce vehicle theft or burglary in a particular area: in some cases the subject of an intelligence-led policing or 'problem-oriented policing' initiative. Either way, it is essential that the agency which is then going to try to answer the question with intelligence understands exactly what is required and where the information gap lies. (Very often, the real underlying requirement can be something subtly different from the question originally posed.)

Pitfalls in this area concern whether the original requester of the intelligence understands how intelligence gathering can help to answer his or her questions. In a survey of police intelligence analysts in Britain, Cope noted that some felt their intelligence products were sometimes described as 'wallpaper' by others in the force, and were 'demanded at the end of an operation to summarize the outcomes or used to justify an operation that was already planned'.[23] In this instance, the importance of intelligence as a critical factor meeting an information requirement appears not to be understood.

Once the intelligence-analysis function has established the question or questions it is charged with answering, it then needs to undertake a process

---

[23] N Cope, 'Intelligence Led Policing or Policing Led Intelligence? Integrating Volume Crime Analysis into Policing' (2004) 44 *British Journal of Criminology* 188, 192.

of gathering or identifying sets of information and data which will go towards providing a suitable solution to the problem: the **Information/data gathering** stage. (In some representations of the Intelligence Cycle, a stage of **Planning** exists prior to this stage.) Often this information will already exist within databases (eg a search through existing criminal records) and it is merely a question of extracting the appropriate pieces of data. There might also be judgements to be made about how to combine pieces of data from different repositories, assuming this is possible (there will often be practical and political reasons why it is complicated, especially if the relevant pieces of data reside in different agencies). In other cases, a decision might be made to undertake extra operational data gathering to collect new data on the question in hand. This may entail difficult resource and logistics questions, such as whether and how to deploy a surveillance team, for example, or the need to apply for search or interception warrants. (A further stage of **Processing/Collation** of data is also sometimes inserted into the cycle at this stage of the process, whereby gathered data and information has to be organized and processed before it can be properly analyzed.)

This is the area in which differences in 'information' and 'intelligence' become crucial. Information or just data alone, and the collection thereof, is not necessarily intelligence if it does not take the readers of it any further forward in their thinking. As Warner noted:

> Think of how many names are in the telephone book, and how few of those names anyone ever seeks. It is what people do with data and information that gives them the special quality that we casually call 'intelligence'.[24]

Thus, there are dangers in analysts supplying intelligence products to others which are little more than collections of data, without any analytical value added. In many scenarios, and particularly in the terrorist context, there is sometimes a pitfall in the belief that relentless gathering of information is an end in itself, and will eventually lead to evidence of suspicious activity or crime.[25] The risk is made greater by the ever-growing availability of information.

Aside from this process being inefficient, there are difficult political and ethical questions arising over the gathering of information, and the boundary between this information and 'intelligence'. An intelligence-gathering process called 'Rich Picture' in the UK perhaps best encapsulates the difficulties.[26] Launched after the July 2005 terrorist bombings in London, 'Rich Picture' is a joint activity between the Security Service (MI5) and the police which aims to gather a wealth of information about Muslim communities in the UK, with a view to identifying the small percentage of individuals within those communities who may be

---

[24] M Warner, 'Wanted: A Definition of "Intelligence"' (2002) 46/3 *Studies in Intelligence* 15, 17.

[25] RV Clarke and GR Newman, 'Police and the Prevention of Terrorism' (2007) 1 *Policing* 9, 12.

[26] J Bennetto, 'MI5 conducts secret inquiry into 8,000 al-Qa'ida "sympathisers"', <http://www.independent.co.uk/news/uk/crime/mi5-conducts-secret-inquiry-into-8000-alqaida-sympathisers-406435.html>, accessed 30 December 2009.

on a dangerous path to radicalization. At its core, therefore, Rich Picture is an intensive *information*-gathering exercise, which leads on to *intelligence* following subsequent analysis. The two terms are often blurred in their usage, however, with the security services often referring to 'community intelligence' as a catch-all phrase for the product of the whole process.

In many ways this process is no different from standard intelligence-led polic-ing activities across a range of problem areas. In analyzing antisocial behaviour within a city, for example, the police would gather data about where pubs and bars were located, which had extended licences, and which were likely to be the source of problems in the evening. An approach to examining drugs traffick-ing would attempt to gather information on late-night gathering areas where groups of young people congregated. In the terrorist context described above, however, the information-gathering process—which is often referred to as com-munity *intelligence* gathering—focuses on a particular community. In one town in the UK, a pressure group has been formed within the Muslim community which is lambasting the exercise as unfairly targeting and victimizing the Mus-lim community.[27] The radical Muslim organization Hizb-ut Tahrir has described the government's Preventing Violent Extremism programme as 'Macarthyist' and an underhand way of asking local authorities to 'spy on Muslim youth'.[28] In the terrorism context therefore, and particularly where it interfaces with local community issues, the uses of the terms 'information' and 'intelligence' and the meanings ascribed to them can become critically important and politically very charged.

It is interesting in this case how Hizb-ut Tahrir's message reflects the way in which intelligence is often equated with negative images and notions: spies, espionage, and covert activities are rendered in popular culture in confusingly complex ways. Sometimes the images are romantic (eg James Bond), but more often than not the association is negative, particularly in countries and cultures in which intelligence agencies have held a lot of unaccountable power (think of the KGB, the Stasi, or 'Big Brother'). Ratcliffe notes that in the US in the period between the 1950s and 1970s, when the FBI had a remit for counter-subversion and was found to have interpreted this very broadly in covertly targeting domes-tic political figures, an anxiety over the connection between a domestic police service and 'intelligence' grew to considerable proportions, and still shapes the language of policing today.[29]

The next phase in the cycle, that of **Analysis**, is a crucial one to the picture. In this stage, a process is applied to the gathered information which makes it more than just a set of pieces of apparently unrelated data. Analysis of the data

---

[27] The Reading PVE [Preventing Violence Extremism] Crisis Group: see <http://pvecrisisgroup. com>, accessed 30 December 2009.

[28] Hizb-ut Tahrir UK, 'Hazel Blears threatens to get heavy as councils are unconvinced by her Macarthyist agenda', 2009, <http://www.hizb.org.uk/hizb/press-centre/press-release/hazel-blears-threatens-to-get-heavy-as-councils-are-unconvinced-by-her-mccarthist-agenda.html>, accessed 30 December 2009.   [29] J Ratcliffe, *Intelligence-Led Policing* (Cullompton: Willan, 2008) pp 27–8.

may establish a hypothesis that says something about what is happening under the surface, or what may be about to happen. Purchase of very specific uranium enrichment equipment, for example, could mean that a country is at an advanced stage in nuclear weapons development, especially when combined with indicators from other sources. Often this process entails combining different sets of data to form a more complete picture of what might be happening, and is the very essence of intelligence in that it delivers something more than just a bald set of information: essentially, a *hypothesis*.

In a policing context, the crime analyst Deborah Osborne describes intelligence as 'knowledge derived from careful analysis of the total information-rich environment'.[30] This implies the appropriate assumption that intelligence 'product' or 'output' needs to be a value-added process, which assists policy-makers in their deliberations.

A deeper definition of the central role of analysis to intelligence was provided by Ribaux et al, as follows:

> It is generally recognized that intelligence is the timely, accurate and usable product of logically processed information. In the context of the criminal justice system the information pertains to crime and the context in which it occurs. For instance, from a series of crimes, a hypothesis about where the criminal lives or when and where he will next offend can sometimes be inferred from the available data. These judgements provide leads that are then translated to operative measures like surveillance or targeted police patrols. . . . This interpretation step, called analysis, is often considered as the heart of a process embodying the whole treatment of data, from its collection to the practical implementation of the intelligence itself.[31]

In this context, the critical step that translates information into intelligence is the creation of 'leads' which can be hypothesized from the data and taken forward practically into further operational activities.

Having established a particular intelligence hypothesis, however, the value of so doing is negligible or even lost altogether if the information cannot be disseminated appropriately to the people who really need to know and can benefit from it: the **Dissemination** phase. Very often, the significance of a piece of intelligence is lost, under-emphasized or even over-emphasized because of the way in which it was circulated and communicated to the relevant consumers. In a tactical context, this can include situations in which a piece of intelligence is delivered too late to have a bearing on a situation, or not delivered at all to the relevant people who could have acted upon it. This, in turn, can warp the significance of that piece of intelligence in every direction.

---

[30] D Osborne, 'Intelligence-led policing: it's not in your intelligence files', LawOfficer.com, 11 June 2008, <http://www.lawofficer.com/news-and-articles/columns/Osborne/intelligence_led_policing.html>, accessed 30 December 2009.

[31] O Ribaux et al, 'Forensic Intelligence and Crime Analysis' (2003) 2 *Law, Probability and Risk* 47, 49.

The final phase in the cycle is that of **Policy/action**. This, also, is a crucial phase, whereby the intelligence has a bearing on real-world outcomes, either by influencing high-level policy on a particular issue, or by allowing an executive arm of government to take some assertive action, whether it be military action in the field, the arrest of a particular individual, or any number of other interventions. For many, this is the defining process in turning something that was just information, or data, into actual *intelligence*, because it had a bearing on the world rather than just being background noise.

Marrin suggests that national security policy-makers generally follow an intelligence decision-making framework described by Harvard University historian Ernest May, whereby the 'so what?' question is eventually followed by 'what to do?'[32] Sims neatly articulated the problem by defining intelligence as 'information collected, organized, or analyzed on behalf of actors or decision makers'.[33]

In the policing context, the President of the International Association of Law Enforcement Analysts, Lisa Palmieri, suggests that the very definition of intelligence is that it influences policy-makers, otherwise it is not really intelligence at all, rather like the question of whether a tree falling over in the middle of the Amazon forest can be said to make a sound, if no one hears it.[34]

While this makes a lot of sense, it offers some dangerous hostages to fortune for intelligence analysts and the agencies in which they work, particularly in the aftermath of intelligence failures. Odom notes that members of intelligence oversight committees in the US after the 9/11 period have often ascribed a heavy responsibility to intelligence agencies. In the wake of the Intelligence Reform and Terrorism Prevention Act 2004 in the US, one senator said that the US had to have intelligence 'that does not allow the president to make wrong decisions about going to war'.[35] Some on the committees even demanded that punitive action be taken against staff in the intelligence agencies who were responsible for supplying the President with erroneous intelligence leading to the invasion of Iraq.[36] Aside from the intelligence process having clearly failed in the case of Iraq, it implies a somewhat political shifting of blame for such mistakes away from the President himself. It also suggests a failure to recognize the inherent uncertainty of intelligence assessments and judgements, such that they can rarely provide policy-makers with cast-iron options on how to proceed, based as they are almost always on imperfect or lacking data.[37]

Finger-pointing between policy-makers and intelligence analysts is not the preserve of state intelligence actors alone, nor is it only an issue in major strategic situations. The case of the fatal shooting of Jean Charles de Menezes by the

---

[32] S Marrin, 'Intelligence Analysis Theory: Explaining and Predicting Analytic Responsibilities' (2007) 22 *Intelligence and National Security* 821, 829.

[33] J Sims, 'What is Intelligence? Information for Decision-Making' in R Godson, ER May, and G Schmitt (eds), *US Intelligence at the Crossroads* (London: Brassey's, 1995) p 4.

[34] L Palmieri, cited in Ratcliffe, *Intelligence-Led Policing*, n 29 above, p 152.

[35] WE Odom, 'Intelligence Analysis' (2008) 23 *Intelligence and National Security* 316, 317.

[36] Ibid.   [37] Odom, 'Intelligence Analysis', n 35 above, p 321.

police in London in the summer of 2005 is an illuminating one in a much more tactical context. The inquest into how the police came to shoot dead an innocent man instead of the fugitive terrorist they had assumed him to be, discovered that the issue was more than just a simple misidentification. One aspect of the enquiry found that a management discussion about the fast-moving intelligence picture led to a decision to order the police officers on the scene to take action and shoot the man, but that this was not a course of action on which everyone in the management team agreed.[38] Here we can see that, while there were problems with the intelligence itself (in that de Menezes had been erroneously identified as someone else), the key factor which led to his fatal shooting was a decision by the policy-makers (on which they did not all agree) to take a particular course of action on that intelligence. This in turn determines who ends up being 'in the dock' of the investigation (in this case the front-line officer who acted on the intelligence rather than the decision-makers above him).

Problems with the Intelligence Cycle Model

As discussed, it is increasingly the case that a particular intelligence requirement will not flow neatly and carefully through each of these stages. There are often switch-backs and deviations whereby transactions between players in the cycle will vary, repeat, or be changed. Interim returns to the requirement phase will often happen throughout the cycle, for example, whereby a particular intelligence case will build up in several different directions and the original 'customer' will need to provide an input as to whether the analysis is proceeding in the right direction. Often this may lead to a different question being answered from that initially posed. This may happen a number of times before the 'finished' intelligence product emerges from the end of the cycle. Similarly, the end of the cycle is often not the end, but the middle, in the sense that each delivered and assessed piece of intelligence will immediately and seamlessly lead to further questions and investigations, and so the cycle repeats.

In his extensive analysis of the intelligence process primarily in the US state sector, and proposing a new model for a more 'target-centric' approach (rather than the function-centric approach implied by the traditional intelligence cycle), Robert Clark noted that:

> Over the years, the intelligence cycle has become almost a theological concept: No one questions its validity. Yet when pressed, many intelligence officers admit that the intelligence process 'really doesn't work like that'. In other words, effective intelligence efforts are not cycles.[39]

---

[38] S Laville, 'Special Branch officer cleared of deceiving de Menezes Inquest', *The Guardian*, 26 May 2009, <http://www.guardian.co.uk/uk/2009/may/26/menezes-police-ipcc-cressida>, accessed 30 December 2009.

[39] Clark, *Intelligence Analysis: A Target-Centric Approach*, n 22 above, p 11.

It is increasingly important, therefore, not to see the intelligence process as a strictly formulaic one, which always follows certain procedures in a certain order. This is important when thinking about how the intelligence function and process can be taught to new analysts, and whether it is a 'science' or an 'art'. We will return to this question later, but we can certainly establish at this stage that the process is not necessarily a strictly defined scientific process. This also has managerial implications in terms of where intelligence analysts sit within the organization, and how intricately they are connected to other parts of the business.

We have used the intelligence cycle model to identify the key elements within the process, by way of emphasizing the key touch points in the process. This provides a certain understanding of intelligence, and where its boundaries lie. However, there are other dimensions to the process of intelligence which are important to its definition, but which are not adequately explained by the intelligence cycle model. These are the question of whether secrecy is an inherent aspect of intelligence; differences in types of intelligence analysis and product; and the question of what the full extent of the intelligence process is or should be, and whether it includes 'covert action' as well as passive analysis.

Secrecy

There has been much academic debate about whether the element of secrecy is another defining characteristic of intelligence. Schulsky and Schmitt note that, without what the grandfather of intelligence analysis at the CIA, Sherman Kent, calls 'clandestinity', intelligence is essentially little different from social science.[40] Intelligence is about examining situations and behaviours in adversaries which the subject wishes to keep secret, and which are generally very difficult to uncover. Warner went further in claiming that

> secrecy is the key to the definition of intelligence . . . Without secrets, it is not intelligence. Properly understood, intelligence is that range of activities—whether analysis, collection, or covert action—performed on behalf of a nation's foreign policy that would be negated if their foreign 'subjects' spotted the hand of another country and acted differently as a consequence.[41]

Thus, for intelligence activities to be effective and remain so, it is essential for them to be conducted without the knowledge of the subject. To do otherwise is to invite changes in behaviour which render the intelligence-gathering operations less effective, or worse—defunct. The obvious examples lie in the military sphere, and relate as equally to 'counter-intelligence' (ie activities aimed at thwarting or misleading the offensive intelligence-gathering activities of another country or agency) as to intelligence itself.

---

[40] AN Schulsky and GN Schmitt, *Silent Warfare: Understanding the World of Intelligence* (Dulles VA: Potomac, 2002) pp 171–2.

[41] Warner, 'Wanted: A Definition of Intelligence', n 24 above, p 20.

We have seen that intelligence is sometimes a tool to influence policy on sensitive matters of national security, or crime. It is also sometimes given the power to provide 'foreknowledge' of the intentions of an individual, or organization, or government. In this sense it makes sense for it usually to be hidden behind closed doors, otherwise its power to influence policy could be diminished. In some cases, particularly in parts of Europe, it is seen as right and proper that a national intelligence agency should issue to the public assessments of security threats, much in the way that the CIA issues the National Intelligence Estimates. In this context, the intelligence agency sometimes carries out a function akin to a news agency, or policy research institution. The Dutch civil intelligence agency, the AIVD, is a good example, as is the Danish Security and Intelligence Service, the PET. The AIVD in particular makes a virtue of issuing comprehensive, well-researched—and unclassified—assessments of issues such as extremism, radicalization, espionage, and so on.[42] In the Netherlands, an intelligence agency is seen not only as a gatherer and trader of secret information, but also a market leader in high quality analysis of security threats within the public domain. In many other countries, intelligence as academic research is anathema.

Of course, things that are supposed to be secret do not always remain so, despite the best intentions of the originator. In the UK, the intelligence agencies do not issue publicly available assessments in any formal way, other than through occasional statements from high-ranking personnel, or as a result of leaks. Both are situations that have proliferated considerably in recent years. A case of a conscious placing of information into the public domain was the statement delivered by the then Director-General of MI5 on the current terrorist threat in Britain in 2006. Without providing specific details of targets, Dame Eliza Manningham-Buller said that MI5 were working on thirty terror plots and had approximately 1600 individuals under surveillance.[43] Although the Director-General was obviously not going to reveal any more specific details, this was a level of sensitive intelligence information whose release would have been unthinkable just a few years previously. It could be argued that political forces were at play in the statement, in that it was judicious at the time to stress that the security threat from terrorism remained at a heightened state following a peaceful year after the London bombings, and that the intelligence and security agencies needed to continue receiving the enhanced levels of investment that had been flowing their way. The public also needed to remain vigilant to help the agencies in their work.

An example of an intelligence leak was that of August 2008, whereby *The Guardian* newspaper published details of an MI5 report, classified 'UK Restricted', which examined the terrorist radicalization pathway in the UK and

---

[42] See, eg the list of publications on the AIVD website at <https://www.aivd.nl/english/publications>, accessed 30 December 2009.

[43] 'MI5 tracking "30 UK terror plots"', *BBC News*, 10 November 2006, <http://news.bbc.co.uk/1/hi/uk/6134516.stm>, accessed 30 December 2009.

assessed that there is no standard template for the process.[44] Aside from the surprise factor of seeing the cover of a classified document on the front page of a national newspaper, there was some conjecture as to whether the report's release was again engineered in some way to get certain security messages out into the public domain. Whatever the validity of this theory, it is interesting to note that secret intelligence does not always remain so, and again, that it can be used to influence public opinion and, indirectly, government policy, in complex ways.

A further, and in some ways more bizarre example, is the inadvertent exposure of classified operational details concerning a counter-terrorist operation in April 2009 in the UK, whereby the Assistant Commissioner of the Metropolitan Police emerged from the Prime Minister's office with uncovered classified papers under his arm, in full view of photographers. The leak of tactical details concerning terrorist suspects almost certainly led to a hasty acceleration in the arrest of the suspects in question (who were later either deported or released without charge) and the resignation of the police Assistant Commissioner. In this case, the policy-maker was the casualty of the mishap, and the policy/action outcome of the secret intelligence being made public was a rapid change in the tactical direction of the operation.

Any offensive intelligence activity carries risks if it is discovered, the main one being that it is quickly negated. In a human intelligence (Humint) context, the risks can be physically disastrous for a 'source'. In a signals intelligence (Sigint) context, the risk is a complex combination of sometimes highly intelligence-bearing interception capabilities (such as the Enigma code-breaking in the Second World War) set against the ease and speed with which the target can change its activities if the intelligence capability is discovered. Herman depicted the situation as a 'pyramid of source sensitivity, quantity and value'.[45] At the top of the pyramid is decipherment, as this is capable of producing high-value intelligence in large quantities if conducted effectively, in the sense that diplomatic channels of traffic are often those carrying the most sensitive and interesting communications. But the source sensitivity is also high, and can be quickly negated if the target realizes its communications have been compromised. One of the great successes of the Enigma decipherment activities was that they were protected with rigid secrecy, which prevented the German navy from discovering the real reason for their change of fortunes in the war.

In a more modern context, Aid described the example of Al Qaeda's changes in communications behaviour after the launch of their campaign in the 1990s. Initially, Osama Bin Laden used a satellite phone extensively when in Afghanistan (not least because no other communications infrastructure was available) until

---

[44] A Travis, 'MI5 report challenges views on terrorism in Britain', *The Guardian*, 20 August 2008, <http://www.guardian.co.uk/uk/2008/aug/20/uksecurity.terrorism1>, accessed 30 December 2009.

[45] Herman, *Intelligence Power in Peace and War*, n 11 above, p 71.

news reports suggested that the National Security Agency (NSA) was monitoring those communications. It was reported that NSA could use its intercepts to pinpoint installations such as the Khost training camp, which was bombed by the US following the East Africa Embassy bombings by Al Qaeda in 1998. Evidence suggests that Bin Laden and other senior members of Al Qaeda ceased using electronic communications shortly after this period, preferring thereafter to relay messages by hand.[46] Compromise of the secrecy in this instance led to a fairly easy change of behaviour by the target, and the abrupt end of a line of previously very fruitful intelligence. (Although, in this case, kinetic action on the back of the Sigint gave it a natural shelf-life—the target would have soon equated missile attacks on its installations with satellite phone activity.)

Very often, the word 'secret' is conjoined to the word intelligence, suggesting a symbiotic relationship between the two. A recent example concerned the question of the controversial 'control orders' in the UK, which are a tool of the counter-terrorism strategy equating broadly to house arrest for certain categories of suspects. Control orders can be applied to certain terrorist suspects where the only evidence of wrongdoing is contained within 'secret intelligence', whose disclosure to the public would be damaging to national security.[47] Here, the whole issue is about the secrecy of the information which supports the case against the suspects in question: the European Court of Human Rights, and the Law Lords in the UK subsequently, ruled that, while it was understood that certain intelligence needed to remain secret for the protection of sources and techniques, it breached the human rights of individuals not to be privy to the evidence against them when charged.

Gill describes a breakdown of contemporary 'security networks' that has entailed both a deepening of levels of security threat between domestic and international sectors, and a broadening of sectors beyond just state security actors.[48] In this way, intelligence can be gathered not just by elements of the state itself, such as the police or state intelligence agencies, but also by non-governmental and private sector agencies (such as the media, or private security companies), and by the 'communitarian' sector, ie the public.

Intelligence actors are not the only ones to recognize the opportunities here. It is interesting to note how major news agencies, when a story is breaking overseas, will increasingly issue appeals for 'anyone in the area' to provide details of what they have seen, including images and accounts. This is particularly so where an incident happens in a far-off place in which correspondents may not

---

[46] M Aid, 'All Glory is Fleeting: Sigint and the Fight Against International Terrorism' in Andrew et al (eds), *Secret Intelligence: A Reader*, n 3 above, p 52.

[47] A Travis, 'Terror control orders breach human rights, law lords rule', *The Guardian*, 10 June 2009, <http://www.guardian.co.uk/politics/2009/jun/10/control-orders-breach-terror-suspects-rights>, accessed 30 December 2009.

[48] P Gill, 'Not Just Joining the Dots but Crossing the Borders and Bridging the Voids: Constructing Security Networks after 11 September 2001' (2006) 16 *Policing and Society* 27, 29.

be in place but travellers and tourists—armed with camera-phones—will be. In an age of instant mass media across the globe, this is a method of harnessing the public effectively to make the news themselves.

In a security context, a good example of where this happened was 'Operation Crevice', an investigation in the UK into a terrorist cell which resulted in the successful conviction of five men in April 2007 for the preparation of a terrorist attack. One of the most crucial pieces of intelligence during the operation was a tip-off from a vigilant member of the public, who was concerned about a lock-up garage being used by the group.[49] In this case, the intelligence came willingly, but the intelligence agencies will sometimes try to make it easier by publicizing confidential phone lines or email addresses to which information can be sent, or, in the case of Northern Ireland, pasting the information phone line number on the side of patrolling military vehicles. Interestingly, the intelligence received from the public through such mechanisms cannot be 'secret' in the official governmental sense of formal classification (because the information comes from the public domain), but it is clearly intelligence nonetheless and can be extremely valuable.

Secrecy, therefore, is not an inherent aspect of intelligence, but the exclusivity of the information can be critical and can make the difference between openly available data and 'intelligence' which helps policy-makers take significant action. This exclusivity can relate to information provided in confidence by members of the public, or can be a time factor, that is, information received early and possibly in advance of other parties. The question of secrecy remains pertinent in the context of the nature of modern threats to national security. Terrorists, organized criminals, proliferators of weapons of mass destruction, and other contemporary targets of intelligence, are all working in situations in which they are seeking to hide and obfuscate their activities and communications as far as possible. They are generally well aware that the authorities are working their hardest to uncover their clandestine activities, and will be very quick to change behaviour when things appear to go wrong. In many ways, terrorist planning activities are much less visible among the 'noise' of general public activity than was the case with high-profile military targets of the past, and deliberately so. For this reason, it may well be the case that intelligence in these contexts has to be secret by its very definition to avoid failure—it, too, has to be 'below the radar' of the targets. Johnson and Natarajan described the example of organized drugs dealers, who deploy an array of counter-intelligence activities to try to mitigate the risk of police intelligence penetration of their networks, including surveillance and counter-surveillance, careful information sharing between buyers and sellers, and use of elaborate linguistic codes.[50]

---

[49] 'Five get life over UK bomb plot', *BBC News*, 30 April 2007, <http://news.bbc.co.uk/1/hi/uk/6195914.stm>, accessed 30 December 2009.

[50] BD Johnson and N Natarajan, 'Strategies to Avoid Arrest: Crack Sellers' Response to Intensified Policing' (1995) 14/3 *American Journal of Police* 49, 54.

Boundaries of Intelligence—Passive Collection or Covert Action?

In considering the question of ethics and intelligence in the post-9/11 'war on terror' world, the celebrated academic analyst of intelligence, Michael Herman, noted that:

> Intelligence is information and information gathering, not doing things to people; no-one gets hurt by it, at least not directly. Some agencies do indeed carry out covert action, which confuses the ethical issues, but this is a separable and subsidiary function.[51]

Herman was referring primarily to the British intelligence system, noting that the intelligence agencies there do not have a covert action function. The model in Britain is one in which intelligence agencies provide assessments and judgements to other executive bodies, such as the police or military, who then decide whether to take action: they do not have executive arms themselves, nor indeed do they directly comment on government policy. (This is notwithstanding the cases of whistleblowers David Shayler and Richard Tomlinson, formerly of MI5 and MI6 respectively, who spoke of 'Special Operations' and a purported plan to assassinate Colonel Ghadafi of Libya in 1995/96. Such claims cannot be corroborated and Shayler has been prosecuted under the Official Secrets Act, but it may at least be the case that 'disruptive action' is available in some circumstances, if heavily shrouded in secrecy.[52]) This is generally true across most other European countries. In the case of the US, the row over covert action by the CIA since the advent of the War on Terror, and the political fallout in European countries over their collaboration with the US in these polices, is indicative of the differing ways in which covert action is seen as part-and-parcel of the work of an intelligence agency. In June 2005, a judge in Milan issued arrest warrants for thirteen US intelligence officials believed to have been involved in the extraordinary rendition of terrorist suspects from Italy to Egypt; several further arrest warrants have been issued subsequently in Italy.[53]

The mandate for covert action has waxed and waned in the US. The 1948 National Security directive 10/2 authorized the CIA to engage in:

> Propaganda; economic warfare; preventive direct action, including sabotage, anti-sabotage, demolition and evacuation measures; subversion against hostile states, including assistance to underground resistance movements, guerrillas and refugee liberation groups, and support of indigenous anti-Communist elements in threatened countries of the free world.[54]

---

[51] M Herman, 'Ethics and Intelligence after September 11' in LV Scott and PD Jackson (eds), *Understanding Intelligence in the Twenty-First Century: Journeys in Shadows* (London: Routledge, 2004) p 180.

[52] L Scott, 'Secret Intelligence, Covert Action and Clandestine Diplomacy' (2004) 19 *Intelligence and National Security* 322, 325.

[53] Gill and Phythian, *Intelligence in an Insecure World*, n 1 above, p 80.

[54] Cited in C Andrew, *For the President's Eyes Only: Secret Intelligence and the American Presidency from Washington to Bush* (London: HarperCollins, 1995) p 173.

Over subsequent years, activities internationally such as the assisted overthrow of the Mossadeq and Allende governments in Iran and Chile respectively, the backing of anti-communist guerrilla movements such as the Contras in Nicaragua, and the bungled attempts to assassinate Fidel Castro in Cuba, cast a shadow over the effectiveness and moral legitimacy of such covert action. Domestically within the US, the FBI's counter-intelligence programme (COINTELPRO) which ran from the mid 1950s to 1971, was found, as we have seen, to have stepped over the mark in its scrutiny of dissidents and critics of the government, and instilled a national anxiety over the proximity between law enforcement bodies and intelligence gathering.

A drawing-back from covert action with the advent of the fall of the Soviet Union and the peace dividend in the 1990s was somewhat brought to a halt with the 9/11 terrorist attacks in the US. Cogan notes that the New Strategic Doctrine of President Bush in this period extended the Presidential Finding and Congressional oversight mechanism for the CIA's covert action, in place since 1970, and gave it the remit aggressively to hunt down and capture or kill high-level terrorists perceived to be threatening the security of the US. This included a much closer cooperation between the CIA and Special Forces in the field abroad.[55] Just over a year after the 9/11 attacks, an unmanned Predator drone fired a Hellfire missile in Yemen, killing six Al Qaeda terrorist suspects, on the basis of operational intelligence supplied by the CIA. This was the first time such a device had been used offensively by the US outside a war zone,[56] and was reminiscent of the Israeli policy of targeted assassination of high-ranking Palestinian militant leaders. Numerous further attacks have subsequently taken place, especially in the border region of Afghanistan and Pakistan, to a mounting degree of domestic unrest within Pakistan, in particular, over apparent disregard of its sovereignty.

We have already mentioned the case of extraordinary rendition of terrorist suspects to third countries where they will often be subjected to torture, and use of interrogation methods bordering on torture by the CIA itself, such as 'waterboarding'. For the US administration immediately post 9/11, these were seen as integral and important parts of the CIA's activities, yet for many European partner agencies they pose serious and difficult questions about the reasonable bounds of an intelligence agency's remit. The position seems to be complex. In an interview in 2006, former UK Ambassador to Uzbekistan, Craig Murray, expressed his belief that MI6 had knowingly used intelligence obtained under torture from the Uzbekis in terrorist cases, but that the Foreign Secretary had agreed with the head of MI6 that this did not contravene the UK's position on the issue of torture since Britain did not torture suspects directly itself.[57] Murray

---

[55] C Cogan, 'Hunters Not Gatherers: Intelligence in the Twenty-First Century' (2004) 19 *Intelligence and National Security* 304, 316.

[56] Gill and Phythian, *Intelligence in an Insecure World*, n 1 above, p 79.

[57] Europe-NU.nl, 'Former British ambassador says CIA and MI6 use testimony obtained under torture', 21 April 2006, <http://www.europa-nu.nl/9353000/1/j9vvh6nf08temv0/vh9z222zqpze?ctx=vg9hnwn4qtyz>, accessed 30 December 2009.

was therefore stating his belief that, in the UK, an intelligence agency can define itself as not having the mandate directly to undertake certain nefarious aspects of covert action (at least not openly) but can, it seems, draw on the intelligence dividends delivered by others who have.

The twin issues of covert action and secrecy draw out the fact that intelligence is a multi-layered activity, with different applications in different situations. At one level, it is important to draw the distinctions between 'tactical', 'strategic' and 'operational' intelligence, since they will be conducted by different agencies in different ways, at different times. In the policing sphere, in a survey of crime analysis in the US, O'Shea and Nicholls found a strong preference for 'tactical' applications of intelligence analysis, ie those that directly impacted on crime control policies.[58] Similarly, in the military and active counter-terrorist scenario, such as in the firing of missiles at high-ranking terrorist targets described above, the intelligence behind the action (such as a locational fix on a target) is intensely 'tactical'. Covert action is generally tactical, although it can be part of a much wider strategic view: this was certainly the case in the major anti-communist proxy warfare activities across Latin America, Africa, and Asia during the Cold War.

'Strategic' intelligence is the sort of intelligence presented in the National Intelligence Estimates, which aims to be more forward-looking and predictive. In many ways this is the hardest type of intelligence, as it aims to use analysis of fragmented information and modelling of past activities and behaviours to predict what might happen in the future. As we will see in the next chapter, this process has frequently got it wrong, and the stakes can be very high in so doing. In essence, while strategic and tactical intelligence-gathering activities and their processes of analysis look and feel very different, they entail use of basic analytical skills that have much in common.

'Operational' intelligence is that which is aimed less at policy-makers and 'customers' of intelligence within government, but that which supports the agency itself in carrying out its activities. Thus, different parts of the intelligence community will increasingly need to share pieces of intelligence with each other to improve their overall performance on difficult security and crime targets. In the context of Sigint, Aid notes that international terrorist targets are very difficult ones on which to gather and interpret intelligence, even when there is plenty of information and data available.[59] Operational sharing and 'fusion' on intelligence between agencies will strengthen performance.

The language used to describe different types of intelligence is broadly universal, although the policing sector will sometimes use a finer-grained set of definitions for intelligence products. The NIM in the UK identifies four sets of intelligence product: strategic assessments, tactical assessments, target profiles

---

[58] TC O'Shea and K Nicholls, *Crime Analysis in America: Findings and Recommendations* (Washington DC: Office of Community Oriented Policing Services, 2003) p 13.

[59] Aid, 'All Glory is Fleeting', n 46 above, p 60.

and problem profiles. In very general terms, the profiles occupy the more tactical, target-specific space, while strategic assessments will take a broader view in terms of detail, context, and time. As Gill and Phythian point out,[60] law enforcement bodies are generally drawn to the tactical sphere rather than that of 'high' strategic assessment, as the former is where the results are to be found in terms of crime reduction on the ground, and the latter is left to agencies which work more closely on longer-term mapping, such as the Serious and Organised Crime Agency in the UK.

Conclusions

Notions of intelligence, and intelligence gathering, are as old as time, yet attempts to define clearly where the boundaries of intelligence are to be found, remain problematic. At one level, this does not matter greatly: perhaps we all know important intelligence when we see it, and there is a risk that attempts to develop theoretical models of intelligence will not have great relevance to the day-to-day reality of law enforcement or protecting national security. On another level, however, the matter is an important one, since governments and bureaucracies need to make decisions on how to allocate resources to best effect in developing intelligence capabilities to tackle the security threats of the modern world.

Increasingly, the problem needs to be seen as one in which the law enforcement analyst works hand-in-glove with the state security intelligence analyst. Since the end of the Cold War, the nature of security threats and interconnectedness of those threats across sectors and borders have meant a natural coming-together of intelligence analysts. This is not without its problems, or without anxieties in certain sectors, but it is an increasing reality.

We have seen how intelligence is both an output, and a business process, the elements of which can be conceptualized as a cycle of activities, although care needs to be taken to recognize that the flow of the process is increasingly less cyclical and more networked. In terms of a product, intelligence signifies a spectrum of analyzed and assessed outputs, from tactical intelligence on very specific threats and targets, to more strategic assessment of trends and likely future events. Both, in their own way, are the 'foreknowledge' advantage against the enemy that Sun Tzu recognized many centuries ago.

We have also seen how the whole question of intelligence and how it is organized can become a distinctly political question, with different parts of the process jostling for position and pointing fingers when things go wrong. In planning intelligence activities and attempting to maximize their effectiveness, it is important to consider how things can go wrong, and how they can go right. It is to the question of intelligence success and failure that we turn in the next chapter.

---

[60] Gill and Phythian, *Intelligence in an Insecure World*, n 1 above, p 85.

Key Points

- Attempts to develop theories of intelligence are important, because intelligence is both a theoretical concept and a practical activity, and thinking in the former can help maximize the effectiveness of the latter.

- Intelligence requirements are central to statecraft and national security, and definitions of state security requirements have changed substantially through the turn of the century.

- Increasingly, modern security threats and intelligence priorities have meant a merging of the law enforcement with the state security intelligence functions.

- Intelligence is both a product, and a business process. The elements of the process can be conceptualized using the 'intelligence cycle', although it is important to remember that the intelligence process is increasingly more networked and dynamic than linear.

- Most observers define intelligence as the output of the process of analysis applied to information. They also define the purpose of this process as to supply intelligence to help policy-makers in government do their job.

- Some observers suggest that intelligence inherently has to be secret, to avoid being just 'information'. This is a complex definition in an environment where some crucial intelligence comes from the 'communitarian' sector.

- Intelligence often means both the information resulting from the analysis process, and the actors conducting that analysis. There are crucial differences between societies and periods of history as to those agencies that include 'covert action' in their remit, and those that do not.

- Distinctions can be drawn between tactical, operational, and strategic intelligence, although similar issues and skills requirements can apply across each of these activities.

2

Intelligence Failure and Success

Woodrow Kuhns noted, a short while after 9/11, that the study of intelligence failure is perhaps 'the most academically advanced field in the study of intelligence'.[1] Much of this area of study focuses on military strategic surprise, drawing on a large body of examples from Pearl Harbor in 1941 up to and beyond the Falklands War in 1982. The repeated failure of major intelligence powers to foresee major strategic developments through history has led many to conclude that failure is an inherent risk in the intelligence function, for a host of reasons which we will explore. When Betts wrote his much-quoted article 'Why Intelligence Failures are Inevitable' in 1978, he noted that 'case studies of intelligence failures abound'.[2]

At the beginning of the twenty-first century, the strategic shift in security threat represented by Al Qaeda led to a further set of major 'intelligence failures', and perhaps more importantly, a rigorous and extensive set of official enquiries into what had gone wrong and how the situation could be improved in the future. The invasion of Iraq in 2003 in pursuit of weapons of mass destruction (WMD) unleashed yet more official investigations into intelligence failure from the US to Australia, once it became clear that the pre-war intelligence had been comprehensively wrong. These examples deal with major strategic and military situations, but their findings offer generic lessons for intelligence practitioners across the sector. The enquiries into 9/11 in the US and the 7 July 2005 attacks ('7/7') in the UK, both of which deal with failures of the state security and police intelligence infrastructures on both sides of the Atlantic to pre-empt major terrorist attacks, take us closer to the more tactical nuts and bolts of the day-to-day intelligence machinery, and how it can get things badly wrong.

---

[1] WJ Kuhns, in RK Betts and TG Mahnken (eds), *Paradoxes of Strategic Intelligence: Essays in Honor of Michael I. Handel* (London: Frank Cass, 2003) p 80.

[2] RK Betts, 'Analysis, War and Decision: Why Intelligence Failures are Inevitable' (1978) 31 *World Politics* 61.

In this chapter we examine the literature and case studies on intelligence failure and present a model for understanding the failing process in terms of the 'intelligence cycle' model presented in the first chapter. In particular, we note that case studies and official enquiries often tell us that failure occurs in one or both of two parts of the intelligence arena: in the cognitive and analytical processes undertaken by intelligence analysts in approaching and assessing the material available to them; and in the organizational structures and process-flows of the intelligence machinery itself.

It should also be observed that, as Kuhns and Betts both noted, studies of intelligence failure seem to be far more abundant than any studies of intelligence success. This is perhaps understandable, in that the consequences of major intelligence failure can be very grave indeed, and it is natural for a state to try to examine what went wrong afterwards in an effort to perform better in the future. Additionally, as we have seen, intelligence is by its very nature something that strives to predict the future and steer states and societies along courses of action that avoid danger. Intelligence success is sometimes represented by the absence of security threat rather than by the presence of any thing or incident. In essence, the successes of intelligence are often invisible when the failures are emphatically not.

To begin our analysis of intelligence failure and success, it is worth briefly looking at the historical examination of intelligence failure and 'strategic surprise'.

Analysis of Intelligence Failure and 'Strategic Surprise'

Much of the early analysis of intelligence failure centred around instances of military surprise. While not necessarily of direct relevance to many of today's security threats and intelligence requirements, it is well worth reviewing many of these cases, as they provide us with a number of observations and conclusions about the intelligence machinery in general and where some of its key weaknesses are situated.

The failure of the French in the First World War to predict that the Germans would advance north of their main defences and through Belgium is a much quoted example,[3] as is the German feat in outflanking the Russian forces at Tannenberg by intercepting their unencrypted military communications, and the infamous Operation Barbarossa in the Second World War which saw German forces penetrating deep into Russian territory.

Through the 1960s and 1970s, a number of strategic intelligence failures occurred despite the rapidly growing size and capability of the US intelligence

---

[3] JK Tanenbaum, 'French Estimates of Germany's Operational War Plans' in ER May (ed), *Knowing One's Enemies: Intelligence Assessment Before the Two World Wars* (Princeton NJ: Princeton University Press, 1986) p 171.

machine. These included the failure of the Bay of Pigs invasion of Cuba in 1961 (which had miscalculated the strength of the Cuban resistance to an invasion), the Tet Offensive in Vietnam in 1968 (for which there had been intelligence indicators but the US military had underestimated the size and intent of the offensive), and the Soviet invasion of Czechoslovakia in the same year.

The 1973 Yom Kippur war in the Middle East was an important and much-examined example of strategic surprise. The coordinated invasion by Israel's Arab neighbours, Jordan, Egypt, and Syria, was itself a response to a major strategic failure by Egypt in particular in 1967, in which Israel had conducted a devastating pre-emptive strike on the eve of an Arab invasion and virtually quashed the operation before it had begun. The problem in 1967 could be partly ascribed to Egypt's naïve and very public preparations for invasion, a lesson it learnt in 1973 by choosing the time of attack more carefully. Interestingly the problem for Israel in 1973 was one of intelligence 'noise', that is, a period of repeated warnings and threats of mobilization of its neighbours' forces which turned out to be false alarms. Between January and October 1973, the Egyptian army mobilized nineteen times without launching an invasion.[4] Tired of mobilizing in response and wary of crying wolf to senior policy-makers, the Israeli army presumed the latest mobilization to be a false alarm, an assessment which proved to be disastrously wrong.

Further major strategic surprises in more recent history include Saddam Hussein's invasion of Kuwait in 1990 (despite clear evidence of his amassing of forces on the border), the Indian nuclear tests in 1998, the 9/11 attacks, and a miscalculation over Iraq's WMD capabilities prior to the invasion by Western forces in 2003.

Marrin notes that the study of strategic surprise within the field of security studies really developed after the Second World War and in conjunction with the expansion of the Western intelligence capability, with a view to determining if lessons of history could be learnt and future Pearl Harbors prevented.[5] Analysis of many of the above events noted a range of reasons for the strategic failure. In her major study of Pearl Harbor,[6] Wohlstetter argued that the problem was not a lack of data (there had been several pieces of intelligence which, had they been pieced together, would have pointed towards a major attack by the Japanese), but rather in how that data was assessed and perceived. In this analysis, Wohlstetter introduced a concept of 'signal to noise' ratios in intelligence, originally taken from mathematics, whereby important pieces of intelligence could be buried in a welter of information and data.[7] We have seen how a similar problem applied to the Yom Kippur war in 1973: again, there was not a lack of information, but if anything, too much information, and the Israelis were not

[4] M Gladwell, 'Connecting the Dots: the paradoxes of intelligence reform', *The New Yorker*, 10 March 2003, p 83.

[5] S Marrin, 'Preventing Intelligence Failures by Learning from the Past' (2004) 17 *International Journal of Intelligence and CounterIntelligence* 655, 658.

[6] R Wohlstetter, *Pearl Harbor: Warning and Decision* (Stanford CA: Stanford University Press, 1962).

[7] Marrin, 'Preventing Intelligence Failures by Learning from the Past', n 5 above, p 659.

able to determine which were the significant pieces of intelligence and which were not.

In other cases, the strategic surprise can be ascribed to a decision by senior policy-makers to interpret the intelligence in a particular way, or to ignore what it appeared to be telling them. We have already seen that this was the case with Stalin and the German invasion of Russia in 1941.[8]

The Hizbollah-authored truck bombing of French and US army barracks in Beirut in 1983 marked another interesting case, which suggests that the strategic shift in terrorist methodology may have started much earlier than 9/11. The attacks marked a new methodology involving greatly enhanced vehicle-borne improvised explosive devices (VBIEDs), deployed by drivers committing suicide, which delivered a much more devastating blast than had been seen in previous VBIED attacks. In the case of the US marine barracks, 241 people were killed and hundreds more injured. The attacks achieved a rare strategic victory for their perpetrators in that the US and its Western allies decided soon afterwards to remove themselves from Beirut and from direct involvement in the civil war that was underway in Lebanon at the time.

Erik Dahl notes that the attacks were the subject of a number of official enquiries, which asked how the US military could have been 'so completely surprised' by the attack.[9] He goes on to observe that

> a re-examination of the Beirut disaster contradicts both the traditional view of intelligence failure and the conventional explanation of terrorism as a starkly different type of problem for intelligence. Put simply, military intelligence personnel and national intelligence agencies all did a poor job of helping decision-makers prepare for what should have been a foreseeable danger. . . . But far more significant is the lesson for today: this case shows that intelligence officials in Beirut suffered from many of the same failings now being discussed concerning the 9/11 attacks, and suggests that these lessons have yet to be learned.[10]

In this analysis, it was not so much the policy-makers who were to blame for ignoring or misinterpreting the intelligence warnings and data they were receiving, but also the intelligence analysts themselves for not understanding the strategic shift that was occurring in Hizbollah's methodology in the region (the US Embassy in Beirut had been attacked with a massive car bomb earlier the same year).

Notwithstanding the events in Beirut in 1983, the 9/11 attacks were interpreted by many as a paradigm-shifting strategic surprise par excellence. It was also initially seen as a monumental intelligence failure, not only because sixty years of investment and development of intelligence capability had happened

---

[8] DP Steury, 'Joseph Stalin, British Intelligence and Strategic Surprise in 1941' (1998) 42/2 *Studies in Intelligence* 4.

[9] EJ Dahl, 'Warning of Terror: Explaining the Failure of Intelligence Against Terrorism' (2005) 28 *Journal of Strategic Studies* 31.   [10] Ibid, p 32.

since Pearl Harbor, but also because the attacks were planned in a way that was far from clandestine in many respects. As Sims describes:

> While the terrorists' plans were indeed close-held, their operations were boldly open. Most used their true names in making airline reservations, used common addresses and communicated on the Internet—not through privileged diplomatic pouches or hidden radios.[11]

These were not, then, the actions of a well-organized military, or clandestine intelligence officers employing counter-surveillance and deception, unlike many of the previous instances of strategic surprise we have examined. Does the international terrorist threat spearheaded by Al Qaeda at the turn of the century mark a wholly new strategic shift, therefore, and more importantly a fundamentally new challenge to Western intelligence that it seems poorly provisioned to tackle?

We will return to the official analyses of the 9/11 attacks and their conclusions as to the causes of the intelligence failure, but it is worth dwelling on the questions of how much of a strategic surprise these attacks represented. Returning to the literature on strategic surprise, Kam suggested that surprise attacks are constituted by three elements: the attack being contrary to expectations, a failure of advanced warning, and a lack of preparation for the nature of the attack.[12] On the question of the modality of the 9/11 attacks, in terms of using civil airliners as an improvised explosive device, while the scale of the attacks was surprising, Gunaratna noted that Algerian terrorists had planned to crash a hijacked airliner into the Eiffel Tower in Paris in 1994 but were thwarted at the last moment by a successful counter-terrorist operation by the French special forces during a refuelling stop.[13] While this remained an isolated case of such an operation, it did set a potential precedent some years before 9/11.

This was the time that the 'new terrorist' paradigm shift was occurring across Islamist militant terrorism,[14] in which mass casualty attacks against civilians came to the fore as the preferred methodology. Al Qaeda's first major successful operation, namely that of the bombings of the US embassies in Nairobi and Dar es Salaam in August 1998, marked the movement of Al Qaeda to the helm of the Islamist new terrorist wave. It also appeared to be an intelligence failure in two respects: the leaders of the newly-announced Al Qaeda organization, and particularly Ayman Al Zawahiri, had been saying repeatedly on various media that the world would soon see the seriousness of the organization's intent following their announcement in 1996 of a 'World Islamic Front for Jihad Against Jews and Crusaders'.[15] More specifically, intelligence about a potential

---

[11] J Sims, 'Intelligence to Counter Terror: The Importance of All-Source Fusion' (2007) 22 *Intelligence and National Security* 38, 41.

[12] E Kam, *Surprise Attack: The Victim's Perspective* (Cambridge MA: Harvard University Press, 1988) p 8.   [13] R Gunaratna, 'Terror from the Sky' [2001] *Jane's Intelligence Review* 6.

[14] W Laqueur, *No End to War: Terrorism in the Twenty-First Century* (New York: Continuum, 2004) p 143.   [15] J Burke, *Al Qaeda: The True Story of Radical Islam* (London: Penguin, 2004) pp 175–6.

bombing operation had also been gathered in the region by the CIA, and the US Ambassador in Nairobi, Prudence Bushnell, had apparently made repeated requests to Washington for more security.[16]

After the 9/11 attacks, a number of major attacks were perpetrated against Western civilian targets in the name of Al Qaeda, including the 2004 attacks on trains in Madrid, the 2005 attacks on the underground train system in London, and bomb attacks in nightclubs in Bali in 2002 and 2005. All of these re-emphasized the major strategic change that had occurred in terrorist methodology towards mass-casualty attacks, and all of them were, to some degree, intelligence failures. They are also united in that they have all been subject to intense official scrutiny after the event as to what happened, how the intelligence agencies were caught off-guard, and how such attacks could be prevented in the future.

On a more tactical, policing level, the changes in security threat represented by the emergence of mass-casualty terrorism have led to a number of intelligence failures. These have included a combination of misidentifications or erroneous pieces of intelligence on specific threats, coupled with continued failures to deliver forewarning of instances of terrorist attack. In the case of the latter, the failed car-bombing of a London nightclub and Glasgow Airport in 2007, and suicide-bombing attempt in an Exeter restaurant a year later, could have been major attacks of the scale of 7/7 in London had they not been bungled by the attackers. Both cases were similar to 7/7 in that they came 'out of the blue' and involved individuals apparently not at the centre of the intelligence services' radar, suggesting that tactical intelligence failures in these cases continue, even if major attacks have been avoided.

We looked in Chapter 1 at the case of the fatal shooting of Jean Charles de Menezes in London in 2005 following a mistaken piece of intelligence that he was a fugitive Islamist suicide bomber. Approximately one year later, the Metropolitan Police raided a property in the Forest Gate area of London with a view to arresting a group of individuals believed to be plotting a terrorist attack. In the melee of the arrest, one of the suspects was shot and wounded. The case against the two men arrested was subsequently found to be wanting and they were released without charge some days later, presumably as a result of erroneous or underdeveloped lead intelligence. Aside from the intelligence failure, such situations are very damaging to community relations and make the job of the police even harder thereafter. A report at the time noted that, of 895 arrests made under the Terrorism Act 2000 up to September 2005, only 23 had resulted in convictions.[17] It may be that this is an acceptable proportion from a counter-terrorism point of view, but it suggests that tactical intelligence failures—for whatever reasons—are a major factor in the contemporary struggle against terrorism.

---

[16] Gladwell, 'Connecting the Dots', n 4 above, p 85.

[17] A Gillan, R Norton-Taylor, and V Dodd, 'Raided, arrested, released: the price of wrong intelligence', *The Guardian*, 12 June 2006, <http://www.guardian.co.uk/uk/2006/jun/12/terrorism.politics> accessed 30 December 2009.

Points of Failure in the Intelligence Cycle

In the previous chapter we conceptualized the process of intelligence by looking at the constituent parts of the intelligence cycle, noting along the way that the cycle needs to be viewed with care, particularly in the context of modern, more networked threats and security responses. With the same caveats, the cycle also provides a useful framework for understanding where and how intelligence, and the process of gathering it, can go wrong. It can be argued that problems can happen in any part of the cycle leading to unsatisfactory outcomes including tactical or strategic 'surprise', but a useful conceptual model is to view the process as involving two key actors in the process: the intelligence analyst, and the policy-maker. Figure 2.1 depicts where some of the problems and stresses can be found in the interface between these two actors (the list is not an exhaustive one, but generally indicative of the key issues).

The model depicted in Figure 2.1 shows where the policy-makers interface with the intelligence analysts, whether this is between agencies, or within them if an intelligence function exists as a part of overall business. The line between the two dissects the cycle at two key points. First, intelligence analysts will act on an intelligence requirement received from, or discussed with, a 'customer', who is usually a policy-maker in some shape or form. In the case of state intelligence agencies, the customer could be the military or Ministry of Foreign Affairs. In the case of the police, an internal intelligence unit could be providing intelligence to managers or to other officers in the context of an intelligence-led policing

Figure 2.1 Potential points of failure in the Intelligence Cycle

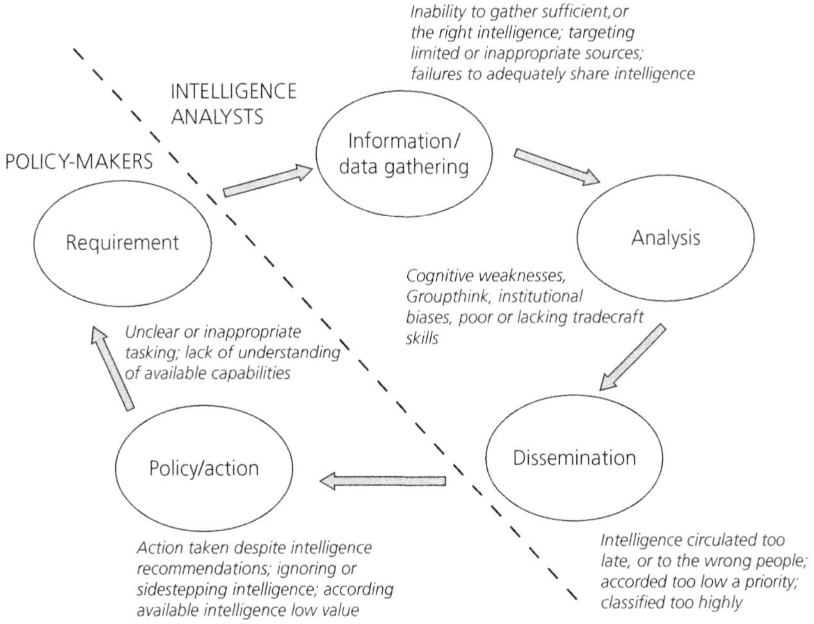

project. As with any transactional process—and it is transactional to differing degrees, even if there is plenty of interplay and communication between the two—the outcome from the intelligence process will be dependent on the input provided. This is the first point at which things can go wrong, and particularly relates to an intelligence requirement being levied which does not adequately or fully represent the true, underlying intelligence need. Often the requirement is not so much for intelligence, as for a very specific pre-ordained piece of information or 'data', in a belief that this will be the answer to the question. This failure to express the true requirement appropriately is often, in turn, the result of a lack of awareness among the policy-makers of the full range of the intelligence analyst's capabilities and sources. Both of the latter will develop over time, and probably at an ever increasing rate as information technology marches forward and intelligence functions make use of new opportunities, so it is not surprising that policy-makers may sometimes be left behind in their understanding of capabilities—essentially, of the 'right questions to ask'. Very often, the result is that policy-makers will ask for the same things they have always requested, in something of a production line process, since it is difficult and time-consuming to challenge norms and processes, and human nature (particularly in bureaucracies) has a preference for doing things the way they have always been done.

The intelligence analysts may therefore provide faulty or lacking intelligence because they have been asked the wrong question in the first place, or not been given enough good quality information about the true underlying intelligence gap they are being asked to address. The second key point in the process at which the analysts and policy-makers interface is in the dissemination stage: here, the results of the intelligence analysis are provided to the policy-maker in some shape or form. There are potential problems at this stage of both content, and organizational weakness. In the case of the former, if the original intelligence requirement was lacking, limited, or inappropriate, the resulting intelligence will often be similarly flawed. The policy-maker may be surprised or disappointed at the results he or she receives, but if the original problem of a lack of awareness of capability exists, then the policy-maker may not know that anything else is possible. The policy-maker may blithely accept the intelligence as the answer, or as 'all there is to know' on the question in hand.

This is where organizational weaknesses can have an effect. The mitigation of poor requirements resulting from limited awareness of capabilities is, as ever, good communication. As Robert Clark noted:

> Intelligence analysts should accept partial responsibility when their customer fails to make use of the intelligence provided, and also accept the challenges to engage the customer during the analysis process and ensure that the resulting intelligence is taken into account when the customer must act.[18]

It is incumbent on intelligence analysts to work hard at communicating with their customers and making sure they are aware of the latest capabilities and

---

[18] RM Clark, *Intelligence Analysis: A Target-Centric Approach* (Washington DC: CQ Press, 2007) p 4.

the various ways in which intelligence questions can be tackled. In turn, it is incumbent on policy-makers to challenge and question what is possible and not take the easy option of levying another data request in production-line fashion. Very often, a whole host of organizational barriers and weaknesses both within and between agencies will cause this interface to be strained and dysfunctional; a point to which we will return.

On the right-hand side of the diagram are situated the intelligence analysts. Having received an intelligence requirement from the policy-makers, it is the analyst's task to consider how best to gather the right information to provide the raw materials for analysis; to subject that information to analysis once it is gathered in; and then to make judgements and assessments on what the information is telling the analyst in terms of an intelligence outcome, and communicate this appropriately to the original customer. At every stage in that process, both 'soft' and 'hard' issues will come into play and provide potential issues that could affect the intelligence outcome adversely. In the case of the former, the training and skill of the analyst is critical, and particularly his or her awareness of cognitive pitfalls that may affect judgement, which we will explore below. In the latter, issues such as resourcing and prioritizing, technical capabilities, and 'bureau-organizational' factors within the intelligence function itself, can play a key role in knocking a situation off course.

Organizational issues within the intelligence function include training and exercising of analysts to improve their tradecraft. The 9/11 Commission report on the attacks in the US noted, among other problems, a 'failure of imagination' in the intelligence and security community to consider ways in which international terrorists would develop their attack methodology (and, indeed, to assess properly the strategic threat posed by Al Qaeda generally). This observation supports the post-event analysis concerning the 1983 bombings in Beirut, which could be ascribed to a failure by intelligence analysts to model Hizbollah's shifting strategy. The 9/11 Commission report suggested it was 'crucial to find a way of routinizing, even bureaucratizing imagination'.[19] In this observation we see the manner in which intelligence analysis is probably both an art (in terms of effectively applying 'imagination') and a science, in terms of making sure the intelligence organizations and departments are structured and run in rigorous ways which ensure analysts are properly trained and can apply their skills to best effect.

Two Dimensions of Intelligence Failure: Analysis and Organization

We have established that problems can emerge at several different stages within the intelligence cycle, and that there are two key actors within this process. To analyze the essence of intelligence failures more deeply, it is worth viewing the situation on a different functional plane. Parker and Stern, in analyzing the

---

[19] National Commission on Terrorist Attacks Upon the United States, *The 9/11 Commission Report* (Washington DC: Superintendent of Documents, US Government Printing Office, 2004) p 344.

enquiries that emerged in the US after 9/11, broke the problem down into three categories: psychological, bureau-organizational, and agenda-political factors. They concluded that the failure to anticipate the attacks was

> due in large measure to a number of interrelated psychopolitical processes that produced a pattern of denial and distraction. Psychological factors contributed to the overvaluation, overconfidence, insensitivity to criticism, and wishful thinking regarding existing US policies and practices.[20]

The wishful thinking had emerged from a number of successful counter-terrorist operations, including the successful thwarting of the 'Millennium' bomb plot that was targeted at Los Angeles but foiled by vigilant security staff. There had also been, as we have seen, a strategic failure to understand the extent of the Al Qaeda threat.

This analysis can be further refined into two key functional processes in which intelligence failures occur: the process of *analysis* itself (which encompasses the psychological factors above), and *organizational* factors, which encompass Parker and Stern's bureau-organizational and agenda-political factors.

Analysis

One of the most influential writers on the question of intelligence analysis tradecraft in recent years has been Richards J Heuer, who was a 45-year veteran of the CIA. His 2005 paper, 'Limits of Intelligence Analysis', provides a very useful practical framework for considering some of the key shortcomings in intelligence analysis which can lead to failure. Although based primarily on his experience of a state intelligence agency, the basic conclusions are fairly generic and applicable to any agency working in intelligence.

Heuer's conclusions are summarized in Figure 2.2. In common with much of his writing, he concentrates particularly on psychological factors within the process of analysis itself (Heuer's own academic background was in philosophy). The first conclusion, concerning the inherent limitations and uncertainty of the intelligence process itself and the need for all involved to adjust their expectations accordingly, applies not only to the producers of intelligence but to its consumers also. We have seen in a number of enquiries following major intelligence failures such as 9/11, the case for the Iraq War of 2003, and the 7/7 terrorist attacks in the UK, that the finger of blame is pointed at the analysis process itself. In the UK, the very comprehensive Butler enquiry following the Iraq War focused on analytical difficulties within the intelligence agencies (while clearing the intelligence assessment process amongst the policy-makers in the shape of the Joint Intelligence Committee of 'active politicisation'), noting that:

> There is ... the risk of 'group think'—the development of a 'prevailing wisdom'. Well-developed imagination at all stages of the intelligence process

---

[20] CF Parker and EK Stern, 'Blindsided? September 11 and the Origins of Strategic Surprise' (2002) 23 *Political Psychology* 601, 621.

Figure 2.2 Summary of Heuer's conclusions in 'Limits of Intelligence Analysis'

- Occasional intelligence surprise is inevitable: policy-makers and the public need to adjust their expectations.
- Human beings have cognitive limitations, which are as important as incompetence or groupthink for causing wrong judgements to be made. The limitations concern:
  - *Perception*
  - *Impressions resist change*
  - *People find it difficult to look at the same information from a different perspective*
  - *People form strong impressions on the basis of very little information, then need solid evidence to change their mind.*
- Mindsets are critical in intelligence analysis (a fixed attitude or state of mind).
- Intelligence analysts do not communicate uncertainty very well.
- Hindsight bias is very powerful.
- Analysis can be improved. Suggestions include:
  - *Red Cell analysis*
  - *Devil's advocacy*
  - *Brainstorming*
  - *What if? analysis*
  - *Alternative futures analysis*
  - *Analysis of Competing Hypotheses*

is required to overcome preconceptions. There is a case for encouraging it by providing for structured challenge, with established methods and procedures, often described as a 'Devil's advocate' or 'red teaming' approach. This may also assist in countering another danger: when problems are many and diverse, on any one of them the number of experts can be dangerously small, and individual, possibly idiosyncratic, views may pass unchallenged.[21]

Lord Butler called for a greater degree of professionalization of the intelligence activity, which led to the creation of a Professional Head of Intelligence Analysis based within the Cabinet Office.[22] As Glees noted in a review of the earlier Hutton enquiry, while 'the use made of intelligence is political', the nature of the Joint Intelligence Committee system in the UK makes it extremely difficult for politicians to exercise undue pressure on the nature of the intelligence assessments they receive.[23]

---

[21] *Review of Intelligence on Weapons of Mass Destruction,* Report of a Committee of Privy Counsellors chaired by The Rt Hon Lord Butler of Brockwell (London: TSO, 2004) p 16.

[22] Intelligence and Security Committee, *Annual Report 2006–2007* (London: TSO, 2008) p 23.

[23] A Glees, 'Evidence-Based Policy or Police-Based Evidence? Hutton and the Government's Use of Secret Intelligence' (2005) 58 *Parliamentary Affairs* 138.

In the US, the Silberman-Robb Commission similarly found much of the root of the intelligence failure in analytical shortcomings. It noted that:

> Most of the major key judgments [reached by the intelligence community] ... either overstated, or were not supported by, the underlying intelligence reporting. .... A series of failures, particularly in analytic trade craft, led to the mischaracterization of intelligence.[24]

Problems were further identified as failures of analysts to question assumptions and apply their tradecraft correctly, and errors in technical and factual analysis.[25] Basic errors were made on technical questions where the answer should have been 'knowable', such as whether the aluminium tubes that Iraq was seeking to acquire were indeed suitable for a gas centrifuge within a nuclear weapons production facility.[26] Separately, the Senate Select Committee report in the US also picked up on Lord Butler's point about the failure to use 'devil's advocacy' and hypothesis-challenging methodologies within the intelligence community at the time.[27] We will conduct a deeper analysis of these specific methodologies in later chapters.

Tradecraft questions in the Iraq case included reliance on isolated and untested sources of human intelligence (Humint), and particularly the infamous Curveball source, who was later identified as a notably unreliable Iraqi defector with plenty of interest in seeing Saddam's regime removed.[28] When he was found to be a fabricator, the problem of intelligence 'layering' came into play, whereby subsequent unchallenged judgements were made on this original erroneous intelligence.[29] Tactical intelligence errors of this kind can be made in the terrorist context, particularly where a source provides information pertaining to a potential current threat to life and there is not the time to verify the source. In January 2002, police in north-east England raided a number of properties looking for a batch of suicide vests on which a Humint source had provided information. Rather like the case of Forest Gate in 2006, the information turned out to be false and the six people arrested were all released without charge some days later.[30] The damage done in this case was political, while in the case of Curveball and Iraq the ramifications were immeasurably greater.

The 'cognitive limitations' identified by Heuer are all things that affect every human being when they are perceiving the world around them and making judgements based on available information, but in the case of intelligence analysts, the task is to raise awareness of these natural limitations of the human

---

[24] D Jehl, 'Report Says Key Assertions Leading to War Were Wrong', *The New York Times*, 9 July 2004, <http://www.nytimes.com/2004/07/09/national/09CND-INTEL>.html?pagewanted=1>, accessed 25 January 2009.

[25] The Commission on the Intelligence Capabilities of the United States Regarding Weapons of Mass Destruction, *Report to the President of the United States* (2005), pp 52–3.

[26] M Phythian, 'The Perfect Intelligence Failure? US Pre-War Intelligence on Iraqi Weapons of Mass Destruction' (2006) 34 *Politics and Policy* 400, 408.   [27] Ibid, p 413.

[28] B Woodward, *State of Denial: Bush at War, Part III* (London: Simon and Schuster, 2006) pp 216–7.   [29] Phythian, 'The Perfect Intelligence Failure?', n 26 above, p 409.

[30] Gillan, Norton-Taylor, and Dodd, 'Raided, arrested, released', n 17 above.

brain and to mitigate and challenge them wherever possible, as the conse-quences of such limitations can be very grave. Most of the techniques that Heuer recommends for improving analysis accordingly, such as Red Cell analysis and competing hypotheses, are in essence about 'challenge'. Returning to our intel-ligence cycle model, challenge can be introduced at every stage of the process to improve the intelligence outcome. This can be conceptualized in terms of the asking of a number of questions by the intelligence analyst as the intelligence cycle unfolds, namely:

- **Requirement**: is the request being levied really the root of the problem? What is the underlying intelligence gap? Is the request really one for a specific piece of information, rather than for intelligence? How certain is the customer of what they really need?

- **Information/data gathering**: am I targeting all the right and best sources of information to help form a judgement on the intelligence question (or am I just collecting the usual material as always)? Could I obtain more or different sources of information with some development work? Do any other agen-cies or partners hold some of the information I need, and could they share it with me?

- **Analysis**: have I tested and checked my assumptions and hypotheses? Are there alternative readings of the information which could be just as valid? Could I have inadvertently exercised bias or selective perception in forming some of my judgements? Have I properly and thoroughly examined all the available data? Do I have enough to form a judgement at this stage? Have I properly assessed uncertainty in the information in forming my judgement?

- **Dissemination**: is the intelligence I have given the customer an appropriate response to their requirement? Have I provided it in a form that is useful for their purposes? Has it reached the right people, at the right time? What further intelligence requirements does it prompt? If there is uncertainty or judgement in my analysis, have I communicated that effectively and appropriately?

- **Policy/Action**: does the intelligence support the action being taken as a result? Has any uncertainty or ambiguity been taken properly into account? Are the policy-makers fully and properly aware and understanding of what the intelligence is saying in coming to their judgements?

These are just examples, and clearly such questions will not always be appro-priate and can run the risk of bureaucratizing or slowing the process if not implemented appropriately, but the idea is that the analyst needs constantly to challenge his or her actions and judgements while moving through the intel-ligence cycle, to provide assurance that cognitive and other limitations have not been allowed to exercise undue influence on the process without being spotted. Challenge, in short, needs to be an integral part of the intelligence process.

A second, very useful analysis of limitations in the intelligence analysis process is provided by Hendrickson in his 2008 paper, 'Critical Thinking in Intelligence

Analysis'.[31] In it, Hendrickson offers a 'new foundational paradigm' for defining critical thinking and addressing the 'unique challenges of intelligence analysis'.[32] He notes that intelligence analysis is essentially about reasoning in the face of available data, and, as Heuer observed, reasoning is affected by generic cognitive challenges. He further notes that 'analysis occurs through navigation in multiple directions on a "network of analysis" with four major nodes: data, information, knowledge, and understanding'.[33] The key point here, is that the analysis process is not a linear 'production line', but something that moves back and forth between data and understanding, and all points between, as an analysis is built up. In this model, the cognitive methods of critical thinking will be crucial in successfully moving an analyst through to knowledge and understanding. Hendrickson notes that 'four central problems of reasoning in intelligence derive from the place of knowledge in the network of analysis'.[34] These are characterized as:

- **'Not Usually Enough'**—an **Insufficiency** of data on which the analyst bases his or her judgements usually exists both in terms of the data's scope and its reliability.

- **'Not Always Relevant'**—there is usually an **Irrelevancy** in much of the information and data that the analyst has available in forming a judgement, but which parts are relevant and which are not will not always be easy to define, especially in the early stages of an analysis.

- **'Not Ever Inevitable'**—the problem of **Indeterminacy** of data is that life, and human beings, do not always act and do things in logical or 'deterministic' ways. Much of the gathered information about the words and actions of a terrorist, for example, will not necessarily form any sort of useful indicator as to what that terrorist is planning to do next. Unfortunately, it is a common and flawed mindset experienced by intelligence analysts that information on a target is naturally deterministic and builds up to an overall picture, like the pieces of a jigsaw. In reality, this will often not be the case.

- **'Not Always Useful'**—the fourth problem of **Instrumentality** is a subtle variation on the problems above, and concerns the fact that analysts will acquire data and knowledge in an attempt to address very specific questions, often under time constraints, and they will want and need that knowledge to be instrumental to forming a judgement on the question in hand. This runs the risk of placing constraints on which knowledge and data is gathered and how useful it is ultimately to the final judgement.[35]

Again, if Hendrickson's paradigm is taken as a potentially useful model for structuring and testing the intelligence analysis process, it can be usefully rendered in

---

[31] N Hendrickson, 'Critical Thinking in Intelligence Analysis' (2008) 21 *International Journal of Intelligence and CounterIntelligence* 679.

[32] Ibid, p 679.   [33] Ibid, p 680.   [34] Ibid, p 680.   [35] Ibid, pp 681–2.

the process as a number of 'challenge' questions that the analyst asks of him or herself while moving towards an intelligence judgement, such as:

- Have I got enough data to form a suitable judgement here, or are there still too many gaps?
- Is all of the information I have used to support my judgement actually relevant?
- Is the way in which I have chained together pieces of data and events a reliable indicator of a particular 'story', or are some of those events potentially unconnected and irrelevant to one another?
- By answering a specific question, have I been unduly constrained in the data I have gathered, and could I have gathered some other more useful data which could have allowed me to form a better intelligence judgement in the time available?

Much of the analysis of intelligence failure has been centred around psychology. This has highlighted the fact that human beings, as Frühling describes them, are 'limited in their cognitive, mental and psychological abilities to process information'.[36] Moreover:

> Human nature leads to cognitive traps—blunders and lapses as well as errors, i.e purposeful action on the basis of wrong assumptions or faulty reasoning. In a social context, it leads to translational uncertainty if information has to be exchanged between individuals, and the reinforcement of incorrect mental models through 'groupthink' and similar processes.[37]

Thus, intelligence analysts, like all human beings, are not built very well to be able to process large amounts of complex information and derive accurate judgements. They suffer from a number of cognitive limitations and flaws, which can become amplified when analysts work together on a problem and build a collaborative judgement of a situation. The danger with this assertion is that it can lead one to think there is nothing that can be done about it—we are just built that way. Clearly we cannot change the way our brains work and must be alive to their processing weaknesses, but we can assist them with techniques and sophisticated data handling and mining mechanisms, and we can ensure that analysts are 'self aware' of the cognitive pitfalls they can fall into, and go into situations with their eyes open. We have seen how a number of official enquiries into intelligence failure on both sides of the Atlantic have suggested professionalization of the analytical trade, and the deployment of hypothesis-challenging techniques such as devil's advocacy. These will not take away the uncertainty inherent in intelligence analysis, but they may help to improve performance.

---

[36] S Frühling, 'Uncertainty, Forecasting and the Difficulty of Strategy' (2006) 25 *Comparative Strategy* 19, 23.   [37] Ibid, p 23.

Organization

However effective or otherwise the intelligence analysts are at their job, we have seen that intelligence is more than just an information product: it is also a process and a system of agencies which interact in sometimes complex ways. For this reason, major intelligence failures have often been followed with intense scrutiny of the organization of the intelligence function, and whether the structure can be organized differently.

Returning to the question of the case for the Iraq War, the question of the limited Humint source Curveball was indeed an analytical tradecraft failure, but we are reminded by the deputy chief of the CIA's Iraq Task Force, who provided testimony to the Senate Select Committee enquiry at the time, that the failure was also that of the policy-makers. When the question of Curveball's reliability was raised, he was quoted as saying:

> Let's keep in mind the fact that this war's going to happen regardless of what Curve Ball said or didn't say, and that the Powers That Be probably aren't terribly interested in whether Curve Ball knows what he's talking about.[38]

One of the leading academic researchers of intelligence failure, Richard Betts, noted that:

> Observers who see notorious intelligence failures as egregious often infer that disasters can be avoided by perfecting norms and procedures for analysis and argumentation. This belief is illusory. Intelligence can be improved marginally, but not radically, by altering the analytic system. The illusion is also dangerous if it abets overconfidence that systemic reforms will increase the predictability of threats. The use of intelligence depends less on the bureaucracy than on the intellects and inclinations of the authorities who use it.[39]

Betts observed that major intelligence failures are often met with analyses of the intelligence structure and machinery, and often produce recommendations both for reorganization and for 'changes in operating norms'.[40] Turner has noted that there is a growing debate in the US about whether the historical development of a decentralized and fragmented intelligence sector, with a strict delineation between foreign and domestic intelligence gathering, is not fit for purpose in the face of contemporary security threats. A particular focus is the possible creation of a domestic intelligence agency along the lines of the Security Service (MI5) in the UK, centred on countering espionage, terrorism, and threats to the national security of the state.[41] Experience in the UK and other modern democratic countries has shown that domestic intelligence gathering does not necessarily have to compromise civil liberties and freedoms if it is mandated and

---

[38] US Congress, Senate Select Committee on Intelligence, *The US Intelligence Community's Prewar Intelligence Assessments on Iraq*, 108th Congress, 2nd session, S-Report 108-301 (Washington DC: US Government Printing Office, 2004) p 249.

[39] Betts, 'Analysis, War and Decision', n 2 above, p 61.   [40] Ibid, p 63.

[41] M Turner, *Why Secret Intelligence Fails* (Dulles VA: Potomac Books, 2006) pp 59–60.

managed correctly (this is the primary fear militating against the formation of such an agency in the US).

In the UK, one of the key controlling factors is that MI5 does not have its own powers of executive action; its role is merely to generate intelligence leads for other law enforcement bodies to take forward in appropriate—and lawful—ways. This is not the case in a number of other countries where such a structure can lead to abuses of power by agencies which both gather the intelligence and act on it, with weak authority or oversight of the whole process.

The question is an important one for the US to consider in the light of changing threats and strategic issues, although experience suggests that creation of yet another competing and overlapping agency may compound problems if it is not combined with a fundamental root-and-branch reform and rationalization of the whole intelligence structure and oversight process. This will be a hard proposal to design, let alone to sell, in the US, even in the light of incidents such as 9/11 and the Iraq War.

In the UK, as in many other countries, various experiments have been conducted in the organizational structure of the intelligence function, particularly in the policing and national security arena. The National Criminal Intelligence Service (NCIS) was launched in the UK in 1992 in the immediate aftermath of the post-Berlin Wall era, when the national security picture in the West was changing rapidly. The new agency brought together seconded officers from the police, HM Customs and Excise, and small numbers from other departments such as the Home Office, with a remit to collate and share intelligence on key security threats emerging from serious and organized crime. The cultural shift towards sharing of information and cooperation across agencies was a huge one, and proved to be something of a hurdle to overcome in the early years. In 2006, NCIS was merged into another new body, the Serious Organised Crime Agency (SOCA), which brought together intelligence-gathering and investigative functions from NCIS and other departments such as HM Revenue and Customs, and provided an executive law enforcement function. SOCA—the much heralded 'British FBI'—has yet to make a major mark at the time of writing, and there have been reports in the press of the agency having 'serious problems'.[42]

Aside from a natural but sometimes misguided instinct to reorganize when things go wrong in the intelligence world, many observers have noted a number of 'organizational pathologies' which are built into the intelligence structure, and which inevitably lead to failures. In the US context, Turner noted that 'structural pathologies permeate the entire intelligence process, making them the most significant barriers to successful intelligence'.[43] In a study of intelligence-led policing across several countries in the West, Sheptycki produced a structured model of 'organizational pathologies in Police intelligence systems', which is

---

[42] A Davies, 'SOCA's "major problems"', *Channel 4 News*, 23 January 2007, <http://www.channel4.com/news/articles/uk/socas%20major%20problems/187620>, accessed 30 December 2009.

[43] Turner, *Why Secret Intelligence Fails*, n 40 above, p 53.

Figure 2.3 Sheptycki's 'Organizational Pathologies'

- Digital divide
- Linkage blindness
- Noise
- Intelligence overload
- Non-reporting
- Intelligence gaps
- Duplication
- Institutional friction
- Intelligence-hoarding and information silos
- Defensive data concentration
- Differences in occupational subculture

worth dwelling on here.[44] Figure 2.3 summarizes the list of pathologies in the model which hinder the successful production of intelligence and can lead to failures.

Sheptycki noted that the process of intelligence production within a policing environment is fundamentally about the way in which information moves around within and between departments and agencies:

> What cannot be contested is that intelligence systems models are based on hierarchies of information flow. Indeed, one diagram used to illustrate the intelligence process in the Dutch police system depicts a pyramid with three 'levels' (read from the top; national files, regional files and investigations files).[45]

Numerous examples have illustrated how blockages in the flow of information can lead to serious intelligence failures. In the UK, a case concerning failures to share information between police districts, and between different sectors of government (in this case between social services and the police) was that of the 'Soham murders' of two young girls in 2002. The resultant Bichard enquiry found there to be serious failures in sharing information on the killer, Ian Huntley, between Humberside and Cambridgeshire police constabularies, which may have contributed to him being able to secure a job as a school caretaker in the latter district despite having been accused of sexual offences in the former area. In the case of Humberside, the Bichard report noted that:

> One of the key failings was the inability of Humberside Police and Social Services to identify Huntley's behaviour pattern remotely soon enough. That was because both viewed each case in isolation and because Social Services failed to share information effectively with the police.

---

[44] J Sheptycki, 'Organizational Pathologies in Police Intelligence Systems' (2004) 1 *European Journal of Criminology* 307.   [45] Ibid, p 312.

It was also because, as the Humberside Chief Constable admitted in his evidence, there were 'systemic and corporate' failures in the way in which Humberside Police managed their intelligence systems.[46]

Sheptycki's organizational pathologies, identified through the findings of a UK Home Office study, plus interviews with the Royal Canadian Mounted Police, Swedish police and customs, and Dutch National Police Service, can be summarized as involving volumes of information, how that information moves around, and cultural issues. Specifically:

- **Volumes of information**: in some cases there can be too much information gathered, leading to failures to discern what is relevant as intelligence (noise). Intelligence overload can place a bureaucratic burden on the intelligence function. In other cases, there is not enough information allowing an intelligence judgement to be made (intelligence gaps).

- **How information moves around**: some of the problems here are technical, such as incompatible computer systems between departments, agencies, or even between different sets of data within the same agency (digital divide), while some are procedural (such as non-reporting, which often arises from the act of logging information being too burdensome a process and thus often ignored or sidestepped by intelligence officers). The problems that arise from these issues can be linkage blindness (where incompatibilities between data or lack of sharing mean that connections are not easily spotted) or duplication, where the same data and information is wastefully reproduced in different places. The former problem was essentially at the root of the Bichard observations in the case of the Soham murders.

- **Cultural issues**: these are often still rife in many intelligence sectors, and can operate at many different levels. Within the police, there is some evidence that civilian intelligence officers are sometimes viewed differently and not altogether favourably by seasoned police officers.[47] Between agencies, rivalries and perceived equities over sources of data can cause all manner of difficulties in sharing and pooling that data for collective intelligence gain. This can lead to such problems as defensive data concentration and information hoarding.

It is clear from this analysis, therefore, that while there may often be problems in the analytical process itself, intelligence failures can often not be explained away by addressing these issues alone. This is why so many of the post-failure government enquiries have focused on both analytical and organizational factors.

Betts argued that 'producers of intelligence have been culprits less often than consumers'.[48] Yet we have seen how, in a number of major enquiries into contemporary intelligence failures, such as 9/11, the 7/7 bombings in London, and the hunt for

---

[46] *The Bichard Inquiry Report* (London: TSO, 2004) p 2.
[47] J Ratcliffe, *Intelligence-Led Policing* (Cullompton: Willan, 2008) p 161.
[48] Betts, 'Analysis, War and Decision', n 2 above, p 67.

WMD in Iraq, fingers of blame of varying degrees of assertiveness have been pointed at the intelligence analysts themselves and their processes of investigating and assessing the intelligence before them. Lowenthal is critical of this process, noting:

> Connecting the Dots. This is one of the post 9/11 phrases that has entered into popular lexicon as one of the ways to judge intelligence. It is also one of the most unperceptive, misleading, demeaning and mean-spirited things ever said about any intelligence organization.[49]

A former member of the intelligence community himself, Lowenthal argues that the suggestion that the task prior to 9/11 was a 'simple' one of piecing together the various intelligence indicators that existed and making sure they were shared across the community, was a gross under-estimation of the difficulties faced by the intelligence sector in anticipating a strategic shift of the nature and scale of 9/11, and the tactical task of positing exactly where and when Al Qaeda would attack. Ironically, the problem a few years later with Iraq was the opposite one of 'connecting too many dots, or of connecting dots that were not there'.[50]

In the UK policing sector, one of the responses to a recognition of the importance of organizational factors in intelligence performance was the establishment of the National Intelligence Model (NIM), launched by NCIS in 2000 and mandated as the process for handling criminal intelligence across all constabularies in England and Wales. Despite some examination of specific analytical techniques and products, ranging from network analysis to operational intelligence assessments, the NIM does not offer any guidance on the core analytical process and the cognitive aspects central to it, and is perceived by most users and observers as fundamentally a 'management tool'.[51] The NIM is much more about how intelligence is processed and moved through the police management machinery than about how analysts conduct their tradecraft, reflecting the importance of organizational issues in improving intelligence performance.

Conclusions

It is appropriate to consider the analytical capabilities of analysts in the intelligence community, and to ensure that they are as skilled and professional in their work as they can be, given the consequences of sloppy or uneducated analysis. This process involves raising awareness of natural cognitive limitations of the human brain in processing and assessing information, and constantly challenging hypotheses and judgements. This was broadly the recommendation of Lord Butler in the UK following his review of intelligence gathering on WMD targets. We will see in later chapters how exercise and techniques can be developed to hone these skills among intelligence analysts and to counter the cognitive weaknesses of the human brain in the face of large amounts of complex data.

---

[49] MM Lowenthal, 'Towards a Reasonable Standard for Analysis: How Right, How Often on Which Issues?' (2008) 23 *Intelligence and National Security* 303, 306.   [50] Ibid, p 306.

[51] Ratcliffe, *Intelligence-Led Policing*, n 46 above, p 113.

It is also appropriate, however, to consider organizational issues in tandem with an examination of the analytical process, since these can represent a number of inbuilt institutional problems which will ensure that intelligence failures still happen, even if the analytical function is improved. Chief among these damaging 'organizational pathologies' is the question of how data is moved around, and particularly how it is shared within and between datasets and agencies. Despite this repeatedly emerging as an issue in every major enquiry into an intelligence failure, it is still a very present issue in just about every intelligence structure across the world.

In the context of modern security threats such as terrorism, some have argued that the performance of intelligence analysts can be improved by 'effective information technology' to gather, process, mine, and extract large amounts of complex data relating to target behaviours, and by deepened subject-matter expertise to understand the nature of targets in detail.[52] In the case of the latter, many in the intelligence profession have realized the growing importance of 'Open Source intelligence' such as media, technical, and academic reporting and analysis, which is much more abundant and more available than ever before. This underpinned the decision by the Director of National Intelligence in the US, whose post was created in the light of recommendations following 9/11, to open a major new Open Source Centre in 2006 to support the work of the intelligence community.[53] Others have looked to other professions, such as medicine, to determine if useful comparisons could be made and lessons learnt from improved performance in that area, noting that intelligence analysis is similar at a generic level to analyzing a set of symptoms and developing a diagnosis.[54]

Whether this will prove to be a fruitful avenue of enquiry remains to be seen, but a measure of its success will be how well it deals with the very particular problems and challenges posed by the international terrorism threat, as it is faced by intelligence agencies at the beginning of the twenty-first century. It is to this issue that we now turn.

Key Points

- Intelligence failure is one of the most prolific areas of study within Intelligence Studies.
- Initial analysis of intelligence failure was focused on the military and political 'strategic surprise' dimension, and grew particularly after the Pearl Harbor attack in the Second World War.

---

[52] MJ Cook, 'New Uses of Intelligence Needed to Counter Terrorism', *RUSI/Jane's Homeland Security and Resilience Monitor*, 1 May 2004, p 3.

[53] 'DNI aims to boost intelligence analysis', *Oxford Analytica*, 10 January 2006.

[54] S Marrin and JD Clemente, 'Improving Intelligence Analysis by Looking to the Medical Profession' (2005) 18 *International Journal of Intelligence and Counterintelligence* 707, 708.

- Generic lessons can be learnt about these examples of failure, and the official enquiries that followed many of them, for all intelligence practitioners.

- The Intelligence Cycle model points to stress areas in the process in the interface between the two main actors in the cycle: the policy-makers and the intelligence analysts. These occur at the requirement and dissemination points.

- Further analysis identifies two key dimensions within the Intelligence Cycle, which account for most of the examples of weakness and failure. These are the analysis, and organizational dimensions.

- Heuer and Hendrickson identified useful models for understanding cognitive and information-flow limitations which affect intelligence analysis and its chances of failing.

- Sheptycki described a useful model for categorizing and understanding organizational weaknesses which can lead to failure in the intelligence process, in the shape of his 'organizational pathologies'.

- Strategies for confronting these weaknesses and limitations include the introduction of 'challenge' at all stages of the Intelligence Cycle.

3

From Third Reich to Al Qaeda: Changing Intelligence Targets, Evolving Challenge

We have seen in previous chapters how intelligence is linked to concepts of national security, in terms of the targets on which the agencies are mandated to gather information, and the way in which the intelligence sector is structured and operates. We have also seen how the concept of national security has changed considerably over the years, and particularly since the end of the Cold War with the emergence of 'transnational' threats such as international organized crime, and terrorism.

From a policing perspective, these changes have posed questions as to the difference between 'high' and 'low' policing—terminology which we will examine in more detail—and how intelligence can and should span the divide. More generally, the changes have included questions of changing sources of intelligence and data, offering both threats and opportunities; the increasing imperative of sharing intelligence across boundaries; and difficult questions of ethics and proportionalities posed by a modern intelligence and security structure in the twenty-first century.

In this chapter we examine the changing security paradigm in more detail, and relate it to how the definitions and processes of intelligence gathering have changed and developed in the years leading up to the present. We take a particular look at the question of the terrorist threat, which has evolved to become one of the highest priority subjects for intelligence and security at the beginning of this century. The emergence of international terrorism has also brought law enforcement and state security agencies closer together in complex ways.

To begin, it is worth recapping on the key developments in security threats over history and the implications of this narrative for the unfolding intelligence picture.

The Evolving Threat

We have mentioned that, in the UK, counter-terrorism work as we understand it today effectively began in 1883 with the formation of the Special Irish Branch by the Metropolitan Police in London, later renamed simply the Special Branch as it took on a wider range of work against extremist and terrorist activity. The Special Irish Branch was formed in response to a number of improvised bomb attacks in the capital by Irish Republicans in the shape of the Fenians. Intelligence gathering at this time was primarily in the shape of human intelligence (Humint), as the police attempted to cultivate sources close to the terrorists who could provide tactical information on terrorist movements and plans.

The two world wars

At around the same time, the prospect of war in Europe was looming. As the twentieth century began, all of the major European powers were keen to gather intelligence on each other's military capabilities and intentions, as a struggle for power and control began to emerge across the continent. It was in 1909 that the Secret Service Bureau was formed in London, with a particular focus on counter-espionage against German spies believed to be operating in Britain at the time and gathering information on the size and nature of her military forces, but it also had an offensive overseas espionage role. The two branches of the Bureau were headed by Captain Vernon Kell (counter-espionage within the UK) and Captain Mansfield Smith-Cumming (espionage overseas). Kell's department later became the Security Service (MI5) and Cumming's, the Secret Intelligence Service (SIS, or MI6).

Interestingly, the model of an internal security service has been followed in many countries, notably France, Germany, Canada, and Israel, many of them because of an internal terrorist threat. In other countries, very notably the US, there is no such internal security service, although developments in the world of terrorism have increasingly led to calls for there to be one, a point to which we will return. Returning to the UK model, however, we can already see in the parallel formation of the Security Service and the Special Branch in the police what Swallow calls 'the archaic and confused nature of the British response to terrorism'.[1] The former head of the Security Service, MI5, noted that it took twenty years after the first IRA bomb went off on the British mainland for the Security Service and Special Branch to resolve divisions of responsibility over

---

[1] P Swallow, 'Proactive Terrorist Investigations and the Use of Intelligence' (2003) 10 *Journal of Financial Crime* 378, 381.

the terrorist threat within Britain.[2] The interface between state security agency and law enforcement on the question of terrorist intelligence, particularly in the case of a domestic threat such as that from Northern Ireland in the UK, is clearly complex and not without potential for confusion and stress.

Returning to the First World War, Humint operations were the main focus, although they were achieved with highly variable degrees of success. Kennedy notes that the British received most of their intelligence on German military capabilities prior to the war from newspapers and reports from the British ambassador in Berlin.[3] The efforts of defence attachés to uncover useful information were 'amateurish' at best, and much more resource was put into trying to find what was believed—erroneously as it transpired—to be a large army of German spies in Britain.[4] Technical intelligence gathering was not highly developed at this stage, with the exception of some interception of telegrams and radio traffic, and observation of border areas, sometimes using overflights from aircraft, to observe military preparations and strategic activities such as the building of new railway lines to bring troops to the front line.

With the arrival of the Second World War, intelligence gathering became much more industrialized and more central to the state's security activities. In Britain, the SIS became the sole agency responsible for foreign intelligence gathering, and from 1923 it was also responsible for the Government Code and Cipher School (GCCS), a forerunner to the GCHQ signals intelligence (Sigint) agency, which was responsible for intercepting and deciphering military and diplomatic radio communications from enemy countries. The performance of these intelligence capabilities in the run-up to the Second World War was patchy, with some successes at anticipating Hitler's intentions balanced by some successful deception operations by the Third Reich's *Abwehr* agency in Germany, and structural weaknesses within the British military and intelligence structure. Watt identifies these weaknesses to consist of many of the issues we have seen in the previous chapter, namely a combination of imperfections in intelligence-gathering apparatus (including a lack of radio communications for relaying messages back from the field), imperfections in the process for communicating intelligence up through government, and 'psychological or other barriers to the appreciation of such intelligence by the policy-makers'.[5] On the latter point it was often the case that the intelligence was viewed with suspicion and scepticism by some in senior positions, especially if it did not fit with information normally gained from diplomatic circles.

---

[2] M Herman, *Intelligence Power in Peace and War* (Cambridge: Cambridge University Press, 2008) pp 308–9.

[3] PM Kennedy, 'Great Britain before 1914' in ER May (ed), *Knowing One's Enemies: Intelligence Assessment Before the Two World Wars* (Princeton NJ: Princeton University Press, 1986) p 179.

[4] D French, 'Spy Fever in Britain, 1900–1915' (1978) 21 *The Historical Journal* 355, 362.

[5] D Cameron Watt, 'British Intelligence and the Coming of the Second World War in Europe' in May, *Knowing One's Enemies*, n 3 above, p 261.

During the war itself, covert and technical intelligence-gathering techniques took a huge step forward, and became central to tactical and strategic success in the war. The jewel in the crown was the developing capability to break high-grade military cipher traffic, both in Europe in the case of the German 'Enigma' enciphered communications, and in the Pacific in the case of the 'Magic' decrypts of Japanese military and diplomatic traffic. In Britain, the work of the GCCS against Enigma communications, based in Bletchley Park, scored a major breakthrough in strategic capability and turned the tide in the naval war in the Atlantic, against the Germans. At the height of its activities, some 10,000 personnel are believed to have been working at Bletchley Park.[6] The Colossus machine that was built at the station to process intercepts and deliver decrypts, kept secret for many years afterwards, is now believed to have been the first computer to be used in an operational capacity.

In addition to Sigint, photo-reconnaissance or Imagery Intelligence (Imint) received a further boost in significance during the war, allowing observation of troop movements on the ground, and of the development of installations such as the radio-beam systems used by the Germans to guide bombers to targets in England.[7] In military situations, where penetration of human agents on the ground can be difficult and highly dangerous, such technical methods of intelligence gathering can become much more significant.

The Cold War

With that said, it was the post-war period, and the freeze of capabilities in the Cold War, that gave even more credence to technical intelligence-gathering techniques. For much of the Cold War, the West suffered a pitiful lack of human intelligence capabilities behind the Iron Curtain, with the exception of some much welcomed dissident sources such as Oleg Gordievsky. Signals intelligence may also have been difficult due to military and diplomatic ciphers, relying heavily on 'traffic analysis' of the externals of communications,[8] although, as Herman points out, 'neither side has revealed its Cold War successes and failures'.[9] What does seem apparent is that the Soviet Union invested a great deal in Sigint, developing a capability said to be five times larger than that of the US.[10]

Partly for reasons of Humint being very difficult during the Cold War, Imint derived from U-2 flights proved to be a critical capability, until the Soviets shot down one of the aircraft over its territory in 1960, capturing its pilot, Francis Gary Powers, and recovering a valuable insight into the technology of the plane. Nevertheless, imagery taken by a U-2 over Cuba in 1962 proved to be a pivotal piece of intelligence for the US at the height of the Cuban Missile Crisis, allowing President Kennedy to confront Soviet President Krushchev over the placement

---

[6] M Smith, *Station X: The Codebreakers of Bletchley Park* (London: Channel 4 Books, 1998) p 176.

[7] AN Shulsky and GJ Schmitt, *Silent Warfare: Understanding the World of Intelligence* (Washington DC: Potomac Books, 2002) p 23.   [8] Ibid, p 28.

[9] Herman, *Intelligence Power in Peace and War*, n 2 above, p 68.   [10] Ibid.

of strategic ballistic missiles in Cuba, despite denials, and eventually to reach an agreement which defused the crisis. This was an example of highly critical covert technical intelligence product serving and influencing the policy-makers at the highest level.

By this time, the U-2 capability was already in the process of being supplemented by satellite imagery capabilities. The programme in the US was headed by the National Reconnaissance Office, whose existence was highly secret until relatively recently. The multi-billion dollar programme to develop and launch ever more capable satellites to conduct Imint has continued apace, and delivered important pieces of intelligence on remote military installations, troop movements and build-ups, missile testing, and even such issues as massacres in Bosnia and Rwanda. Yet, the case of the 'first Gulf war' in 1991 showed the limitation of these technical intelligence capabilities. Imagery had shown that Saddam Hussein was amassing troops on the border with Kuwait in the summer of 1990, but the intelligence did not offer any clues as to what he planned to do next. That he followed through and invaded Kuwait was something of a strategic surprise to the West. As Gill and Phythian noted:

> employing satellite reconnaissance to compensate for an absence or lack of HUMINT can induce a false sense of confidence. There is a limit to what satellite reconnaissance can reveal, particularly with respect to intent.[11]

As events a decade later proved with the ill-fated second expedition against Iraq, all the technical intelligence might in the world could not unravel the mystery of Iraq's WMD capability. Images of installations and factories did not supply the intelligence needed, and in the end, the case for the war was built on a flimsy set of Humint intelligence which proved to be fundamentally flawed. The limitations of imagery are not least because every country in the world is now well aware of the satellite capabilities of the US, and knows the ways to avoid revealing secrets, whether it is through building sensitive installations underground, restricting activities to periods in which the well-known orbits of the satellites are not overhead, or deploying deliberate deception techniques (although it appears that, in the case of Iraq, there was nothing to hide).

For the overseas intelligence agencies in the West, the Cold War marked a prolonged period of work against an essentially static and in many ways predictable target. The job was to uncover military capabilities and movements, and map these to any clues of expansionist intent. The target was very large, did not move very much and was clear to see, even if it made proactive technical intelligence gathering difficult, and the chance of gaining Humint access to top-level decision-makers was very thin. For the intelligence agencies, the protracted nature of the Cold War allowed a long period of expansion and development in technical capability, which Rathmell describes as an 'intelligence factory',

---

[11] P Gill and M Phythian, *Intelligence in an Insecure World* (Cambridge: Polity, 2006) pp 74–5.

showing similarity to 'Fordist modes of production'.[12] In this sense, items of intelligence on the current disposition of Soviet forces in Eastern Europe, and their movements at times of exercise and deployment, would roll off the production line and be provided to military customers in the West. The contrast between this situation and the rapidly unfolding events unleashed by the collapse of the Berlin Wall in 1989 were a considerable shock to the Western intelligence powers, from which it is not clear if they have yet recovered.

Post-Cold War

Writing shortly after the strategic shock of 9/11 in the US, Bruce Berkowitz examined many of the aspects of intelligence failure in the US system which could have led to the disaster, and particularly to the manner in which the intelligence challenges had changed with the arrival of Al Qaeda. He noted that

> whereas the Cold War enemy was big and noisy, today's terrorist organisations have 'small signatures' and a 'low signal-to-noise ratio'. . . . As a result, intelligence agencies must be fiercely proactive in collecting information on terrorists and must rustle the bushes to find a threat that is hiding. That requires different methodologies and a different operational mindset than prevailed during the Cold War. It also requires new sorts of relationships between intelligence analysts and intelligence users.[13]

Berkowitz examined three key areas in which the US intelligence machinery, and particularly the CIA, had changed (or rather not changed) in step with the evolving intelligence challenges it faced. These were:

- 'An alleged American infatuation with technology, especially satellite imagery and intercepted communications signals (IMINT and SIGINT)'.[14]
- Difficulties over understanding the manner in which counter-terrorist intelligence crossed over with law enforcement intelligence, and structural difficulties in the US intelligence machinery in making these interfaces work.
- An old paradigm of intelligence tradecraft, which had focused for years on diplomatic circles and locations, either in cultivating direct Humint sources in foreign governments, or cultivating sources in relevant ministries and agencies who could provide second-hand intelligence on the real targets.

On the first issue, we have seen how the particular challenge of the Cold War target had meant both that Humint was very difficult, but also that technical intelligence-gathering methods could be extraordinarily effective, such as U-2 flights or satellite imagery. The enormous stakes of falling out of step with the adversary also meant that huge investment was available to develop such technical intelligence-gathering methods, especially in the US. On the second issue,

---

[12] A Rathmell, 'Towards Postmodern Intelligence' (2002) 17/3 *Intelligence and National Security* 87, 91.   [13] B Berkowitz, 'Intelligence and the War on Terrorism', *Orbis*, Spring 2002, pp 291–2.
[14] Ibid, p 294.

we have seen in the previous chapter the organizational difficulties, especially in the US where there is no domestic security agency as such, which have led to obstacles being placed in the way of agencies such as the FBI communicating effectively with the likes of the CIA.

The question of over-reliance on technical methods of gathering intelligence is interesting when considering the most effective ways of tackling organizations such as Al Qaeda. We saw in the previous chapter the analysis of the Hizbollah bombings in Beirut in 1983, in the context of strategic surprise and intelligence failure. Some of the experts who analyzed the intelligence indicators for the bombings post-incident, such as Brian Jenkins, concluded that one of the key failures was the lack of Humint on the terrorist group, and that this is an inherent problem with contemporary terrorist organizations which are very close-knit and extremely difficult to penetrate.[15] Dahl notes that the importance of Humint to counter-terrorism operations is identified by many analysts both of terrorism and of intelligence.[16] In the light of intelligence 'noise' representing a blizzard of unfocused threats and predictions, a source close to the operational thinking of the terrorist group would help to identify the key pieces of intelligence to note. However, over-emphasis of the Humint issue can risk downplaying the importance of raw intelligence analysis skills deployed against what is available.[17]

In an analysis of Sigint deployed against terrorist targets, Matthew Aid reported mixed results.[18] Some notable intelligence successes appear to have been had in the 1980s by the US National Security Agency and GCHQ against state-sponsored terrorism in the Middle East. But the Al Qaeda organization proved to be much more difficult, despite some early successes after 2001 against the core leadership's satellite phones being used in Afghanistan.[19] As a target, Al Qaeda proved to be much more difficult than the state-sponsored terrorist groups such as Hizbollah, in that it is much more loosely structured, and has more diffuse and less organized channels of communications.

The former head of Mossad, Ephraim Halevy, noted that Sigint had become 'the high priest of intelligence' in the US and blinded analysts to other possibilities.[20] Aid further notes that:

> The Israeli military's experience fighting Hizballah in southern Lebanon during the 1990s only serves to reinforce the notion that Sigint is no substitute for good Humint in counter-terrorist operations, especially when the terrorist groups in question limit their use of telecommunications in order to preserve operational security.[21]

---

[15] B Jenkins, *Lessons of Beirut: Testimony Before the Long Commission* (Santa Monica CA: Rand, 1984), <http://www.beirut-memorial.org/history/long.html>, accessed 31 December 2009.

[16] EJ Dahl, 'Warning of Terror: Explaining the Failure of Intelligence Against Terrorism' (2005) 28 *Journal of Strategic Studies* 31, 36.   [17] Ibid.

[18] MM Aid, 'All Glory is Fleeting: Sigint and the Fight Against International Terrorism' (2003) 18/4 *Intelligence and National Security* 72.   [19] Ibid, pp 87–8.

[20] Ibid, p 95.   [21] Ibid, p 95.

In the UK, one of the factors being considered by the government in its constantly evolving counter-terrorism strategy is the question of the use of domestic intercept as evidence in court[22] (at present, unlike some other European countries, intercept cannot be presented evidentially in open court in the UK). One of the arguments against this is that, in terrorist cases, intercept is often not the smoking gun that many assume it to be. The case of Rabei Osman El-Sayed Ahmed, a defendant in the trial following the Madrid train bombings of 2004, is a sobering one in this instance. Despite evidence being presented in court of taped phone conversations by Osman in which he appeared to brag about being the mastermind of the attacks (the conversations were taped in Italy, where intercept is admissible in court), the case against Osman ran into trouble over allegations that his conversations were translated from Arabic incorrectly.[23] In counter-terrorism trials, questions of language and interpretation mean that Sigint intercept will not always be the answer.

A possible dangerous over-reliance on Sigint and other technical examples of tradecraft may relate to the difficulties of conducting Humint on modern terrorist targets. Berkowitz examines the 'case officer model' deployed by the CIA, which tended to mean that overseas intelligence stations were located in country capitals and within the diplomatic quarter. The model dated back to when Allen Dulles, the first civilian director of the CIA, was a station chief in Bern during the Second World War. Under this pattern of tradecraft, the CIA could not easily cultivate 'unsavoury' sources at lower levels of the social hierarchy, especially if they were involved in unlawful activities and were located away from the capital, and the CIA officers generally did not have the skills (including the necessary language) to do so. Their targets were generally 'not a terrorist, but another intelligence officer or an official from a neighbouring embassy or organisation that might have access to a terrorist'.[24] When the terrorist organization in question is a non state-affiliated group such as Al Qaeda which operates in remote areas far away from national capitals, the problem starts to look like a deep and structural one of ineffective tradecraft.

The age of terror

At this stage, it is worth examining the nature of the terrorist threat in more detail and the changing security and intelligence challenges it has posed. One of the more useful theoretical frameworks is that of David Rapoport's 'Four Waves of Modern Terrorism',[25] updated in the immediate aftermath of the 9/11 attacks.

---

[22] 'Intercept evidence may be permissible—PM', *Number10.gov.uk*, 6 February 2008, <http://www.number10.gov.uk/Page14491>, accessed 31 December 2009.

[23] C Brayton, '"Traduttore Traditore": Italian translation throws Curveball at 11-M trial', 31 May 2007, <http://cbrayton.wordpress.com/2007/05/31/traduttore-traditore-the-italian-translation-throws-curveball-at-11-m-trial>, accessed 31 December 2009.

[24] Berkowitz, 'Intelligence and the War on Terrorism', n 13 above, p 296.

[25] D Rapoport, 'The Four Waves of Rebel Terror and September 11' (2002) 8/1 *Anthropoetics, art. 1*, <http://www.anthropoetics.ucla.edu/ap0801/terror.htm>, accessed 31 December 2009.

Table 3.1 Rapoport's Four Waves of Terror

Wave	Timeframe	Characteristics
1. Anarchist Wave	1880s–1920s	Small-scale, popular, anti-state, characterized by assassinations of political figures. Example: Narodnaya Volya in Russia.
2. Anti-Colonial Wave	1920s–1960s	Large, popular resistance movements primarily aimed at ejecting colonial powers from their colonial possessions. Examples: Malaya, Algeria, arguably Vietnam.
3. New Left Wave	1960s–1990s	Ideologically-motivated rebel and terrorist movements. Examples: various leftist Latin American groups, and European groups such as Red Brigades and RAF (Baader-Meinhof group).
4. Religious Wave	1990s–present	Fanatic, religiously-motivated terror groups, with new boundaries to their violence. Examples: Aum Shinrikyo, Al Qaeda.

For Rapoport, those attacks were the archetypal expression of the fourth wave of terror, which had placed itself very firmly on the map. Table 3.1 provides a summary of the four waves.

The advent of each wave represents a major structural shift in the dominant expression of terrorism across the world, and leads to certain conclusions, such as the theory that a major wave of terrorism has generally only survived for thirty to forty years before running out of steam and being replaced by other expressions of political violence.

As a general historical model, Rapoport's theory is a useful conceptual framework, and emphasizes the fact that Al Qaeda-style terrorism is fundamentally different in very significant ways from earlier expressions of terrorism. As ever with such models, however, things do not always fit neatly into the boxes and there is a blurring of lines around the edges. One example is the question of 'nationalist' terrorism, much of which emerged in the anti-colonial wave but has simmered on throughout history to varying degrees. Examples include the Liberation Tigers of Tamil Eelam (LTTE) in Sri Lanka, who emerged in the 1940s, as a reaction not to the British colonial power but to the Sinhalese-dominated independent administration which followed, and which was perceived to be discriminatory towards the Tamil community. LTTE terrorism has persisted stubbornly throughout the twentieth and early twenty-first centuries, experiencing a major road-block only in 2009 through overwhelming Sri Lankan military action—whether this will be the end of the LTTE remains to be seen.

Irish Republican terrorism emerged right at the beginning of Rapoport's model, with the Fenian terrorist acts in Britain in the late nineteenth century, and has again persisted to varying degrees well into the twenty-first century, with fissiparous splinter groups within the movement carrying out attacks as late as 2009. The Basque terrorist group Euskadi Ta Askatasuna (ETA), mean-while, emerged in the 1950s with a new claim for national independence from Spain, and has again persisted well into the twenty-first century despite periods of calm, with fresh attacks carried out within Spain in 2009.

Leftist terrorism still persists in the twenty-first century in some parts of the world, notably in Latin America (eg with FARC in Colombia and Sendero Luminoso in Peru) and in Mediterranean Europe, as Richards notes, with some evidence that it might be gathering fresh steam under the anti-globalization and anti-US banners.[26]

A notion of the fourth, 'religious' wave grew out of literature identifying a shift towards 'new terrorism' in the 1990s, which Walter Laqueur was one of the first to describe.[27] It identified that apparently religiously-motivated ter-rorism such as that of Al Qaeda broke new ground in terms of the scale of its ambitions, the indiscriminate nature of its targets, and the globally networked nature of its organization and operations. This posed fundamentally new and very challenging questions for the security and intelligence actors ranged against it, particularly in such areas as tradecraft, as we have seen in the case of the CIA. Table 3.2 summarizes the differences between 'New Terrorism' and previous forms of modern terror movements.

Again, not every situation or example neatly fits the model. Older terrorist groups have occasionally displayed characteristics of 'new' terrorist groups, either by targeting civilians indiscriminately for attack (as has been the case with the IRA, or Palestinian terror groups on occasion, for example), or by use of sui-cide attack methods (eg as in the case of some Palestinian groups, or the LTTE in Sri Lanka). Northern Irish terror groups have also shown a propensity for ran-dom sectarian attacks on occasion, in addition to specifically targeting members of the British state. Similarly, groups which would normally be labelled as new terror groups, such as some of the Kashmiri militant groups (eg LeT and JEM), have often confined their operations to military and police targets rather than necessarily always towards civilian targets. Nevertheless, the table below use-fully shows how some of the goalposts have shifted substantially in the counter-terrorism battle and placed new strains on the effectiveness of the security and intelligence structure.

Al Qaeda embodies this process and the new threats that can emerge from it in so many ways. The ideological underpinning of Al Qaeda is that the post-colonial network of nation-states that have been mapped across the world should be swept away in favour of a Global Caliphate that unites the global

---

[26] J Richards, 'Europe and the nature of the terrorist threat in 2007', Grupo de Estudios Estratégicos, <http://www.gees.org/articulos/europe_and_the_nature_of_the_terrorist_threat_in_2007_4272>, accessed 31 December 2009.

[27] W Laqueur, *The New Terrorism: Fanaticism and the Arms of Mass Destruction* (Oxford: Oxford University Press, 1999).

Table 3.2 Characteristics of pre- and post-'new' terrorism

Modern terrorism prior to the 1990s	'New' terrorism
Movement goals: specific, regionally-bounded, politically detailed, potentially negotiable in some aspects.	**Movement goals:** millennial, transnational, often vague and variable in detail, generally non-negotiable in any way.
Organization: usually well organized on hierarchical, military brigade-style lines, with clearly identified leadership.	**Organization:** cellular, dispersed, sometimes 'inspirational' and virtual.
Targets: usually figures of the state (military, police, government, or royalty).	**Targets:** indiscriminate towards state and civilian targets, often sectarian rather than individual.
Modus operandi: conventional (shootings or conventional explosives), protagonists usually aim to escape arrest.	**Modus operandi:** large-scale mass casualty attacks for maximum effect, some evidence that unconventional techniques and methods would be used (in terms of chemical/biological/radiological methods, or use of unconventional methods such as airliners in 9/11); attackers prepared to kill themselves in the act.

ummah of Muslim believers. Roy noted of 'neofundamentalist' movements such as Al Qaeda and the Taliban in the immediate aftermath of 9/11:

> these movements are supranational. A quick look at the bulk of bin Laden's militants killed or arrested between 1993 and 2001 show that they are mainly uprooted, western educated, having broken with their family as well as country of origin. They live in a global world . . . While Islamists do adapt to the nation-state, neo-fundamentalists embody the crisis of the nation-state, squeezed between infrastate solidarities and globalization . . . Using two international languages (English and Arabic), travelling easily by air, studying, training and working in many different countries, communicating through the Internet and cellular phones, they think of themselves as 'Muslims' and not as citizens of a specific country. They are often uprooted, more or less voluntarily (many are Palestinian refugees from 1948, and not from Gaza or the West Bank; bin Laden was stripped of his Saudi citizenship; many others belong to migrant families who move from one country to the next to find jobs or education).[28]

Roy notes the distinction between political 'Islamist' groups such as Hamas or the Muslim Brotherhood, which do fight for an essentially orthodox nationalist goal (ie the establishment of an independent Palestine), and more 'fundamentalist' Islamist movements such as Al Qaeda, which are at odds with such groups for participating in the Western-designed democratic process and nation-state framework.[29]

---

[28] O Roy, 'Neo-Fundamentalism', Social Science Research Council, <http://essays.ssrc.org/sept11/essays/roy.htm>, accessed 31 December 2009.   [29] Ibid.

The point here is that the international terrorist threat embodied by Al Qaeda explicitly rejects concepts of 'national' and 'international', and in its modus operandi makes considerable use of the benefits and modalities of globalization. The threat is therefore very different from the state-sponsored terrorist threats of the 1970s and 1980s, which represented some degree of focus around specific nation-states in the Muslim world which covertly sponsored the terrorists through diplomatic channels. The current threat has its roots in existential issues of identity, society, and economic development—indeed, many of the broader sectors of security threat we have seen emerging since the former preoccupation with the politico-military nexus.

The case of Younis Tsouli provides a compelling description of some of the new challenges posed by the latest wave of terrorism. Police in London arrested Tsouli in October 2005 in the aftermath of 'Operation Praline', which had centred around two young Muslim men of Scandinavian nationality interdicted in Bosnia in possession of suicide vests, weapons, and martyrdom videos. Tsouli had been one of their contacts in the UK.[30] On analysis of computer media seized during his arrest, police discovered that he was none other than 'Irhabi007', the online presence of 'Terrorist 007', who had been a highly significant webmaster for the Al Qaeda organization, and particularly for Al Qaeda in Iraq, at a time when they were struggling to get their message out onto the internet.

Tsouli had come to the attention of Al Qaeda in 2004 when he had joined two key password-protected extremist forums on the internet, which Al Qaeda had been using to convey propaganda and operational information. Tsouli had quickly built up an online relationship with Al Qaeda through Iraq's official spokesman, Abu Maysara Al-Iraqi, and soon emerged as a key source of expertise for the jihadist organization. He ensured videos and messages were hosted successfully across the internet despite efforts to stop them, and provided a wealth of expert IT advice to fellow jihadists. Many of the postings were found to have been placed covertly on servers located in the US, including those of the state of Arkansas and George Washington University, and payment was made using stolen credit cards. Within a relatively short space of time, Tsouli had become a hacker and webmaster par excellence for Al Qaeda, and received an open expression of support online from a member of the Iraqi extremist group, Ansar Al-Islam. While his period of involvement with Al Qaeda before his arrest was relatively short, his expertise and knowledge sharing across the online jihadist community would be difficult to underestimate.[31]

Tsouli's story was a truly transnational one, involving a bewildering array of national identities and locations: Iraq, Bosnia, the US, Britain. And yet, this was almost immaterial, as all of his activities were centred around cyberspace, which

---

[30] R Pantucci, 'Operation Praline: The Realization of Al-Suri's Nizam, la Tanzim?' (2008) 2/12 *Perspectives on Terrorism* 11, 12.

[31] R Katz and M Kern, 'Terrorist 007, Exposed', *The Washington Post*, 26 March 2006, <http://www.washingtonpost.com/wp-dyn/content/article/2006/03/25/AR2006032500020.html>, accessed 31 December 2009.

recognizes no borders. The fact that postings were placed on servers in the US is largely of no particular consequence—they could just as easily have been posted anywhere else in the world with a few clicks of the mouse. That he posted some of them on US government servers was surely deliberately ironic. From a recruitment point of view, Tsouli made his approach to the Al Qaeda organization and began serving them entirely over the internet: there was no formal application process or period of vetting—he proved himself to be of use to them by doing what he did, and doing it well. It is highly likely that he never met in person any core Al Qaeda members with whom he was communicating, or that they knew his real identity, or he theirs. There was no need: he was just a 'brother' working for the cause.

His expertise was key, and he showed that such expertise can be found from wherever it may be situated in the world and put to use immediately. His instincts for knowledge sharing were impeccable, and highly effective. His level of IT expertise was so high that to monitor and counter his activities would presumably require similarly expert-level degrees of skill and knowledge on cutting-edge technologies and internet security. Indeed, like many good spies in history, he was eventually interdicted through a chance connection and not as a result of his core activity. Interestingly, his activities were also intermingled with an element of old-fashioned crime: in this case credit card fraud which allowed online payments for server space to be made. Thus, to work effectively against a target of this nature, intelligence agencies would need to work closely with their law enforcement colleagues and identify the intelligence connections between the two respective worlds.

How effectively have intelligence agencies responded to the terror challenge? Britain's response to terrorism in Northern Ireland has sometimes been seen as a model of success, although Campbell and Connolly, for one, dispute that it should be seen as such when thinking about models for the contemporary 'war on terror'.[32] What is true is that the long struggle with the terrorism threat in Northern Ireland during the second half of the twentieth century went through three stages: an initial military-led stage, partly necessitated by the local police force, the Royal Ulster Constabulary, being seen to be inappropriately partisan; a second police-led stage from 1977 when a policy of 'criminalization' was adopted towards the terrorists; and a final stage from 2007 when the Security Service, MI5, took over 'primacy' in the battle against the terrorist threat (although it had been operating in the province for some years before). It is also the case that intelligence and security policies waxed and waned throughout these periods, between aggressive operational military strategy against IRA perpetrators, to police-led action against criminal figures, and finally to political engagement with the Sinn Fein party.

Throughout these periods, the British intelligence sector developed a number of elements of tradecraft in their activities in Northern Ireland. These comprised

---

[32] C Campbell and I Connolly, 'A Model for the "War Against Terrorism"? Military Intervention in Northern Ireland and the 1970 Falls Curfew' (2003) 30 *Journal of Law and Society* 341.

Humint, both from the use of agents and informers; interrogation of arrested individuals; and various forms of surveillance, from the use of human agents to various intrusive technical means. The latter ranged extensively in sophistication and audacity. The Four Square Laundry operation was part of the mobile reconnaissance strategy of the military in the early phase of the intelligence war, and constituted a legitimate laundry business covertly gathering intelligence among the Catholic community in Belfast. It proved reasonably successful, until it was inevitably uncovered and ended abruptly with an ambush, killing the laundry-van driver.[33] More technical methods of surveillance became increasingly sophisticated, as evidenced by the occasional discovery of various bugging and tracking devices, such as that discovered by the Sinn Fein leader, Gerry Adams, in his car in 1999.[34]

Probably the most effective method deployed against the IRA in particular was the use of Humint sources, which had a doubly negative impact on the terrorists. Mark Urban noted that

> the effects of the informer war are profound: the level of violence is reduced; the republican community is rendered increasingly paranoid and must eliminate a proportion of its own membership in an attempt to retain its integrity.[35]

With successful penetration of terrorist cells and structures by the intelligence gatherers, the terrorists must spend a large proportion of their energies and efforts flushing out the informers and trying to keep control of their organization, which deflects them from actually planning terrorist operations. In many ways this is the corollary of the kinetic war against the Al Qaeda leadership in the Afghanistan/Pakistan border region since 2001 (spearheaded by missile attacks from unmanned aerial drones), which may have had the effect of pinning Al Qaeda down and forcing them to concentrate on survival rather than planning and executing major terrorist attacks.

Throughout the counter-terrorist struggle in Northern Ireland, the difficult balancing act that the British state had to achieve was between taking a hard line on the terrorist perpetrators, including a covert surveillance war, while retaining the trust and support of the local community and minimizing the risk of radicalizing young people and driving them into the ranks of the terrorists. At various stages, hardline tactics adopted by the state were seen as potentially counterproductive. These particularly included aggressive interrogation techniques employed by the military, including the infamous 'five techniques' of sensory deprivation, which, Bamford notes, 'were successfully exploited by [Provisional]

---

[33] B Bamford, 'The Role and Effectiveness of Intelligence in Northern Ireland' (2005) 20 *Intelligence and National Security* 581, 588.

[34] 'Who might have bugged Gerry Adams?', *BBC News*, 8 December 1999, <http://news.bbc.co.uk/1/hi/uk/555715.stm>, accessed 31 December 2009.

[35] M Urban, *Big Boys Rules: The SAS and the Secret Struggle Against the IRA* (London: Faber and Faber, 1993) p 245.

IRA propaganda and caused damage to Britain's international reputation as they clearly impinged on human rights'.[36] Again, similarities with the debates currently raging in the contemporary 'war on terror' are striking, notably the question of whether apparent Western complicity in the torture of terrorist subjects through rendition and general collaboration with unsavoury foreign intelligence agencies, will play into the hands of the terrorist recruiters. (The former Director General of MI5, Dame Stella Rimington, claimed in a recent interview with a Spanish newspaper that this risk was being realized).[37]

Looking at the situation in previous terrorist threats, such as Northern Ireland, or the ETA problem in Spain, the danger is that there will be a failure to recognize the operational differences between the 'new' terrorist threat and more traditional nationalist and ideological terror threats from the past. Bamford noted that the Provisional IRA was initially structured (ironically) around the model of a British Army brigade, with clear, hierarchical lines of authority and tasking.[38] The British clearly understood this structure, and were able to exploit its weaknesses in working upstream into the organization through lower-level informants and suspects. Later, the IRA reorganized into a more dispersed cellular network structure, which lessened the threat of one interdicted individual or group having many connections with the rest of the organization.

Al Qaeda has taken the cellular network structure to a new level. Innes aptly describes Al Qaeda as 'morphing, fluid and de-centred'.[39] Although there is—or at least was—a senior leadership of Al Qaeda which planned and authorized major operations, this may increasingly no longer be the case, with regional franchises and local 'self starting' groups carrying out attacks in the Al Qaeda name without the need for central direction. For the intelligence agencies, this means there may be little or no 'organization' in the traditional sense of the term to attack or penetrate, but rather an amorphous ideology and mindset embedded throughout the international community. This makes planning and spotting emerging operations and strategic direction an extraordinarily difficult thing to achieve without very widespread penetration of the community by surveillance and intelligence gathering. We will return to the ethical difficulties of so doing in the following chapter.

In another sense, however, the intelligence challenge posed by the terrorist threat in Northern Ireland was similar to that faced today in many parts of the world, and particularly in Western Europe. This is the case with respect to the question of how to unearth intelligence from deep within a community as to

---

[36] Bamford, 'The Role and Effectiveness of Intelligence in Northern Ireland', n 33 above, p 589.

[37] J Booth, 'Ex-Spy Chief Dame Stella Rimington says ministers have turned UK into a police state', The Times, 17 February 2009, <http://www.timesonline.co.uk/tol/news/politics/article5750713.ece>, accessed 31 December 2009.

[38] Bamford, 'The Role and Effectiveness of Intelligence in Northern Ireland', n 33 above, p 591.

[39] M Innes, 'Policing Uncertainty: Countering Terror Through Community Intelligence and Democratic Policing' (2006) 605 ANNALS, AAPSS 222, 224.

who is moving towards the terrorists, who those terrorists are, and how far individuals within that community will be willing to provide such intelligence to the police or to other organs of the state. Intelligence can be gathered covertly through various technical means or through informants and agents, but it also needs to be gathered overtly through open engagement with the local community on the ground, as they will be the first and best source of when things are going wrong. However, too much covert activity—or at least discovery thereof—can affect the success of overt intelligence gathering through cooperation with the community.

For the police and its intelligence function, this is the point at which 'high' and 'low' policing come together. This terminology was coined by Jean-Paul Brodeur in the 1980s with reference to policing in France.[40] Brodeur notes that there is an 'asymmetrical' relationship between the everyday activities of the police in delivering 'community security', and those involving intelligence gathering and intelligence focused on major strategic security threats such as organized crime or terrorism—he further conceptualizes the difference from an intelligence point of view as that between criminal intelligence (low policing) and security intelligence (high policing).[41] A further nuance in the difference between these types of policing is that the former is primarily concerned with collecting evidence for criminal prosecution, while the latter tends to be much wider and moves more into the area of understanding or interpreting a situation, without necessarily producing actionable evidence that could be used in a court of law.[42]

This difference across the spectrum of intelligence becomes a major problem with the advent of international terrorism, because the international security dimension suddenly becomes intricately connected with the local community situation to a degree that was never quite the case before. Brodeur noted that numerous enquiries after 9/11 in the US and in Canada repeatedly stressed the difference and disconnect between high and low policing as being one of the major contributory factors in the intelligence failure.[43] Waddington further outlined the issue:

> Whilst it is currently fashionable for intellectuals to pour scorn on President George W Bush's characterization of American foreign and domestic policy as the pursuit of a 'War on Terror', there is reason to consider seriously the distinction between criminal acts, on the one hand, and warfare, on the other. For this distinction mirrors that between the police and military as the joint custodians of the state's monopoly of legitimate force. Implicit in this distinction is that the military fights wars, whereas the police enforce the law and pursue criminals. Terrorism blurs that distinction.[44]

---

[40] JP Brodeur, 'High and Low Policing: Remarks about the Policing of Political Activities' (1983) 30 *Social Problems* 507.

[41] JP Brodeur, 'High and Low Policing in Post 9/11 Times' (2007) 1 *Policing* 25, 27.

[42] Ibid.   [43] Ibid, p 29.

[44] PAJ Waddington, 'Policing Terrorism' (2007) 1 *Policing* 1, 2.

We have seen how, in the British struggle against terrorism in Northern Ireland through the latter part of the twentieth century, the security policy shifted over the years from the 1970s to the 1990s from the military, to the police, and ultimately to the security intelligence agency, MI5. With international Al Qaeda-style terrorism, a new international dimension is added which makes it even more complicated, especially in the case of 'home-grown' terror threats.

Any number of cases illustrate the point, but the story of Richard Reid is particularly illuminating. Born in south-east London in 1973 to an English mother and Jamaican father, Reid fell into a life of petty crime after his parents split up and his father moved away. He spent a number of periods in a young offender's institution in West London after a spate of muggings. During one of his stays at this institution, Reid—an impressionable and vulnerable young man—converted to Islam with the help of fellow inmates. On his release, he became a visitor to Brixton mosque, then fell in with a more extreme faction who operated on the fringes of the mosque. Gradually, he drifted towards violent extremism, and undertook a number of trips abroad, including, almost certainly, to Afghanistan to receive terrorist training with Al Qaeda. Further trips to various countries in Europe and elsewhere appear to have been 'scouting' exercises to test airline security. On 22 December 2001, just weeks after the 9/11 attacks, he was overpowered by passengers on a flight between Paris and Miami while attempting to detonate an explosive device concealed in his shoe.[45]

As the infamous 'shoe-bomber' of 2001, Reid's story is one of how a simple local issue of petty crime and offending can develop, through connections with radical elements on the fringes of certain communities and institutions, to the heart of the Al Qaeda organization in remote training camps in Afghanistan. For the police and the intelligence sector as a whole, understanding and profiling this story—and hopefully being able to do so before it is too late—means connecting intelligence gained on a major international terrorist group and its activities in remote places overseas, with situations within a local community involving crime and youth offending, and dynamics, in this case, within a particular ethno-religious community. To make such connections would involve cooperation and intelligence sharing between a wide range of institutions at several levels, from the police, to social services, to local mosque and community groups, to MI5 and possibly even foreign intelligence liaisons. This poses an extraordinary set of challenges for the intelligence sector as it is currently configured.

In some ways militating against the forging of these intelligence connections has been the policy shift within policing away from performance indicator-led activities, spearheaded by intelligence-led policing projects in the mid-1990s, back towards a concept of neighbourhood, community, or 'reassurance' policing in the early years of the twenty-first century. Ratcliffe notes that police in Britain

---

[45] 'Who is Richard Reid?', BBC News, 28 December 2001, <http://news.bbc.co.uk/1/hi/uk/1731568.stm>, accessed 31 December 2009.

have recently been discussing a 'reassurance gap', whereby 'falling crime rates were not reflected in a correspondingly increased sense of public security'.[46] In this way, policing priorities become driven by particular 'signal crimes' that appear to have a disproportionate impact on public perception of crime and security. In reflecting on the Thames Valley region of which she is Chief Constable, Sara Thornton noted that

> the main concerns are issues such as young people loitering in an intimidating manner and the associated problems of underage drinking, criminal damage, vandalism, and public drunkenness; drug-dealing, fly-tipping and littering; speeding cars, dangerous driving . . . We are not arguing that we simply aggregate these local issues and make them the strategic priorities for the force, with associated targets and performance monitoring. This would miss the point completely about local issues for local people. It would also fail to acknowledge the fact that, while people rarely identify serious crimes as their key concern, something also needs to be done about issues such as organised crime, criminal gangs and terrorism. People want the police to do something about all levels of crime.[47]

The police, therefore, have to cover an enormous range of issues from reassurance policing for local communities on issues they have identified as priorities, to more strategic security issues at a regional, national, and even international level. One of the difficulties is that the two dimensions are seen as separate issues, with a wall between them through which 'intelligence' should not pass. We have seen, however, how modern terrorism can break down these barriers and connect local criminal issues with international security issues.

Cultural problems within the law enforcement community can include the fact that the gathering of intelligence is often viewed, as Stovin and Davies noted, as a 'shady, clandestine or morally dubious activity'[48] which should be confined to those conducting 'high' policing activities rather than the regular police on the ground. Additionally, the police will sometimes not appreciate the connection between information gathered as part of the routine process of daily policing in the local area, and intelligence-led projects within the Special Branch or other departments—effectively not realizing which information is potential 'intelligence' were it to be analyzed or assessed in particular ways. Compounding this problem is a frequent failure to document such information properly and to do so in such a way that it can be shared and cross-referred with information even within a particular force, let alone across force or agency boundaries.[49]

We have seen, therefore, that the dominant security threat has changed radically through the latter half of the twentieth century, away from a set-piece

---

[46] J Ratcliffe, *Intelligence-Led Policing* (Cullompton: Willan, 2008) p 209.

[47] S Thornton and L Mason, 'Local Accountability and the Police Service: The Development of Neighbourhood Policing' (2007) 1 *Policing* 517.

[48] G Stovin and C Davies, 'Beyond the Network: A Crime Science Approach to Organized Crime' (2008) 2 *Policing* 501.

[49] Author's conversation with Special Branch officers in south-west England, 23 July 2009.

Table 3.3 Major security threats, late twentieth and early twenty-first centuries

Major security threats: 1960s onwards	Major security threats, early 2000s
• 'Big ideology' confrontation between East and West. Targets: military entities and communications, state-centred espionage, diplomatic communications. • Nationalist and Leftist terror groups (Palestinian terrorism, IRA, ETA, Baader-Meinhof, etc). Targets: state sponsors of groups, group organization and hierarchy.	• International organized crime. Targets: civilian and commercial entities and networks. • Proliferation of WMD and other sensitive technologies. Targets: covert diplomatic/ commercial entities and networks. • International terrorism. Targets: ideological and community sponsors, movements of individuals internationally and civilian networks, 'virtual' cyberspace activities and communications.

state-centred politico-military threat, to a more networked, amorphous, and disparate threat which is threaded through civil society. Modern international terrorism epitomizes this threat, and the new set of intelligence and security challenges posed for the state in countering the threat. In many ways, the changes are integral parts of the general transformation of society into a more networked, mobile, and de-centred society in which traditional hierarchies and power-structures are blurred. We also saw in the previous chapter how major intelligence failures and strategic surprises can generally be explained by a complex combination of both analytical and bureau-organizational factors within the intelligence sector. Some of the key changes in security threat are summarized in Table 3.3, which compares threats in the latter half of the twentieth century with the sort of threats faced today.

We can see in the above table some of the key differences in threat over time. In summary, the differences as we move into a new century can be characterized as a less defined, and more internationally networked set of activities and targets, which are deliberately covert and complex and are embedded in civilian and commercial sectors as much as in diplomatic, military, or political arenas. The Baader-Meinhof terrorist group was a difficult and very challenging intelligence threat in the 1970s in West Germany, but in retrospect, it was a very defined and bounded group with no real external connections, other than a brief flirtation with Palestinian terrorists which was quickly curtailed by mutual consent. It was embedded in local communities and intelligence was needed by the police on local, civilian networks of sympathizers and collaborators, but there was little or no need to combine this tactical intelligence with wider, strategic intelligence on events or activities outside the immediate locality, which would be held by other intelligence actors. The threat of Al Qaeda today very emphatically emphasizes the need to compare local, tactical intelligence on particular individuals with intelligence from overseas on network connections, or indeed from cyberspace on virtual contacts with information or people elsewhere. It is also as much about community and ideological issues concerning inter-group relations and processes of radicalization as it is about crime; again necessitating a connection between two very different types of information and intelligence.

The changes needed to respond to these challenges in the intelligence community are both those of mindset, and of organizational structures and information flows. Berkowitz noted that the 'greatest tragedy of September 11 is that it not only could, but should have been anticipated'.[50] He explained this statement by referring to organizational problems within the US intelligence sector, and specifically that it 'could not move, process, and analyze information effectively'.[51] Further:

> Many of the steps needed to prepare US intelligence for the terrorist threat are the same measures needed to update the intelligence community in general. In short, intelligence organizations need to become agile, networked organizations, able to respond to threats emerging from many different directions with little warning.[52]

Intelligence organizations need to think and operate in the same ways that make their adversaries peculiarly effective and efficient. Terrorists and other targets, like many businesses and civilians, are capitalizing on the opportunities offered by modern communications, mobility of information, and labour. Intelligence organizations need to derive benefit from the same opportunities. However, certain intelligence failures suggest that they have an inbuilt inertia which is preventing them from doing so to full effect. Berkowitz identified a set of specific factors that the intelligence agencies needed to address in meeting this challenge, namely to:[53]

- reduce bureaucratic barriers between intelligence producers and customers.
- reduce technological barriers to information sharing and mining.
- provide 'sensible approaches to security' which simultaneously protect sensitive information, while allowing intelligence officials to work and share information across boundaries.
- develop better mechanisms for drawing on outside expertise more effectively.
- develop changes in intelligence 'tradecraft' which focus not on traditional 'narrow down' approaches, but are better able to think laterally and spot new emerging threats.

If we think of the adversary in the shape of Al Qaeda, we can see that many of these factors are present and are acting as force multipliers, particularly the ability to share information across barriers (with the internet providing the central infrastructure), the lack of bureaucracy and hierarchy in building networks, and the ability to identify and recruit specific talent and expertise needed for

---

[50] Berkowitz, 'Intelligence and the War on Terrorism', n 13 above, p 298.
[51] Ibid.   [52] Ibid, pp 298–9.   [53] Ibid, p 299.

the cause. An ability to surprise has also been present, with apparently sudden changes in modus operandi catching the intelligence and security agencies on the hop. Somehow, the latter need to reduce their propensity to be surprised by developing their analysis and assessment.

Seven years on from Berkowitz's suggestions, the depressing conclusion has to be that very little progress has been made on most of these factors. A lack of ability to share intelligence across boundaries, capitalizing on modern communications technology, perhaps typifies the depth of the problem. Norris identifies a number of positive developments which are planned in the police sector in the UK, including the Cross Regional Information Sharing Project, which will 'take the Police Service through a process of aggregating its data into local data warehouses which is the starting point for national information sharing'.[54] As laudable as this is, for the police in 2007 to be only just planning for the starting point of being able to share criminal intelligence information nationally at some point in the future, is probably not good enough, and does not feel like agile and proactive capitalization of new information technology. It appears we are still some way off being able to address the critical question of intelligence sharing across boundaries from a technical point of view, let alone from procedural and ethical standpoints. The sad fact of the matter is that further intelligence failures can be expected in the meantime as a result of the continued lack of progress on this front.

Conclusions

There is no doubt that the security threat picture has changed drastically and irrevocably since the events of 1989 in Berlin, when the wall between East and West came down and the Cold War quickly began to thaw. By this time, the Western intelligence structure had developed since the wartime years in the first half of the twentieth century into a modern, industrialized, and almost 'Fordist' production machine; well focused and honed to look at a particular monolithic and largely static threat.

At this stage in intelligence history, the technical tradecraft that had flourished and developed during the Second World War, and particularly Imint, Sigint, and to a lesser extent, covert operations, had become set in the panoply of weapons available to the intelligence agencies.

With the end of the Cold War, a whole array of new threats and security dynamics began to change the picture substantially. In academic security studies, models of threat widened and diversified away from politico-military obsessions to include an array of social, economic, and even cultural issues. In the UK, the Intelligence Services Act 1994 mandated the SIS and GCHQ to supplement their activities on national security threats with those on the 'prevention or

---

[54] C Norris, 'The Intensification and Bifurcation of Surveillance in British Criminal Justice Policy' (2007) 13 *European Journal of Criminal Policy and Research* 139, 147.

detection of serious crime' and 'in the interests of the economic wellbeing of the United Kingdom'.[55] In 1996, the domestic intelligence agency, MI5, formally began intelligence operations against serious crime targets, working with the relatively newly-established NCIS in the UK. Transnational drugs and people smuggling, money laundering, and other financial crimes came into the purview of the intelligence agencies, and accelerated their relationship with the law enforcement agencies.

On the terrorism front, the state-sponsored terrorism of the 1970s and 1980s became supplemented and in some ways eclipsed by a newly emergent threat of international Islamist terrorism, headed by Al Qaeda and its supporting new terrorist groups. Here was a threat closely linked to the whole process of globalization, and in many ways very different from the state-sponsored terrorist threat of before. Suddenly, a threat had emerged which made a mockery of international borders and national jurisdictions, and which was very much at one with the internet age and the knowledge economy that was emerging. The threat had been growing for some years and had been noted with varying degrees of conviction by the intelligence agencies, but 9/11 firmly placed it on the map as a new and much more challenging security and intelligence issue.

For intelligence agencies to work effectively against targets of these types, it can reasonably be presumed that certain corollaries would need to be in place. International collaboration on intelligence sharing and mutual legal assistance would need to be fluid, so that different jurisdictions with different degrees of control over their internet sectors could not be played off against each other. Distinctions between nationalities and jurisdictions, between 'domestic 'and 'international', would need to be largely immaterial, or at least no barrier. (The terrorists themselves would certainly not take heed of such differences.) Degrees of expertise on internet security and communications would need to be high, so that the intelligence agencies could understand what was happening, and preferably get themselves one step ahead. Flexibility and agility to develop and interdict new targets, and to find and deploy new skill leaders, would need to be at least as effective as the abilities of the Al Qaeda organization itself to identify and develop new sources of expertise. These are the questions that Western intelligence agencies are having to ask themselves in the post-9/11 world, and many of the answers will no doubt make uncomfortable reading.

To confront the problem, Robert Clark suggested the answer is to take a comprehensively 'target-centric approach' to intelligence analysis.[56] In essence, this comprises two things: first, intelligence agencies and actors have to tackle the problem in a much more collaborative, and much less stove-piped and hierarchical way. In many ways, the intelligence sector needs to model itself on the flatter structures and greater instincts for knowledge sharing of society at large in the postmodern world than has traditionally been the case with governmental

---

[55] Intelligence Services Act 1994, s 1(2)(b) and (c).

[56] RM Clark, *Intelligence Analysis: A Target-Centric Approach* (Washington DC: CQ Press, 2007).

agencies. In essence, the intelligence sector needs to model its organization on that of its targets. Second, the analytical approaches to contemporary targets need to be much more closely aligned to the nature of those targets' behaviours and attributes than to traditional, technology and process-oriented approaches. Contemporary targets are complex, and they are constantly trying to hide their activities in the noise of daily life. A forensically analytical approach that models itself on the target's behaviour is the essence of target-centric analysis.

Subsequent experience of Al Qaeda after 9/11 has shown it to be flexible, network-oriented, and amorphous. The intelligence actors have responded in many ways, attempting, with varying degrees of success, to increase their collaboration with one another, especially internationally, and grappling with the erosion of the distinction between domestic and foreign. National jurisdictions have also seen, to varying degrees, that the battle is as much one of ideas as of one of military and law enforcement action.[57] This takes intelligence into the realm of local communities and societal dynamics, with all the attendant problems of appearing like a 'police state' at every turn. Such political and ethical problems are now integral to the intelligence process and to the work of the intelligence analyst in the twenty-first century, and it is to these factors that we now turn.

Key Points

- Early intelligence efforts through the World Wars were characterized by a growth of technical intelligence-gathering techniques, supplemented by Humint.

- Moving into the Cold War, further advances were made in technical tradecraft such as Imint, and a static and large target allowed an industrial process of intelligence production to be established in the West.

- With the fall of the Berlin Wall and the emergence of a much more diverse map of security threats, the agility of the intelligence capability and its over-reliance on certain technical techniques were called into question.

- The terrorist threat has evolved from nationalist and leftist threats at the end of the twentieth century, to a more millennial new terrorism at the beginning of the twenty-first century. This is characterized by a more dispersed, de-centred, and amorphous threat.

- Models for how to deal with terrorism are variable and far from clear. The ability to adapt to the new security threats is also a moot question for the intelligence structures in the West. At the moment, the adversary looks more flexible than the intelligence agencies.

---

[57] L Scott and RG Hughes, 'Intelligence in the Twenty-First Century: Change and Continuity, or Crisis and Transformation?' (2009) 24 *Intelligence and National Security* 6, 20.

4

The Intelligence Environment: Political, Cultural, and Ethical Influences on Intelligence Analysis

We have seen in previous chapters how the intelligence cycle needs to be treated with care. While it is a useful conceptual model for understanding the various components of the intelligence process, it is frequently the case—and perhaps increasingly so—that the process is far from being a neat, linear one. One of the key factors throughout the cycle is the effect of external influences on the analytical process. These can be political, bureaucratic, or cultural influences, and all of them can change the flow of intelligence through the system so that what comes out at the end is not necessarily how it started or could have evolved from the beginning. In some cases these influences are slight and are managed by the intelligence actors. In other cases they can have an enormous influence on the process and its eventual outcome.

A secondary set of influences, other than those within the intelligence system itself, are factors that have become arguably more significant as society and security threats have changed. Again, the advent of international terrorism at the beginning of the twenty-first century has caused intelligence actions and reactions to be reconsidered radically, in such a way that difficult questions of ethics and morality have resurfaced in increasingly complex ways. There has always been a debate about the ethics of intelligence, and particularly the role it should play in a liberal democracy, but the need to confront terrorism robustly has brought many of these issues very sharply into focus. The impact of these factors both on intelligence organizations and on individual staff working within them cannot be overestimated, and the long-term effects of such changes are difficult to predict at the time of writing.

In this chapter, we review the range of influences that come to bear on the intelligence process, and consider the debate on ethics for intelligence in the twenty-first century. We begin with recapping on the factors which warp and shape the flow of intelligence through the intelligence cycle.

Factors Affecting the Intelligence Cycle

In the early stage of the intelligence cycle, questions around decision-making as to what the requirement is, and what tasking will be undertaken by the intelligence gatherers, is a complex one which does not always work as envisaged from the outside. We have seen in Chapter 2, in the context of intelligence failures, that the 'customer' supplying the requirement will often have imperfect knowledge as to what is possible, or even what the key requirement actually is. Hulnick notes that 'intelligence managers, and not policy officials, are the real drivers of the intelligence collection process'.[1] From this we develop a sense of the intelligence machine tasking itself, at least in terms of the detail of how to respond to particular intelligence requirements, although this should not be taken to mean that the agencies are rogue elephants who do whatever takes their fancy.

At a more detailed level within the intelligence machinery, Hulnick goes on to note that, in the US at least, the 'collection' process (which we have called the Information/data gathering process), sometimes works in parallel to the analysis process rather than in a transactional relationship with it. Additionally, it does not always work in concert with the analysis function but might short-circuit that stage in the process, whereby policy customers receive 'raw' intelligence from the collectors rather than assessed and finished analysis. This might be the case, for example, where a particularly sensitive or time-critical piece of intelligence was collected and directed 'straight to the White House'. Hulnick notes that 'restrictions of information sharing, psychological barriers, fears of compromising sources, and security concerns' are all factors that can mean the collectors and analysts do not always work in tandem with one another.[2] While these are defensive issues causing problems for intelligence sharing, more nefarious factors such as the importance of claiming credit for the key piece of intelligence on a particular issue, and deliberately withholding intelligence by operating the 'knowledge is power' model, must surely also be factors militating against intelligence sharing between departments and agencies on occasion.

Normally these issues work as barriers and complications between agencies, whether across sectors within one country (eg between the police and a state intelligence agency) or between agencies in different countries attempting to

---

[1] AS Hulnick, 'What's Wrong with the Intelligence Cycle' (2006) 21 *Intelligence and National Security* 959, 961.   [2] Ibid, p 962.

collaborate on intelligence targets. At the supranational level, the EU shows plenty of examples of continuing mistrust between agencies, leading to disappointing levels of intelligence sharing at sensitive levels, despite the laudable establishment of the technical mechanisms to do so.[3] However, these problems can be factors within departments of the same agency in some cases. The outcome of such complications can be that the customer receives an incomplete or fragmented picture, or one that is based on unassessed and faulty intelligence, particularly if it is based on a small number of sources. This was essentially the problem with the case for going to war in Iraq in 2003, a story to which we will return.

Even where the analysis function has had a chance to assess information and make an intelligence judgement, what happens to that judgement in the managerial and policy chain can be very variable and subject to a number of influences. This can relate to cultural factors between analyst and policy-maker whereby the latter feels it is his or her job to make a judgement, rather than for the analyst to suggest a course of action: a situation that Cope observed as a problematic factor sometimes within the police.[4] Thus, an analyst can suggest a particular hypothesis, but it is for the senior manager to decide what action to take, and he or she might choose not to act on the recommendation of the analyst. In other cases, the intelligence may have been presented in such a voluminous way that managers and policy-makers do not have the time to read it, and are thus forced to make decisions based on sketchy or incomplete appraisal of the incoming intelligence.[5]

Most of these issues are procedural ones of process and inter-agency relationship, but technical factors will have a bearing on the cycle also. We have seen in the previous chapter how continued failures to develop interlinked IT systems across the intelligence community—or even within individual agencies in some cases—can cause the intelligence flow to be fractured, interrupted, or limited. But technical intelligence-gathering capabilities can be critical also, and can change as the world of technology at large changes. Sometimes these can be simple gaps in the coverage, which are due to the need to prioritize scarce resources, or to lacking resource or capability. These can be particularly problematic where an issue 'blows up' in an unexpected part of the world, or involves an unexpected change of modus operandi by the targets. Many of the immediate post-Cold War security threats will surely have posed early problems for an intelligence machine that had been pointed towards the Soviet Union for decades. Hulnick notes the example of the Argentinian invasion of the Falklands in 1982, on which the US was unable to help with satellite imagery as its satellites were configured to be over the Soviet Union at the critical times of day.[6] Similarly, tradecraft such

---

[3] JI Walsh, 'Intelligence-Sharing in the European Union: Institutions are not enough' (2006) 44 *Journal of Common Market Studies* 625, 638.

[4] N Cope, 'Intelligence-led Policing or Policing-led Intelligence?' (2004) 44 *British Journal of Criminology* 188, 191.

[5] J Ratcliffe, *Intelligence-Led Policing* (Cullompton: Willan, 2008) pp 161–2.

[6] Hulnick, 'What's Wrong with the Intelligence Cycle', n 1 above, p 960.

as the gathering of human intelligence (Humint) from high-value sources can be lengthy and complex to set up, and can be halted very abruptly if a source decides to retire, is moved within their organization to a position with less access, or worse, is discovered and removed from the picture.

Political Influences

In late 2003, when it began to look distinctly possible that the invading US and British forces in Iraq were not going to find the weapons of mass destruction (WMD) that had formed the bedrock of the case for going to war, a political storm was unleashed on both sides of the Atlantic which accused the political establishment of having 'politicized' and perverted the intelligence analysis running up to the war. As we have seen, the Iraq War was an intelligence failure par excellence, and has been much studied and scrutinized, leading to a number of official enquiries.

Those enquiries that have been held found that the usual organizational problems came into play, particularly in the US where the military lobby, in the shape of its forceful and charismatic chief, the Secretary of Defence, Donald Rumsfeld, jostled for primary position for the President's ear with the chief of the CIA, George Tenet (who was also Director of National Intelligence until 2005, when the role was decoupled from that of CIA chief). Rumsfeld and the military ultimately held sway in the Bush regime. The differences in strategic position were highlighted by a CIA assessment in 2002 entitled 'The Perfect Storm: Planning for Negative Consequences of Invading Iraq', which predicted the sectarian and civil strife and upsurge in anti-Western feeling that would be unleashed by an invasion. Yet the operation went ahead on the urging of Rumsfeld and the military, who downplayed such risks.[7] Here we can see problems in the policy-maker arena, both in terms of their interpretation and assessment of strategic intelligence, and their political disagreements, which could have affected judgements.

Indeed, it increasingly became clear that the decision to invade Iraq was a political and strategic one that had already been made before all the intelligence had been evaluated. In his famous 'Downing Street memo', the chief of the Secret Intelligence Service (MI6) in Britain, Sir Richard Dearlove, reported to the Prime Minister his findings on a visit to Washington prior to the decision to invade that 'the intelligence and facts were being fixed around the policy'.[8] By this stage, it appears that the intelligence cycle was effectively working in reverse.

Interestingly, much of the reaction to the official enquiries in all three countries (the US, Britain, and Australia) was that they shifted the blame away from

---

[7] W Pincus, 'Before War, CIA Warned of Negative Outcomes', *The Washington Post*, 2 June 2007,<http://www.washingtonpost.com/wp-dyn/content/article/2007/06/02/AR2007060200905.html>, accessed 31 December 2009.

[8] Cited in M Fitzgerald and RN Lubow, 'Iraq: The Mother of All Intelligence Failures' (2006) 21 *Intelligence and National Security* 884, 895.

politicians and policy-makers, and back into the intelligence agencies themselves, which had made assessments based on thin and ambiguous intelligence. The Flood report in Australia cleared the Prime Minister of 'politicising' the intelligence case,[9] while the Hutton enquiry in the UK cleared the government of manipulating and 'sexing up' the case for war, and instead brought opprobrium on the media, and particularly the BBC, for wrongly accusing the government of lying to the people, forcing a number of resignations including that of the BBC chairman and director-general.

The very comprehensive Butler enquiry in the UK found that most of the processes for agreeing and assessing intelligence on WMD generally within the Joint Intelligence Committee (JIC) process at senior governmental levels were sound, and that there was no evidence of active politicization. This is an important conclusion, if accepted, because it lends weight to a theory that the British intelligence sector is structured in such a way that it has all the appropriate checks and balances, and that its intelligence judgements cannot be manipulated or subverted by the politicians. Great strides have been made in this area, particularly since the Intelligence Services Act 1994 was placed on the statute books and provided a much higher level of detail and scrutiny around the state intelligence agencies than had been the case before. One of the critical provisions of the Act was to establish the Intelligence and Security Committee (ISC), a cross-party group with a mandate to examine and report on the activities of the intelligence agencies. While this has delivered a greater level of scrutiny, it has not altogether avoided accusations that the intelligence agencies are being protected by the political establishment. A notable example of this is the case of the 7/7 terrorist bombings in London in 2005, which have been the subject of two official ISC enquiries examining the possible causes of intelligence failure, both of which have been rejected by a group called the 7/7 Inquiry Campaign Group as being political whitewash, as the enquiries were held in secret.

At the policing end of the intelligence spectrum, there have not been the same issues of potential politicization of decisions, although the case of the Metropolitan Police's recently outgoing Commissioner, Sir Ian Blair, was political in the sense that he was seen by many as 'the government's man' and was eventually eased out by a new London mayor who was aligned to the political opposition. Blair was embroiled in controversy over the police shooting incident in London in 2005, which we examined in Chapter 1, in which an innocent man was mistaken for a fugitive suicide bomber. Blair's initial insistence that the dead man was 'directly linked to anti-terrorism operations', despite rapidly unfolding intelligence suggesting otherwise,[10] was probably not so much a politicized reading of intelligence as an error of judgement.

---

[9] 'Australia's Iraq war case damned', *BBC News*, 22 July 2004, <http://news.bbc.co.uk/1/hi/world/asia-pacific/3915759.stm>, accessed 31 December 2009.

[10] J Sturcke, J Percival, and H Mulholland, 'Sir Ian Blair resigns as Met Police commissioner', *The Guardian*, 2 October 2008, <http://www.guardian.co.uk/politics/2008/oct/02/ian.blair.resigns>, accessed 31 December 2009.

In the US, as we have seen, the activities of the FBI's counter-intelligence programme (COINTELPRO) in the early years of the Cold War became widely discredited when it was found to have extensively overstepped the mark between monitoring communist subversives, and conducting intrusive surveillance and 'dirty tricks' against a large number of individuals seen to be unsympathetic towards the government, including the civil rights leader, Martin Luther King Jr.[11] Ratcliffe notes of the episode:

> The lack of governance of police intelligence units had a corollary outcome in a degree of abuse of the ethics of the intelligence process. Intelligence files were kept on people who were not criminals but merely politically active and vocal in their objections to government policy. As a result, a number of police departments, either through political pressure, voluntarily, or from court mandate, closed down their criminal intelligence units.[12]

The episode proved to be a deeply traumatic one for the US in considering the role of security intelligence actors within a free democracy, and it would not be an exaggeration to say that it has continued to cause problems for policy-makers after 9/11, when the need to fuse law enforcement intelligence with state security intelligence has become more pressing.

A different kind of political influence on the policing intelligence process has been the question of how policing in general has been something of a 'political football' in many Western countries, particularly since the end of the Cold War as Western societies have evolved and changed. Maguire and John noted that 'policing decisions are influenced by many extraneous factors, including sudden shifts in political priorities or community concerns'.[13] This has meant that policing has often been subjected to a fluctuating set of managerial models and theories, in a way that has not been so applicable to state security agencies, who have largely managed to keep their intelligence activities behind closed doors and away from the political spotlight (notwithstanding enquiries following Iraq and similar episodes). The security issue has increasingly been one on which votes are won or lost, and this has affected the way in which law enforcement intelligence has been structured and deployed. Walsh and Vito noted a 'paradigm shift' in policing models, particularly from the 1980s onwards, fuelled by 'the continued demand for safer, more effective and efficient ways to police communities'.[14]

From the 1970s onwards, the rapid improvements in computer systems and information technology began to open up opportunities for greatly enhanced data handling in all walks of life, and the applications to intelligence were soon

---

[11] Ratcliffe, *Intelligence-Led Policing*, n 5 above, pp 27–8.   [12] Ibid, p 28.

[13] M Maguire and T John, 'Intelligence Led Policing, Managerialism and Community Engagement: Competing Priorities and the Role of the National Intelligence Model in the UK' (2006) 16 *Policing and Society* 67, 69.

[14] WF Walsh and GF Vito, 'The Meaning of Compstat' (2004) 20 *Journal of Contemporary Criminal Justice* 51, 53.

noted. In 1973, the National Advisory Commission on Criminal Justice and Goals in the US called on every law enforcement agency in every state to

> immediately establish and maintain the capability to gather and evaluate information and to disseminate intelligence in a manner that protects every individual's right to privacy while it curtails organized crime and public disorder.[15]

(The emphasis on protecting privacy reflects the anxiety over previous uses of intelligence by the FBI.)

By the 1990s, the New York Police Department (NYPD) broke new ground with a new 'goal-oriented, strategic management process that uses information technology, operational strategy, and managerial accountability to guide police operations'; a model which became known as Compstat.[16] Involving not just the processing and management of criminal intelligence but the whole administration of the policing function centred around extensive use of statistical information, the NYPD started to demonstrate reversals in its crime rates which caught the attention of observers within the US and internationally. The Commissioner of the NYPD at the time, William Bratton, based the model around a four-step process:

- Accurate and timely intelligence about crimes and crime-trends.
- Rapid deployment of resources based on assessment of weekly crime statistics.
- Focusing resources on crime problems that emerge in the analysis as being particularly impactful.
- Relentless follow-up and assessment to refine the strategy.[17]

Compstat was essentially a 'problem-oriented' mode of policing, applying analysis and 'science' to understanding the picture of crime in a particular area, then focusing resources and priorities on the key crimes which stood out as having the biggest impact on the community. This was a different model from old-fashioned neighbourhood or community policing, which merely aimed to provide a presence on the streets and deal with whichever problems arose. A key driver in the model was a focus on targets and statistics: with the police under mounting pressure to reduce crime rates tangibly, they recognized that they needed to target themselves scientifically on the aspects of crime which would show the most effective results. Essentially, this was as much a political issue as one of community safety.

In Canada in the early 1990s, the Royal Canadian Mounted Police (RCMP) established a model called CAPRA (Clients, Analysis, Partnerships, Response, Assessment), which had grown, in part, from a recognition that community

---

[15] Cited in US Department of Justice, Bureau of Justice Assistance, *Intelligence-Led Policing: The New Intelligence Architecture* (Washington DC: BJA paper NCJ 210681, 2005) p 5.

[16] Ibid, p 57.   [17] Ibid, p 59.

policing was not necessarily very effective in penetrating serious criminal or terrorist groups. This realization was born painfully out of the failure to anticipate the 1985 bombing by Sikh extremists of an Air India plane departing from Vancouver.[18] It was not enough, in the RCMP's experience, simply to have good relations with a particular community: a more targeted and analytical approach was needed to get to the root of complex and hidden issues and networks.

Around the same time in the UK, the concept of 'intelligence-led policing' (ILP) began to emerge, through some work conducted by the Kent constabulary, and later replicated in a number of other areas. Initially called the Kent Policing Model, ILP was similar to Compstat in that it reflected a need to drive down crime statistics (and particularly burglary and vehicle theft, which had been rising steadily in the county) at a time when budgets were being squeezed. The model in Kent involved two aspects: first, prioritizing calls for service whereby lower priority calls were pushed down the list or out to other agencies; and second, conducting a detailed analysis of statistics relating to volume crimes in the county, and particularly to burglary and vehicle theft. This analysis showed that a relatively small number of individuals, most of whom were previous offenders, were responsible for a disproportionately large amount of crime. This, in turn, allowed the police force to focus its resources on this small pool of individuals, which quickly yielded results in lowering the crime rates in these specific sectors.

Maguire and John noted that ILP was as much about greater efficiency and effectiveness in public services as about anything else:

> Intelligence led policing, it was argued, offered the prospect of more 'rational' use of scarce resources and potentially better 'value for money'—an argument central to the Audit Commission's (1993) influential exhortation to police forces to make more use of proactive approaches and techniques (especially paid informants).[19]

Intelligence, then, was seen as a critical tool not only in focusing more effectively on the key criminal patterns and trends which would show results in the crime statistics, but also in structuring the resource and priority management within a police force more efficiently and effectively. From the 1990s onwards, this was an increasingly political consideration in many countries in the West, which drove the policing model.

Tilley argues that there is an important difference between problem-oriented policing (POP) and ILP. The former, it is argued, takes a more holistic view of a whole criminal problem and its underlying causes, allowing consideration of how to address problems at their root. ILP, in contrast, can run the risk of just treating the symptoms of a problem and not getting to the heart of it.[20] In other

---

[18] W de Lint, 'Intelligence in Policing and Security: Reflections on Scholarship' (2006) 16 *Policing and Society* 1, 2.   [19] Maguire and John, 'Intelligence Led Policing', n 13 above, p 68.

[20] N Tilley, *Problem-Oriented Policing, Intelligence-Led Policing and the National Intelligence Model* (London: UCL, 2003), <http://www.jdi.ucl.ac.uk/downloads/publications/crime_science_short _reports/problem_oriented_policing.pdf>, accessed 31 December 2009.

ways, both are similar in that they require 'much greater and more systematic use of information'.[21] Generally, at a strategic level, both POP and ILP are similar in critical ways, and indeed are based on the same thinking as 'target-centric analysis' as applied to the state security and intelligence arena. All of them take a more proactive approach using analysis of data, to focus in on the issues and targets likely to be most productive from the point of view of generating an intelligence dividend (or indeed, in the policing context, of having a positive effect on crime). All of them are directed, using analysis, rather than being passive or reactionary, using contacts on the ground or officers on the beat. For the police, there are good efficiency drivers for taking this approach since they have to direct their resources to best effect, but there are also good analytical reasons for using data in this more proactive way, especially as modern information and communications technology allow the analyst to do so in ever more creative and ambitious ways.

In the UK, the National Criminal Intelligence Service embedded a notion of ILP firmly into the whole administrative process of policing with the publication of the National Intelligence Model (NIM) in 2000, which was mandated subsequently as a management model across all police forces in England and Wales. Although the NIM describes a set of intelligence 'products' which the police can produce across the levels of intelligence work, from tactical to strategic assessments, John and Maguire note that the model is primarily a management tool, which is as much about managing and prioritizing resources as about the detail of the intelligence process.[22] Indeed, at a review of the early application of the NIM, John and Maguire noted a number of issues, including those concerning the cross-agency Tasking and Coordinating Groups (TCGs), which are a critical administrative vehicle under the model. It was noted that:

> Where tactical TCGs in particular are concerned, further problems were identified in the variable frequency of meetings, the seniority of Chairs (which in turn could affect attendance) and in some cases the conduct of meetings (which could sometimes ignore analytical evidence and/or come to resemble 'resource bidding' sessions).[23]

Here we can see echoes of some of the bureau-political problems and organizational pathologies examined in the case of intelligence failure, although in this case, the problems are not so much of policy-makers wantonly choosing to ignore the intelligence provided to them, but of being so concerned with the resource allocation problems that the intelligence becomes a secondary consideration. In her research among police intelligence analysts in the UK, Cope

---

[21] Ibid, p 2.

[22] T John and M Maguire, 'Rolling out the National Intelligence Model: Key Challenges' in K Bullock and N Tilley (eds), *Crime Reduction and Problem-Oriented Policing* (Cullompton: Willan, 2003) p 41.

[23] T John and M Maguire, *The National Intelligence Model: Key Lessons from Early Research*. Home Office Online Report 30/04, <http://www.homeoffice.gov.uk/rds/pdfs04/rdsolr3004.pdf>, accessed 31 December 2009.

identified a further problem in some instances, of intelligence products being just 'wallpaper' for managers and senior officers, used to adorn final reports and bulletins but not really digested or acted upon in any meaningful way.[24]

At the beginning of the twenty-first century, a number of societal and political developments around the question of security and policing are shifting the balance subtly away from an entirely intelligence-led approach. These developments are primarily twofold:

- A growing public suspicion of a 'targets culture' in public service in the West, whereby the police, and a number of other sectors such as health and education, are seen to be structuring their priorities around what will deliver the best figures and statistics rather than what will address the real public need.
- A general anxiety in society that policing has moved away from a (possibly mythical) vision of 'bobbies on the beat' watching out for problems in the local community, to faceless officers hidden away in squad cars or back at the station, looking at data on their computers.

Maguire and John describe two further policing models which have come to compete for attention with the NIM, and which, in some ways, 'reflect fundamentally different or even conflicting principles and approaches to policing'.[25] These are:

- Reassurance or Neighbourhood policing.
- 'Narrowing the justice gap'.

The first of these reflects a growing recognition among many communities that they should be important 'stakeholders' in the business of policing and crime reduction, and that the police should be responding to their concerns and priorities rather than chasing government-set targets or esoteric models. Coupled with this is the perplexing problem that fear and perception of crime in the West seem to be rising, in a counter-intuitive way when all the statistics point to crime rates actually falling in many areas and sectors of crime. Maguire earlier noted that, in many ways, these societal developments are manifestations of 'fear and insecurity which are endemic to fragmented communities of later modernity'.[26] As traditional societies and support groups begin to break down and become diluted in an increasingly urbanized and globalized world, many feel that the police are their only provider of fundamental local security.

In political terms, this means that a target-driven intelligence-led model has not been providing the public with the levels of reassurance that it wants, and that policing models which stress a return to more visible and community-oriented models of policing have become more important. In the UK this had

---

[24] Cope, 'Intelligence-led Policing or Policing-led Intelligence?', n 4 above, p 192.

[25] Maguire and John, 'Intelligence Led Policing', n 13 above, p 74.

[26] M Maguire, 'Policing by Risks and Targets: Some Dimensions and Implications of Intelligence-led Crime Control' (2000) 9 *Policing and Society* 315.

led to a number of developments, including the advent of Police Community Support Officers whose main job it is to walk around local communities and be a first line of visible contact for the public. As the Chief Constable of Thames Valley Police noted, however, this means that the public increasingly see the police as responsible for a very wide spectrum of issues and challenges, from local vandalism to the interdiction of international organized-crime groups.[27]

The second issue, of narrowing the justice gap, reflects an increasing concern with the end-to-end outcome of policing, whereby first-line activity, such as complaints to the police or arrests, leads all the way through to successful convictions of offenders. Again, this point is partly linked to public anxiety over targets and metrics, and a suspicion that apparently good performance in a particular metric (eg arrests) is a dangerous smokescreen if subsequent action (convictions of offenders and reduction in crime) is not achieved to the same degree. The corollary in the health sector is the metric of waiting times for certain operations, which can be reduced through careful management of the initial referral process, but this does not mean that more people will be successfully treated.

For the question of intelligence, the implications of these issues are that the development of more effective processes and models for building effective intelligence analysis into the policing system can be deflected or undermined by changes in populist models for policing, but also that, as Ratcliffe noted, the goal should not be intelligence-led policing but rather 'intelligence-led crime reduction'.[28] It is also interesting to note that the intelligence role in policing has been subjected to a sometimes bewildering range of managerial models, each with its own set of acronyms, driven by popular concerns and political reactions to those concerns. The intelligence-analysis function in the state intelligence agencies is, by definition, hidden away, but we can be reasonably confident that it has been subjected to nothing like the same degree of populist discourse and fluctuating managerial theorizing.

Cultural Influences, and 'Surveillance Anxiety'

There is a sense in Western society in which intelligence work has always been seen as something a little shady and of dubious moral essence. As long ago as 1929, the US Secretary of State, Henry L Stimson, captured the mood of many when he closed down the infamous cryptographic bureau in the State Department, called the 'Black Chamber', explaining that 'gentlemen do not read each other's mail'.[29] In the US, we have seen how the FBI's counter-intelligence

---

[27] S Thornton and L Mason, 'Local Accountability and the Police Service: the Development of Neighbourhood Policing' (2007) 1 *Policing* 514, 517.

[28] J Ratcliffe, *Intelligence-Led Policing*, Trends and Issues in Crime and Criminal Justice No. 248 (Canberra: Australian Institute of Criminology, 2003) p 6.

[29] Cited in AN Shulsky and GJ Schmitt, *Silent Warfare: Understanding the World of Intelligence* (Washington DC: Potomac Books, 2002) p 169.

programme in the 1950s and 1960s led to deep distrust of the state's use of intelligence powers; particularly in the domestic arena. Cilluffo, Marks, and Salmoiraghi observed that:

> Understanding the historic relationship between the United States and the necessarily shadowy world of intelligence is important. U.S. citizens have been of two minds about the subject, vacillating between their fascination with intelligence's romanticized, James Bond-like aspects and their repugnance at its reality, in which 'dirty people' engage in 'dirty business'.[30]

Ratcliffe is more pessimistic, noting that 'intelligence seems to summon up the wrong image in just about everyone', and tends to conjure up a sense of 'moral ambiguity'.[31] Certainly within the policing profession in the UK there seems to be a cultural issue whereby intelligence is seen as the specialist province of the detectives and Special Branch, and not necessarily the business of routine police officers.[32]

This has probably always been the case to a certain extent, but there is much evidence that a general anxiety about espionage and surveillance has been growing in Western society, particularly since the end of the Cold War and accelerating since 9/11. This is probably for two reasons. First, as we have noted, the nature of civil society is changing in the postmodern world whereby traditional societies, values, and support networks are perceived to be breaking down, and there is a resultant anxiety among many about the nature of identity and community. Second, we have also examined how the nature of the security threat has changed in the post-Cold War world, to a situation where threats are much more global, mobile, and threaded inextricably though civil society. The security response of the state in the West has been to increase its surveillance and analysis of civil society in an effort to track criminals and terrorists hidden within it, and this in turn has led to a suspicion in some that the central values of a liberal democratic society are being eroded. There have also been elements of the security response post-9/11 which are perceived by many to be on the edge of moral acceptability, such as the use of aggressive interrogation techniques and complicity in abduction and torture.

It is a luxury of repressive, totalitarian regimes that they can exercise extensive surveillance and repression of their domestic populations to ensure the survival of their regime and to quash dissent. The Stasi, at its height, is believed to have employed more than 2 per cent of the entire population of East Germany as informers.[33] By 1989, when the East German state collapsed, it is estimated that approximately 12 per cent of the population had collaborated with the Stasi in

---

[30] FJ Cilluffo, RA Marks, and GC Salmoiraghi, 'The Use and Limits of US Intelligence' (2002) 25/1 *The Washington Quarterly* 61, 62.

[31] J Ratcliffe, 'Intelligence-Led Policing' in R Wortley and L Mazerolle (eds), *Environmental Criminology and Crime Analysis* (Cullompton: Willan, 2008) p 263.

[32] Maguire and John, 'Intelligence Led Policing', n 13 above, p 83.

[33] JO Koehler, *Stasi: The Untold Story of the East German Secret Police* (New York NY: Basic Books, 2000).

some shape or form.[34] Liberal democracies would like to see themselves as the antithesis of such societies, yet developments since the turn of the century have seen many compelled to use such terms as 'police state' and 'Big Brother' to describe the security responses of Western nations. Such an evocation of George Orwell's nightmarish society described in *1984*, in which individual privacy and rights are surrendered to a totally authoritarian state, are a problematic turn of events for those charged with achieving buy-in to their modernized security policies. Examples abound, but it is interesting to examine the sentiments and vocabulary used around the UK's efforts to record in a central database communications data which phone companies and internet service providers are obliged to keep for at least twelve months under new EU legislation. Openly and routinely described as 'the Big Brother database' in much of the media, the system has led many civil rights campaigners in the UK to warn of a huge and disproportionate invasion of privacy.[35]

In examining the thinking within government, at least within the UK, part of the answer can be found in the recently republished Counter Terrorism Strategy (CONTEST). Under the heading of 'The Intercept Modernisation Programme', this notes that:

> The way in which people are communicating with one another is changing rapidly, with greater use of internet-based communications . . . These changes pose a significant challenge to our ability to investigate all forms of crime, including terrorism; if we take no action, our capability to obtain [communications data] and intercept communications will fall. The ability of law enforcement and security and intelligence agencies to protect national security and prevent crime would be severely affected.[36]

The necessity to gather details of internet activity is therefore presented as essential to uncover crime and to protect national security. It is assumed that most law-abiding members of the public would have no problem with that notion, but the question is one of balance and proportionality, and trust over whether the government is sufficiently competent and fair-minded to use and safeguard the data appropriately. (A number of high profile losses of data by government officials and contractors working with them have tended to undermine that trust.)

This was essentially the point that GCHQ tackled in its recent and unprecedented press release on the interception issue, in which it said:

> GCHQ does not target anyone indiscriminately—all our activities are proportionate to the threats against which we seek to guard and are subject to tests

---

[34] A Glees, *The Stasi Files* (London: The Free Press, 2003) p 3.

[35] See, eg R Verkaik, 'Call for safeguards over Big Brother database', *The Independent*, 10 January 2009, <http://www.independent.co.uk/news/uk/politics/call-for-safeguards-over-big-brother-database-1297563.html>, accessed 31 December 2009.

[36] HM Government, *Pursue, Prevent, Protect, Prepare: The United Kingdom's Strategy for Countering International Terrorism* (London: TSO, 2009) p 73.

on those grounds by the Commissioners. The legislation also sets out the procedures for Ministers to authorise interception; GCHQ follows these meticulously. GCHQ only acts when it is necessary and proportionate to do so; GCHQ does not spy at will.[37]

For a state intelligence agency to raise its head above the parapet in this way and enter the media debate is extremely unusual, and shows the desire on the part of the government to explain, while accepting the difficult questions of privacy posed by the new surveillance imperative, that these activities are necessary in the face of the post-Cold War security threats. Furthermore, legal oversight and scrupulous attention to policy controls are re-emphasized. Clearly GCHQ felt there was a need to correct perceived inaccuracies in the reporting of its activities.

In recent analysis by Newcastle University,[38] researchers noted a dichotomy in public perception between a need for privacy, and the need to be protected from the anonymity of others. Most traders and members of the public are supportive of CCTV in town centres and shopping districts, as it provides reassurance that urban anonymity cannot be a cover for crime, even if, in practice, most of the CCTV installations are not installed or used properly. There is a public demand for reassuring surveillance, to which private companies have responded.

Similarly, hotels and apartment blocks are considered safer and more attractive if they have 24-hour security on the door, watching who is coming and going. We are grateful when our credit card company automatically notices unusual transactions in our account and alerts us to possible fraud, and many of us (although not all I suspect) are quite happy when retailers such as Amazon model our online shopping behaviour and make recommendations as to which books we might want to read.

In other cases, even the civil libertarians themselves call for greater security and intelligence, exposing a potential flaw in their argument. When the infamous Soham murders happened in the UK, the resultant Bichard enquiry criticized Humberside police for poor record keeping, and called for a national police database which could exchange information with social services.[39] The argument from the Chief Constable of Humberside Police was that he believed the Data Protection Act would have prevented him keeping and exchanging information on allegations about the murderer's nefarious past, all of which were accusations which had not resulted in any criminal charges. However, even the civil rights pressure group Liberty has implied that the police do not properly understand data retention directives and can get it wrong in the case of 'soft

---

[37] GCHQ press release, 3 May 2009, <http://www.gchq.gov.uk/press/prelease.html>, accessed 31 December 2009.

[38] D Murakami Wood (ed), *A Report on the Surveillance Society* (London: Information Commissioner's Office, 2006), <http://www.ico.gov.uk/upload/documents/library/data_protection/practical_application/surveillance_society_full_report_2006.pdf>, accessed 31 December 2009.

[39] 'Huntley case: Key mistakes made', *BBC News*, 22 June 2004, <http://news.bbc.co.uk/1/hi/uk/3826355.stm>, accessed 31 December 2009.

intelligence', namely sensitive records on minors.[40] This was a telling example of how the question of the necessity for intelligence and surveillance in a modern Western democracy is far from being clearly understood and articulated.

In 2004, the Information Commissioner in the UK, Richard Thomas, famously said that we were 'in danger of sleepwalking into a surveillance society', and initiated a Parliamentary Home Affairs Committee debate into the issue.[41] In 2006, he claimed that 'we are in fact waking up to a surveillance society that is already all around us'.[42] He further noted that:

> Surveillance activities can be well-intentioned and bring benefits. They may be necessary or desirable—for example to fight terrorism and serious crime, to improve entitlement and access to public and private services, and to improve healthcare. But unseen, uncontrolled or excessive surveillance can foster a climate of suspicion and undermine trust.[43]

Herein lies the dilemma—in modern society, we feel we need intelligence and surveillance for certain activities such as fighting crime or terrorism, but we have an inherent suspicion of it getting out of control. The Information Commissioner's report generated a great deal of public debate and interest in the UK, reflecting the levels of concern and anxiety over developments in the field of data sharing and intelligence activity, which can be powerful influences on major programmes of work and policy in these areas. Such developments are being replicated across the Western world to varying degrees. In Sweden during 2008, for example, a proposed law to extend government intelligence-gathering powers over cross-border internet traffic, dubbed the 'Big Brother law', ran up against heavy opposition in Parliament over apparently disproportionate invasions of privacy.[44] The opposition has ultimately proved decisive in quashing the law, given the government's slim majority, at least for the time being.

Ethics of Intelligence

Since 9/11 and subsequent developments, the debate in security and intelligence sectors in the West around the ethics of intelligence activity in responding to the new terrorism threat has heightened. Michael Herman pondered whether there was a need to consider the question of ethics in intelligence, as 'no-one gets hurt by it, at least not directly'.[45] Snooping on people to protect

---

[40] G Crossman, *Overlooked: Surveillance and Personal Privacy in Modern Britain* (London: Liberty UK, 2007) p 64.

[41] R Ford, 'Beware rise of Big Brother state, warns data watchdog', *The Times*, 16 August 2004, <http://www.timesonline.co.uk/tol/news/uk/article470264.ece>, accessed 31 December 2009.

[42] 'Waking up to a surveillance society', *Directgov*, 2 November 2006, <http://www.direct.gov.uk/en/Nl1/Newsroom/DG_064891>, accessed 31 December 2009.   [43] Ibid.

[44] R Boyes, 'Swedish revolt over "Big Brother" law', *The Times*, 17 June 2008, <http://www.timesonline.co.uk/tol/news/world/europe/article4158509.ece>, accessed 31 December 2009.

[45] M Herman, 'Ethics and Intelligence after September 2001' (2004) 19 *Intelligence and National Security* 342.

Table 4.1 Ethical models of intelligence

Ethical model	Characteristics	Implications for intelligence
Realist	Acting in the national interest is paramount, and not to do so would be foolish as it would lay the population open to undue hostile influence from outside.	Intelligence gathering is a fundamental duty of the state and should not be seen as unethical: indeed, not to do so could be seen as immoral as it would expose the population to risk and influence.
Consequentialist	Considers that the ethics of intelligence activity are a balancing act, determined by the effects of the activity; a consideration of the 'ethical balance sheet' resulting from the activity.	Intelligence is allowed where it is demonstrably for the public good or protection, but must always be weighed against its impacts: these may sometimes judge that it is not appropriate or ethical in particular cases.
Deontological	Rejects the necessity for most forms of intelligence gathering as they are fundamentally unethical in essence, and this moral value cannot be compromised.	Can allow for some intelligence-gathering activities where these are not harmful, such as passive monitoring of communications in defence of the state; rejects any activities such as deception which are morally wrong.

the nation's security is essentially a passive and invisible activity. He did accept that intelligence agencies also carry out covert action in some cases, but that this is a different line of activity which requires different considerations. However, as we have seen, many would consider intelligence gathering in all its forms as something carrying 'a baggage of unworthiness', which is essentially about deception, manipulation, and sneaking around.[46]

It is worth considering briefly the academic debate around ethics in intelligence, since many of the issues have become much more significant since the turn of the century and can act as political influences on intelligence policy and programmes. Table 4.1 summarizes the three models of intelligence ethics which have emerged in the analysis in recent years.

To a certain extent, these models can be mapped across to models of changing security paradigms more generally. The 'Realist' model, for example, has also been seen in the field of security studies to refer to traditional military-oriented paradigms of security, whereby a state has the right to arm itself and conduct military operations where another state is threatening military action. From an ethical standpoint, this means that some acts of war can be justified where they are conducted to confront an existential threat from a military foe: this is the argument, for example, around the British air bombardments of German cities during the Second World War, which some have argued were morally

---

[46] Ibid.

unjustifiable. For intelligence gathering, and particularly in peacetime, the perceived existential nature of the modern terrorist threat means that some see that the same rules should apply. 'Neo-realist' and 'Pluralist' models of security threat were essentially extensions of this concept, in that they saw a wider source of threats as potentially determining a state's national security policy, including crime, terrorism, natural disasters, and battles for resources.

The 'Consequentialist' model in intelligence is that followed primarily in the Western world at present, and more particularly in Western Europe. Here, the European Convention on Human Rights (ECHR) has been ratified in most national parliaments, and this protects fundamental civil rights including the right not to suffer invasions of privacy or surveillance. The nations in question have accepted that properly controlled intelligence activity is necessary for the defence of their states, however, but must be carried out through separate legislation which temporarily exempts the nation from the ECHR, providing strict controls and tests of proportionality are put in place. Thus, Herman's 'ethical balance sheet'[47] is presumed to be applied on a daily basis by the intelligence gatherers (as GCHQ stressed in its press release above) to consider if their actions are compliant with an override of the ECHR, providing tests of proportionality have been passed satisfactorily and the action has been properly authorized at the appropriate level (usually government ministerial level).

The terrorist threat since 9/11, and the security responses to it in the West, have, however, led to some fundamentally difficult questions about what is proportionate and appropriate to protect the nation's security in the face of such threats. A return to covert action activities, particularly in the US, has thrown the whole debate into relief and generated a great deal of anguished debate. The epicentre of this discussion has been the question of the use of torture in counter-terrorist operations, to generate tactical intelligence. As Kamiya notes, the Kantian argument is a deontological one, that the moral necessity of treating human beings as ends, not means, signifies that torture can never be justified. The consequentialist or 'utilitarian' argument is that torture has been shown to work sometimes (an assertion made by former defence secretary Cheney in the context of the interrogation of Al Qaeda operatives by the US[48]) and that the infamous 'ticking bomb' scenario might mean that torture of a detainee with crucial information can sometimes be justified if it could lead to the protection of multiple lives.[49]

Generally, counter-terrorism policy is not as simple or as black and white as this. The public might accept that intelligence gathering in the fight against terrorism is wholly necessary to protect the state, but might be more equivocal on whether torture is ever justified. A research programme on world public

---

[47] Ibid, p 345.

[48] 'Cheney enters "torture" memos row', *BBC News*, 21 April 2009, <http://news.bbc.co.uk/1/hi/world/americas/8009571.stm>, accessed 31 December 2009.

[49] G Kamiya, 'Torture works sometimes—but it's always wrong', *Salon.com*, 23 April 2009, <http://www.salon.com/opinion/kamiya/2009/04/23/torture>, accessed 31 December 2009.

opinion on certain policy issues, under the management of the University of Maryland, issued an interesting analysis in 2008 of global public opinion on the use of torture in counter-terrorism policy. A total of 19 countries were polled, and the results showed that, while majorities in all of them favoured a general prohibition on torture, in four of the countries there was a sizeable proportion of respondents who were inclined towards an exception in terrorist cases.[50] The countries in this category (India, Nigeria, Thailand, and Turkey), could reasonably be assessed to have slightly harder opinions on the issue as they were suffering substantial terrorist problems in the run-up to the poll, and that they might vote differently at more peaceful periods in their security history. The results of the poll could be presented negatively or positively depending on the point of view taken, but they do show that some are inclined to take a more consequentialist standpoint on something as controversial as torture, and that they might be more inclined to do so when the threat from terrorists is highest. Clearly this was a factor in US policy shifts and developments post-9/11, and shows that the prevailing security climate can be an important influence on intelligence and security policy.

Just War, and Just Intelligence?

One of the more useful theoretical frameworks for conceptualizing a consequentialist model of intelligence is the 'Just War' model. In military security terms, a notion of a Just War emerges from the dual imperatives that, sometimes, to do something that would normally be morally unjustifiable and repugnant (ie killing people) can be seen as appropriate to safeguard a larger number of lives in certain situations. Added to this, a wholly pacifist policy in which all conflict is avoided can itself be seen as immoral and unethical if it means a population being subjected to tyranny and repression.[51] Thus, to enter into a warlike state can sometimes be seen not only as appropriate but morally imperative, as long as certain constraints and prohibitions are observed to ensure proportionality and basic human rights as far as possible. This was the basis for the signing of the Geneva Conventions in 1949, which govern the conduct of prisoners and populations under occupation during war situations.

Quinlan argues that a similar concept could be applied to the process of intelligence gathering, by recognizing that it is necessary and not fundamentally unethical in certain situations of security threat, but that it needs to be managed within a framework of ethical considerations. (He does, however, note the difficulty that far less is known about the activities of intelligence gatherers, by definition, than is the case with warring armies.[52]) Western states, as we have

---

[50] 'World publics reject torture: but a substantial number make exception for terrorists', World-PublicOpinion.org, 24 June 2008, <http://www.worldpublicopinion.org/pipa/articles/btjusticehuman_rightsra/496.php?lb=bthr&pnt=496&nid=&id=>, accessed 31 December 2009.

[51] M Quinlan, 'Just Intelligence: Prolegomena to an Ethical Theory' (2007) 22 *Intelligence and National Security* 1, 2.   [52] Ibid, p 3.

seen, would see that such a framework exists under the ECHR and similar stat-
utes, and the specified legal structures and processes that allow for exceptions to
be applied. The question is whether sufficient assurance can be provided to the
public that such processes are entirely trustworthy.

In other ways, using models normally applied to situations of war to provide guidance on counter-terrorism is a complicated and controversial business.
Many would argue that contemporary international terrorism is a new type of
security threat which blurs the boundaries between war, security threat, and
crime. This makes it an extraordinarily difficult issue around which to frame
policy. We have seen the criticisms from many quarters about President Bush's
'War on Terror' after 9/11, which was a conscious policy choice to place the
terrorism threat into the military bracket, and thus apply military approaches
and military law to the situation. In other contexts, and particularly in Western
Europe, the threat feels like much more of a domestic and civil issue requiring a
different approach.

Waddington described the problems of Western intelligence and security
actors in responding to terrorist incidents such as 9/11 and 7/7:

> in order to prevent such an 'intelligence failure', the security services become
> hyper-suspicious. Insofar as that suspicion alights on everyone then its intru-
> siveness can be regarded as oppressive and a denial of privacy. Yet, if suspicion
> is directed at those belonging to particular sections of the population (such as
> Muslims), then it can readily be characterized as prejudicial and discrimina-
> tory. Either way, it is a violation of the 'social contract' between the citizen
> and the state.[53]

Nations in the West face the dilemma that a need for more effective and comprehensive surveillance of certain individuals embedded in the population
feels appropriate for national security reasons, yet they need to be able to sell
this imperative and engender trust that they will apply it proportionately and
ethically to the population at large. When their activities are, by definition,
covert and hidden from public scrutiny, the problem is much more challenging and probably one of maintaining a balance and keeping the wolves at bay.
Philosophically, the ironic situation is that modern liberal democracies do not
want to resemble, say, Stasi-governed East Germany in any shape or form, yet
increased levels of covert surveillance of the population and penetration by
Humint sources seem to pull policy in these uncomfortable directions. Added to
this dilemma is the particular nuance identified by Waddington, where the anxiety of covert Big Brother-style surveillance is not necessarily felt evenly across
the population, but is seen as a greater and more targeted activity among certain
sectors of the community. For the police in Western societies, the twin responsibilities of gathering intelligence about the population in local communities,
together with forming a trusting and open relationship with those communities,

---

[53] PAJ Waddington, 'Policing Terrorism' (2007) 1 *Policing* 1, 4.

appears to be a very difficult balancing act which it may be virtually impossible to achieve completely.

Conclusion

Whether or not the shock of 9/11 changed the security paradigm in the West fundamentally (and there are arguments for and against this theory), there is no doubt that the immediate security response in the US was one in which questions of the continuum between intelligence gathering and analysis, and covert action based on its findings, were catapulted back into the forefront of public debate in a way that had not been the case since the 1970s. Cogan notes that the key shift was one of intelligence policy, whereby the nature of the new terrorist security threat meant that US intelligence agencies could no longer be passive collectors of intelligence, installed in their bunkers after the difficulties of the anti-communist COINTELPRO era, but had aggressively to confront and hunt down their enemy. In short, twenty-first century intelligence actors in the West had to become 'hunters not gatherers'.[54]

Cogan was referring particularly to the nexus between intelligence gatherers and the military in the shape of special forces, whose capability had been developed ever since the ignominious disaster of 'Desert One' in 1980 in which the US had attempted to rescue hostages from the US Embassy in Tehran.[55] Since 9/11, we have seen a greatly increased use of trained special forces to carry out offensive operations on the ground overseas.[56] We have also seen targeted assassinations of Al Qaeda leaders using unmanned aerial drones, and the clandestine rendition of terrorist suspects to third countries where many of them have undoubtedly been subjected to torture as part of their interrogation. As uncomfortable as some of the debate has been about such measures, these activities would have been politically impossible to undertake in the years leading up to 9/11.

What all of these developments mean is that the intelligence practitioner in the twenty-first century, particularly when dealing with counter-terrorist issues, needs to have a keen awareness of the new ethical issues that surround the craft of modern intelligence gathering and needs to be aware of the influence these issues have on colleagues, the public, and on the intelligence-gathering process as a whole. Such issues feed into the political landscape and can be extremely powerful external influences. In Western Europe, counter-terrorist intelligence does not necessarily deal with targeted assassinations or torture, but it is working at a heightened level of community surveillance, using both technical and human 'informants', in a way that causes uncomfortable memories of authoritarian regimes both past and present. Such issues, and the political fallout from them, can be powerful

---

[54] C Cogan, 'Hunters Not Gatherers: Intelligence in the Twenty-First Century' (2004) 19 *Intelligence and National Security* 304.   [55] Ibid, p 314.

[56] G Lubold, 'A surge of Special Forces for Afghanistan likely', *Christian Science Monitor*, 23 December 2008, <http://www.csmonitor.com/2008/1223/p01s01-usfp.html>, accessed 31 December 2009.

influences on the policy-makers who have to consider how to form and develop their security and intelligence policy within a politicized landscape.

Part of the problem for those working in intelligence is the cultural issue that it has always been seen as a black, and somewhat unpalatable, art by many people. When Katharine Gun, a linguist working at the British Sigint agency GCHQ, brought her career as an intelligencer abruptly to an end in 2003 by leaking details of a classified operation to the press, she did so under the claim that she could no longer be involved in what she perceived to be a 'dirty tricks' campaign of telephone tapping of UN Security Council delegations, and that she was politically and morally opposed to the developing case for going to war in Iraq.[57] While Gun's case was unusual and involved an unorthodox method of raising a grievance, it illustrated a risk that exists within the contemporary intelligence domain, that ethical issues surrounding current intelligence requirements—and surrounding the intelligence-gathering process as a whole in the West—will be seen by some as fundamentally problematic, and incompatible with the values of a modern liberal democracy. Intelligence officers and their managers have to be keenly aware of these political and cultural issues, and of the influences they can bring to bear on intelligence policy and practice.

Key Points

- The intelligence cycle can be interrupted and affected by varying relationships between 'customers' and intelligence producers, particularly in cases where pressing intelligence goes 'straight to the top' before going through the analysis process.

- Political influences can have a major impact on the intelligence cycle, with the Iraq War of 2003 appearing to be a classic example. The issue here was a complex combination of power struggles within the political structure in the US, and the manner in which political goals were driving interpretation of the intelligence, rather than the other way round.

- In the policing arena, political influences have had an influence on the intelligence process in a different way, by the manner in which law enforcement and security issues have become deeply political issues for voters. This has led to a succession of administrative models for policing and the role of intelligence within it, fluctuating between intelligence-led policing and neighbourhood 'reassurance' policing.

- Changes in society in the post-Cold War era have seen a growing sense of 'surveillance anxiety' in the public, and a resurgence of feelings that intrusive intelligence gathering is somehow unethical. This, in turn, has become a political issue which affects intelligence policy formulation.

---

[57] 'Ex-GCHQ Officer "preventing war"', *BBC News*, 27 November 2003, <http://news.bbc.co.uk/1/hi/uk/3243266.stm>, accessed 31 December 2009.

- The growing terrorist threat in the twenty-first century has led to more intrusive and proactive intelligence-gathering measures in the West, which have brought ethical considerations to the fore. Modern intelligence actors need to be keenly aware of such issues, both in terms of their effect on the public, and also on the workforce within the intelligence-practitioner community.

PART TWO

Art and Science in
Intelligence Analysis

5

Analytical Theory:
The Art of Analysis

In the first half of this book we have focused on the macro picture of the intelligence business, particularly as it pertains to the Western world. We have looked at the end-to-end process of intelligence gathering and dissemination, and the influences and stress factors which come into play and shape intelligence outcomes. We have also looked at how major paradigm shifts in the security threat picture since the end of the Cold War have had a bearing on the intelligence response, and have arguably remained one step ahead, continuing to pose very difficult and not entirely resolved questions relating to state intelligence agencies and law enforcement bodies.

In Chapter 2, in the context of intelligence failures, we briefly examined the analysis process within the intelligence cycle, and looked at the limitations and difficulties which apply to the process, and which can have an adverse affect on its outcome. In the second half of the book, we will delve much deeper into the analysis process itself, and into the cognitive and psychological debates and models which have surrounded it. Such an examination leads to recommendations for how to use exercises and techniques for enhancing and improving the analysis process within the intelligence function, whether it concerns strategic or tactical analysis. We will present these recommendations in Chapter 7.

In this chapter, we focus on the cognitive activities surrounding analysis itself, with a view to raising awareness about these activities (which can be called *heuristics*), and considering how to mitigate their negative aspects. This, in a sense, is the 'art' part of the picture. In the next chapter, we will consider the 'science' part of intelligence analysis, namely the technical and organizational considerations which surround the analysis process, which can help, if used correctly, to enhance the overall effectiveness of the process and mitigate against failures.

Thinking about Thinking

The grandfather of intelligence analysis tradecraft as a specific skill to be developed was Sherman Kent, who started life as a teacher of history at Yale University before the Second World War, and ended up working for the CIA in analytical development. In 2000, his name was given to the Sherman Kent School for Intelligence Analysis, founded by the Directorate of Intelligence at the CIA to sit alongside the Center for the Study of Intelligence. This is effectively the first 'university' (albeit restricted to CIA staff) devoted entirely to the business of intelligence analysis; an institution that has not been replicated anywhere else in the world to date.

Kent's life was devoted to the question of critical thinking, first in academia and later within government. He once noted that:

> Whatever the complexities of the puzzles we strive to solve, and whatever the sophisticated techniques we may use to collect the pieces and store them, there can never be a time when the thoughtful man can be supplanted as the intelligence device supreme.[1]

Although made a long time ago, Kent's observation is a critical one which arguably holds as true today as it did all those years ago. In an age of increasingly complex and capable tools and systems available for use by the intelligence analyst to mine and manipulate data (a subject we will explore in greater detail in the next chapter), the analyst's basic cognitive skills are still as essential as any part of the process, and can mean the difference between intelligence success and failure.

One of the more prolific and celebrated academics working within the CIA on the question of analysis was Richards Heuer, whose seminal 1999 work *Psychology of Intelligence Analysis*[2] (hereafter referred to as *Psychology*) still remains something of a bible of analytical tradecraft analysis, certainly across Anglo-Saxon state intelligence agencies. Heuer's work was a comprehensive analysis of the process of thought, including cognitive weaknesses which affect judgement-making, and a set of recommendations for how to improve cognitive performance. Heuer was less well known within the CIA than his contemporary, Sherman Kent, and rose to less senior levels than some of the other influential writers on analysis within the agency, but his work has subsequently proved to be just as far-reaching and influential across the analytical community both within the US and internationally.[3]

---

[1] S Kent, *Strategic Intelligence for American World Policy* (Princeton NJ: Princeton University Press, 1965) p xviii.

[2] RJ Heuer, Jr, *Psychology of Intelligence Analysis* (Langley VA: Center for the Study of Intelligence, 1999).   [3] J Davis, 'Introduction' in Heuer, ibid, p xix.

Heuer opened *Psychology* with the need to conduct 'thinking about thinking' when first considering the process of intelligence analysis, and what can go wrong with it. He noted that:

> Of the diverse problems that impede accurate intelligence analysis, those inherent in human mental processes are surely among the most important and most difficult to deal with. Intelligence analysis is fundamentally a mental process, but understanding this process is hindered by the lack of conscious awareness of the workings of our own minds ... A basic finding of cognitive psychology is that people have no conscious experience of most of what happens in the human mind. Many functions associated with perception, memory, and information processing are conducted prior to and independently of any conscious direction. What appears spontaneously in consciousness is the result of thinking, not the process of thinking.[4]

Intelligence failures can result from faulty cognitive heuristics being applied to intelligence data, particularly if the analysts do not understand the cognitive traps and pitfalls which are natural characteristics of the human brain when faced with large amounts of complex data, and are generally not 'self-aware'. The first thing the analytical community needs to develop, therefore, is a heightened understanding and awareness of these cognitive weaknesses at all times in their analysis, so that the risks of poor judgement can be mitigated or at least spotted wherever possible. This is essentially a level of 'metacognition', ie cognitive awareness about the process of thinking itself.

'Thinking', however, is too woolly a concept to be of utility for analysts in itself, so we will break it down further here into a number of key components, namely: critical thinking, creativity, powers of judgement, and communication (see Figure 5.1). These can act as a sort of mini-framework within which analysts across the community can 'think about thinking', and specifically think about the skills that they need to develop and hone in order to mitigate mistakes and improve overall analytical performance. We will examine each of these skills in turn, but it is worth recapping on the fundamental cognitive weaknesses that Heuer identified in *Psychology*. As Jack Davis noted, one of Heuer's central arguments is that:

> The mind is poorly 'wired' to deal effectively with both inherent uncertainty (the natural fog surrounding complex, indeterminate intelligence issues) and induced uncertainty (the man-made fog fabricated by denial and deception operations).[5]

More specifically, this problem comprises factors of perception and memory in the human brain (as we saw in Chapter 2), both of which are inherently imperfect, and liable to suffer undue influence from a range of environmental,

---

[4] Heuer, ibid, p 1.   [5] Davis, 'Introduction', n 3 above, p xx.

Figure 5.1 Thinking about Thinking: Core Skills

Critical Thinking

Creativity

Powers of judgement

Communication

historical and cultural influences. Yet individuals are rarely aware of the nature and extent of such dangers. Intelligence analysts are no different from other human beings in being vulnerable to these difficulties, but they should arguably be more attuned to their effect, as their trade is, after all, thinking.

Critical Thinking

The former senior CIA officer and analyst of the intelligence-gathering function, Mark Lowenthal, noted that, while the intelligence community has conducted a great deal of soul-searching about how it conducts analysis, much of this has been concentrated on 'techniques, presentation and outcomes', and relatively little on the intellectual process of thinking in an analytical context itself. The specific skill needed is that of 'critical thinking', which Lowenthal describes as 'thinking about our thinking while we are thinking'.[6]

Critical thinking has been much debated in the educational sector, particularly in the US, since the beginning of the twentieth century. Facione et al note that just about every institution in the higher education sector in the US has for many years embraced the notion of critical thinking as a core skill to be developed in its students.[7] In 1990, the American Philosophical Association completed a two-year study into the essence of critical thinking, and concluded that it consists of two dimensions: a list of characteristics or skills that critical thinkers will naturally display, and 'dispositions', which can be defined as a particular attitude or approach that leads a person to think critically in an effective way.

How is a critical thinker defined? The American Philosophical Association came up with the following description:

> The ideal critical thinker is habitually inquisitive, well-informed, trustful of reason, open-minded, flexible, fair-minded in evaluation, honest in facing

---

[6] MM Lowenthal, 'Foreword' in DT Moore, *Critical Thinking and Intelligence Analysis,* Occasional Paper 14 (Washington DC: Joint Military Intelligence College, 2006) p x.

[7] PA Facione et al, 'The Disposition Toward Critical Thinking' (1995) 44 *Journal of General Education* 1, 2.

personal biases, prudent in making judgements, willing to reconsider, clear about issues, orderly in complex matters, diligent in seeking relevant information, reasonable in the selection of criteria, focused in inquiry, and persistent in seeking results which are as precise as the subject and the circumstances of inquiry permit.[8]

In an educational environment, critical thinking is about conducting learning in a more proactive and involved way, rather than passively receiving information and repeating it by rote: essentially the tutorial model as opposed to the lecture model, whereby students learn to find the answers themselves through skilful enquiry and questioning rather than expect to be told the answer without any action on their part other than memorizing the details. It is also about being prepared to challenge one's own assumptions and biases, and being open to ideas from others. At a more extreme level, many have suggested that critical thinking goes further than the educational realm and into that of politics and society, becoming 'essential for a rational and democratic society'.[9] Authoritarian and totalitarian societies are the anathema of a culture of critical thinking, since the essence of this skill is to have complete freedom to develop ideas and hypotheses without constraint or boundary, and to be prepared to embrace ideas from others. There are a good many non-democratic societies where critical thinking is only allowed on very defined and 'safe' areas of enquiry.

The core characteristics of critical thinking can be described as skills in analysis, inference, interpretation, explanation, self-regulation, and evaluation.[10] Dispositions towards critical thinking, as outlined by the California Critical Thinking Disposition Inventory which flowed from the work of the American Philosophical Association in 1990, can be summarized as being inquisitive, systematic, analytical, judicious, truth-seeking, open-minded, and confident in reasoning.[11] Table 5.1 provides an overview of these two dimensions of critical thinking, as outlined by Facione.

How do these factors relate to the business of intelligence analysis? In his extensive and detailed analysis of this question, David Moore asserted that 'critical thinking extends to the entire intelligence analysis process'.[12] We saw in Chapter 2 that Lord Butler's report on intelligence concerning weapons of mass destruction (WMD) noted that 'well-developed imagination at all stages of the intelligence process is required to overcome preconceptions. There is a case for encouraging it by providing for structured challenge.'[13] We also postulated in

---

[8] American Philosophical Association, *Critical Thinking: A Statement of Expert Consensus for Purposes of Educational Assessment and Instruction*, The Delphi Report, ERIC Doc No ED315-423 (1990) p 3.

[9] PA Facione, *Critical Thinking: What It is and Why It Counts: 2009 Update* (Insight Assessment, 2009) p 20.   [10] Ibid, p 5.   [11] Ibid, p 10.

[12] Moore, *Critical Thinking and Intelligence Analysis*, n 6 above, p 6.

[13] *Review of Intelligence on Weapons of Mass Destruction,* Report of a Committee of Privy Counsellors chaired by The Rt Hon Lord Butler of Brockwell (London: TSO, 2004) p 16.

Table 5.1 Critical Thinking Skills and Dispositions (after Facione (2009))

Core Critical Thinking Skills	Critical Thinking Dispositions
• Analysis	• Inquisitive
• Inference	• Systematic
• Interpretation	• Analytical
• Explanation	• Judicious
• Self-regulation	• Truth-seeking
• Evaluation	• Open-minded
	• Confident in reasoning

Chapter 2 how 'challenge' could be applied at all stages in the intelligence cycle, in the shape of critical questions, from the initial receipt of the intelligence requirement (what is the underlying intelligence gap?) through to the dissemination (has uncertainty in the judgement been appropriately communicated?) and the resultant action taken by policy-makers (have they properly understood any ambiguities and uncertainties in the intelligence?).

Challenge is one component of critical thinking. Analysts need constantly to challenge their own hypotheses and judgements, but also constructively challenge those of others around them, being alive always to the possibility that another alternative hypothesis may be more compelling than their own. The method for conducting this challenge is underpinned by a process called 'Socratic questioning', namely the posing of a set of challenging questions which lead students or analysts to explore the information before them, and their analysis of it, and draw out a deeper understanding which approaches something like the truth (if such a thing can ever be definitively established in intelligence, which is doubtful). In education, the deployment of Socratic questioning is a facilitative form of learning delivery, whereby—if used skilfully—the students conduct their own analysis 'out loud' and come to conclusions themselves, without the tutor having to spell it out. In the field of intelligence analysis, a 'culture of Socratic questioning' ought to be the norm, within and between teams of analysts, constantly to challenge unfolding hypotheses.

Moore took the historical example of the uncertain performance of US intelligence in the period leading up to the Cuban missile crisis, in which an urban myth had developed within the intelligence community that all Humint information emerging from Cuba was always wrong. This became a form of 'groupthink' in which all analysts understood this to be the case. When new Humint emerged concerning a sighting of the Soviets deploying what appeared to be SS-4 Medium Range Ballistic Missiles on the island, a process of 'deductive reasoning' was applied whereby the new intelligence was washed against the rule that all

Humint from Cuba was erroneous, and was thus rejected. It was only later, when imagery was obtained from U-2 overflights of the island, that it was realized that the earlier information had in fact been correct. The implication here is that the situation could have been monitored and managed much earlier, before it had reached the crisis stage, if US policy-makers had made a different reading of intelligence about the missile deployments much sooner in the process.[14]

The obvious modern-day corollary of this situation is the case for going to war in Iraq in 2003, in which something of the reverse happened. Here, a piece of Humint from an Iraqi dissident was developed into a groupthink paradigm across the transatlantic intelligence community that Saddam Hussein was currently engaged in developing an offensive WMD capability, when a more critical reading of the situation and consideration of alternative hypotheses might have quickly shone a light on the frailty of the information and its source.

It is important to note that critical thinking inherently does not mean destructive challenge, point-scoring, or intellectual bullying. If these aspects seep into the analytical and discursive culture, then critical thinking is not being applied appropriately and can actually increase greatly the chances of an analytical or judgemental process going wrong and triggering an intelligence failure. Challenge in critical thinking is all about facilitative questioning, to turn over stones and navigate towards a deeper understanding of a situation, combined with a self-effacing disposition towards accepting that one can be wrong sometimes, and that everyone has a potentially valid point to make, even if it seems crazy or tangential at first. Such ideas should be examined, and, if appropriate, discounted through logical and constructive reasoning.

Creativity

We saw in Lord Butler's assessment of the WMD intelligence failure that the question of a failure of 'imagination' is identified. The 9/11 Commission in the US takes this as one of the central factors that led the intelligence community to miss the potential modus operandi that the attackers would use, namely hijacked civilian airliners, rather than more conventional explosive measures such as truck bombs or remotely detonated devices. Much the same had happened sixty years earlier at Pearl Harbor, where abundant intelligence that a Japanese attack was imminent was not converted into a notion that the attack could happen in Hawaii.[15] The answer, claimed the Commission report, is to 'bureaucratize imagination' and somehow build it into the culture of the intelligence agencies.

---

[14] Moore, *Critical Thinking and Intelligence Analysis*, n 6 above, pp 20–6.

[15] National Commission on Terrorist Attacks Upon the United States, *The 9/11 Commission Report* (Washington DC: Superintendent of Documents, US Government Printing Office, 2004) p 344.

Imagination is effectively synonymous with creativity. To build a culture into the intelligence process whereby imagination about how security threats might develop becomes a frequent and routine activity, analysts need to hone and be able to apply their powers of creativity.

The first question in this area, which has been much analyzed and debated, is the question of what constitutes creative thought in an individual, and is it something that can be 'taught' or nurtured? On the first point, psychologists and neurologists believe, as Claxton outlined, that there are two modes of thought which apply at different times to different effect, namely 'deliberative' and 'contemplative' thought.[16] The former is fast-moving and conscious, and usually the result of immediate perception of the situation before the analyst's eyes. The second is slower-moving and largely unconscious, and is the result of more relaxed and less directed contemplation of a particular issue. Both have their value in operational contexts, and are particularly pertinent to the intelligence business. Deliberative thinking is often significant, as the environment is such in an operational intelligence function that there is usually not the time to sit back and cogitate problems indefinitely: the policy-makers often need answers to their questions quickly. The problem is that this more pressurized and deadline-driven mode of thought, so the research suggests, is inherently less suited to creativity, and more particularly to allowing consideration of alternative hypotheses and theories which may challenge the accepted wisdom and guard against such dangers as groupthink. Contemplative thinking, which is akin to 'letting the mind wander' around a particular problem or issue, can prove to be extraordinarily creative and can unlock difficult problems if deployed effectively.

The logical conclusion is that intelligence analysts need as much time as possible to practise contemplative thinking and enhance their imaginative and creative thinking. Inevitably, this is not necessarily very practical for the intelligence business on a day-to-day basis. Hart and Simon highlight the 'tyranny of a current-reporting culture' in the US intelligence community, whereby short, fast-moving fragments of intelligence are the staple diet, and the community of analysts has little time to turn away from the coalface of operational reporting.[17] Nevertheless, Fishbein and Treverton argue that the managers of the intelligence function need to provide analysts with 'much greater time and freedom to think about problems than is normally allowed by hectic production schedule[s]', to foster a 'state of mental relaxation ... conducive to the playful workings of this contemplative mode'.[18] Building thinking time into the schedule, either at the

---

[16] G Claxton, *Hare Brain, Tortoise Mind: How Intelligence Increases When You Think Less* (New York NY: Harper Collins, 2000) pp 201–26.

[17] D Hart and S Simon, 'Thinking Straight and Talking Straight: Problems of Intelligence Analysis' (2006) 48/1 *Survival* 35, 44.

[18] W Fishbein and G Treverton, *Rethinking 'Alternative Analysis' to Address Transnational Threats*, Occasional Paper 3(2) (Sherman Kent Center, 2004) p 6.

office or in the shape of offsites or retreats, can pay for itself in the shape of more effective and creative approaches to difficult analytical problems.

The second issue concerns the 'nature or nurture' debate around the question of creativity. Heuer firmly believes that good analytical tradecraft, including creativity, can be taught:

> Thinking analytically is a skill like carpentry or driving a car. It can be taught, it can be learned, and it can improve with practice. But like many other skills, such as riding a bike, it is not learned by sitting in a classroom and being told how to do it. Analysts learn by doing. Most people achieve at least a minimally acceptable level of analytical performance with little conscious effort beyond completing their education. With much effort and hard work, however, analysts can achieve a level of excellence beyond what comes naturally.[19]

The debate has been going on for many decades, and particularly in the educational sector, where questions of whether students can be nurtured as more creative and critical thinkers have been keenly discussed. Much of the early work on creativity was pioneered by JP Guildford[20] and E Paul Torrance[21] in the 1950s and 1960s. Both were psychometric theorists and measured aptitudes for creativity using psychometric tests. Torrance claimed robustly in the early 1970s that it was definitely possible to teach children to think creatively.[22] By the 1980s, as Treffinger noted, the general academic consensus was that 'improving students' creative thinking and problem-solving abilities are viable educational goals'.[23] Certainly, the environment in which a child is brought up and specifically whether creative and questioning thought is rewarded and nurtured, or chastised and repressed, can be powerful shaping factors in that individual's approach to problem solving in later life. But the general expectation is that creative talents can be developed and honed through appropriate training and exercise.

The question of environment is critical, not just in terms of the environment that the analyst experienced in earlier life, but in the environment created in the analytical workplace, and whether this encourages or suppresses creativity. This means not only whether analysts have time and space to conduct contemplative thinking, as we have discussed above, and can do so in the knowledge that this is accepted and encouraged by management and colleagues in other departments as an entirely appropriate activity of value to the business, but also whether mistakes and misdiagnoses are accepted as an inevitable outcome of the analytical process. Sternberg concluded that 'creativity is in large part a decision

---

[19] Heuer, *Psychology of Intelligence Analysis*, n 2 above, p 2.

[20] JP Guilford, 'Creativity' (1950) 5 *American Psychologist* 444.

[21] EP Torrance, *Guiding Creative Talent* (Englewood Cliffs NJ: Prentice Hall, 1962).

[22] EP Torrance, 'Can We Teach Children to Think Creatively?', paper presented at the Annual Meeting of the American Educational Research Association, 3–7 April 1972, <http://eric.ed.gov/ERICwebPortal/contentdelivery/servlet/ERICServlet?accno=ED061544>, accessed 2 January 2010.

[23] DJ Treffinger, 'Research on Creativity' (1986) 30 *Gifted Child Quarterly* 15, 16.

that anyone can make but that few people actually do make because they find the costs to be too high'.[24]

A fear of making mistakes, or indeed coming up with a hypothesis which does not fit with established norms, can stifle creativity sharply. Weick and Sutcliffe conducted some very useful research on certain 'high reliability organisations' such as aircraft carriers and nuclear power plants, where the consequences of making mistakes can be very serious. They noted that the first principle of such organizations is a 'preoccupation with failure'.[25] This is not in any sense destructive or stifling, but a realization that continual and deep analysis of failure and mistakes with a view to improving performance in the future is a central and critical part of the organizational culture. In a more commercial context, Weick and Sutcliffe noted that the courier firm FedEx incorporates creativity (in this context around reordering, loading, and delivery schedules on aircraft) as a central cultural element in its organization to increase resilience against 'surprises', which are anticipated as a likely nightly occurrence.[26] It is arguably the case that intelligence organizations should take a similar approach to the utility of inculcating a culture of failure analysis as a crucial and positive element of their organizational culture, since the likelihood of surprises and the seriousness of missing them are similarly applicable in the intelligence function. This, in turn, would allow creativity to flourish.

Treffinger expressed confidence that basic ('Level 1') tools for applying creative thinking can be taught and learnt effectively, and that students who learn these tools 'can improve their performance on measures of divergent thinking and creativity-related attitudes'.[27] Care needs to be taken about universal and one-size-fits-all critical and creative thinking programmes, however, as research also suggests that creativity training programmes do not deliver uniform results across all criteria of age, gender, and so on.[28] It is important, therefore, for intelligence analysis units to tailor their creative and critical thinking training programmes carefully to the particular environment present in their organization. We will discuss training options more in Chapter 7.

To unravel further the nature/nurture debate, it is useful to delve a little deeper into the question of what creativity is, and how it works. From a philosophical perspective, Best notes that creativity is sometimes shrouded in an aura of mystery, which creates misconceptions that 'have harmful, or at least confusing, educational consequences'.[29] The matter has not been helped by leaders of creative thought and activity in history, who have often suggested that 'flashes

---

[24] RJ Sternberg, 'The Nature of Creativity' (2006) 18 *Creativity Research Journal* 87, 97.

[25] KE Weick and KM Sutcliffe, *Managing the Unexpected: Resilient Performance in an Age of Uncertainty* (San Francisco CA: John Wiley, 2007) p 9.   [26] Ibid, p 71.

[27] Treffinger, 'Research on Creativity', n 23 above, p 17.   [28] Ibid.

[29] D Best, 'Can Creativity be Taught?' (1982) 30 *British Journal of Educational Studies* 280.

of inspiration' have come out of the air, or by the grace of God. Perhaps unhelpfully, when asked to explain what creativity was, the painter Picasso declared 'I don't know, and if I did, I wouldn't tell you'.[30]

In a review of academic debate around the nature of creativity, Feldhusen and Goh noted that theories have fluctuated between those that conceive it as a subjective experience or set of experiences (eg as suggested by Getzels[31]), and those who feel that an objective and structured framework around both the product and process can be created.[32]

One important differentiation to make is that between the process and the product of creativity. We can all recognize the latter when we see it, but it is the process that has been somewhat elusive and mysterious. Best argues, however, that both are interlinked, and we can only understand the one by understanding the other.[33] From a neurological perspective, Heuer described the process of memory as a system of information being ordered into a schema or multiple schemata. The brain connects together neurons through pathways of synapses, which are structured around relationships between different pieces of information. Over time, this can create 'mental ruts' of heavy traffic which are difficult to overcome. Thus, to recall a long distant piece of information, or one that is not connected very readily to recent thoughts or memories, is much more difficult than to recall something which has been retrieved recently. Creative thinking is essentially a process of transcending these ruts and making new connections between different pieces of information and memory.[34] In very simple terms, mental techniques can help the recall of more extensive pieces of information (such as ordering a shopping list into grouped items, or creating an easy-to-remember acronym to recall a set of pieces of information), but to transcend mental ruts altogether is a more complex undertaking.

In practical terms, Best notes that creativity is usually bounded by objective criteria, within which most people will confine their thinking. A language, for example, has a set of rules and criteria which need to be observed if one is to be understood. A teacher in school has to apply some objective criteria to the framework of the teaching, if only to be able to measure if the curriculum is being taught and the students are making progress against it. But within those boundaries, an individual can be very creative. Sometimes an individual will transcend such boundaries, however, and be creative at a new level. This is the notion of a 'paradigm shift', where new horizons are drawn. Returning to

---

[30] Ibid, p 281.

[31] JW Getzels, 'Creativity: Prospects and Issues' in IA Taylor and JW Getzels (eds), *Perspective in Creativity* (Chicago IL: Aldine, 1975).

[32] JF Feldhusen and Ban Eng Goh, 'Assessing and Accessing Creativity: An Integrative Review of Theory, Research and Development' (1995) 8 *Creativity Research Journal* 231, 232.

[33] Best, 'Can Creativity be Taught?', n 29 above, p 282.

[34] Heuer, *Psychology of Intelligence Analysis*, n 2 above, p 66.

Picasso, for example, we can argue that his art changed the accepted boundaries present at the time of what was considered 'good art', and this in turn created a new landscape into which other artists could move.[35] It is important not to confuse the two levels of creativity, however, or to think that working within boundaries but not challenging them is inherently not creative.

We ask the question again of how is this relevant to the business of intelligence analysis? When calling for the 'bureaucratization of imagination' (see above), both the 9/11 Commission and the Butler enquiry report in the UK were suggesting that practices and techniques needed to be built into the intelligence analysis process whereby time, space, and training to develop creativity and to create an environment in which it could flourish, were necessary to avoid major strategic surprises and intelligence failures in the future. This could be seen to apply both to the assessment of current intelligence questions, and to a post-mortem analysis of previous events and operations to see if anything could be learned from the judgements and indeed mistakes that were made at the time.

We saw in Chapter 2 the case of the bombing of the French and US marine barracks in Beirut in 1983, which marked a significant step forward by Hizbollah in a new strategic direction towards much more effective and destructive truck bombs. A post-event analysis by the intelligence community in the US suggested that, while Hizbollah was thinking creatively about how it could develop its attack methodology to have a bigger impact on Western interests in the Middle East, the Western intelligence community was not being sufficiently creative in its assessment of the situation. The conceptual problem was multi-faceted, and primarily revolved around the imposition of too great a degree of boundaries around the understanding of how Hizbollah might operate. This included a failure to allow new and potentially significant information, in this case the experience of a massive truck bomb deployed against the US Embassy in Beirut earlier in 1983, to alter the perception across the intelligence community of how Hizbollah would operate and where its boundaries might lie. This fits very well with Heuer's assertion, some years later, that:

- We tend to perceive what we expect to perceive.
- Mind-sets tend to be quick to form but resistant to change.[36]

Similarly, after 9/11, the enquiries concluded that there was a massive underestimation of how and where Al Qaeda might change its attack methodology to strike at the West, despite there being fragments of relevant information. These were present at various levels, from the issue of potential terrorists receiving

---

[35] Best, 'Can Creativity be Taught?', n 29 above, p 284.
[36] Heuer, *Psychology of Intelligence Analysis*, n 2 above, pp 9–10.

training in flight schools in the US, of which the FBI was reputedly aware;[37] to previous near-miss incidents, such as the 'millennium bomb plot' in Los Angeles and the bombing of the World Trade Center in New York in 1993; and to the attempt by Algerian terrorists in 1994 to crash a hijacked jet into the Eiffel Tower. As Falkenrath argues, to say that these things amounted to a major failure of imagination in the intelligence community is perhaps a harsh deployment of hindsight given the uncertainty amidst the welter of intelligence information being received, and the 9/11 Commission report does not necessarily offer clues for how to combat such analytical pitfalls in the future.[38] But it has to be the case that the problem could not have been one of a failure alone to share relevant information across boundaries, as significant as this no doubt was.

In the European arena, we have seen a range of potential methodologies deployed by terrorists since the beginning of the twenty-first century, from 'traditional' remotely-triggered devices on trains or in cars (in the cases, respectively, of the Madrid train bombings in 2004, and the attempted vehicle-borne attacks in London in 2007), to suicide attacks (in the case of London in July 2005, or the failed 'shoe-bomber' in 2001 and the Exeter nail-bomber in 2008). We have also seen a range of devices used, from fertilizer-based explosives (in the case of Operation CREVICE), to self-assembled hydrogen peroxide-based devices, and some evidence that non-conventional substances such as the poison ricin might be considered. We have seen attacks and attempted attacks on land, and on aircraft while in the air. In short, we have seen a large and varying range of real or potential attack methodologies, and these require a high degree of imagination and creativity on the part of the intelligence analysts tackling the terrorists, to be aware of the fact that the modus operandi can easily change in a number of directions and anything may be possible.

In terms of how to build this creative capability into the intelligence process, we have also seen that Lord Butler called for a number of techniques to be considered, which Heuer and many others have described under the general banner of challenge and 'alternative analysis'. We will examine some of these techniques in more detail in the next chapter, but it is worth noting here that the thinking around these issues in the intelligence community has shifted in recent years. Initially, many were attracted by structured techniques outlined by Heuer and others, such as Red Teaming, and Analysis of Competing Hypotheses. In the case of the latter, Heuer outlined an eight-step process, which is shown in Figure 5.2.

---

[37] S Fainaru and JV Grimaldi, 'FBI Knew Terrorists Were Using Flight Schools', *The Washington Post*, 23 September 2001, <http://www.prisonplanet.com/fbi_knew_terrorists_using_flight_schools.html>, accessed 2 January 2010.

[38] RA Falkenrath, 'The 9/11 Commission Report: A Review Essay' (2004) 29(3) *International Security* 170, 179.

Figure 5.2 Analysis of Competing Hypotheses, after Heuer[39]

1. Identify the possible hypotheses to be considered. Use a group of analysts with different perspectives to brainstorm the possibilities.
2. Make a list of significant evidence and arguments for and against each hypothesis.
3. Prepare a matrix with hypotheses across the top and evidence down the side. Analyze the 'diagnosticity' of the evidence and arguments—that is, identify which items are most helpful in judging the relative likelihood of the hypotheses.
4. Refine the matrix. Reconsider the hypotheses and delete evidence and arguments that have no diagnostic value.
5. Draw tentative conclusions about the relative likelihood of each hypothesis. Proceed by trying to disprove the hypotheses rather than prove them.
6. Analyze how sensitive your conclusion is to a few critical items of evidence. Consider the consequences for your analysis if that evidence were wrong, misleading, or subject to a different interpretation.
7. Report conclusions. Discuss the relative likelihood of all the hypotheses, not just the most likely one.
8. Identify milestones for future observation that may indicate events are taking a different course than expected.

We will return to this model in later chapters, and consider how it can be applied. More recently, however, many have seen that such heavily structured processes are not necessarily conducive to the fast-moving and time-pressured reality of the intelligence environment. Fishbein and Treverton noted that:

> Understanding complex transnational issues, such as terrorism and weapons proliferation, requires an alternative analysis approach that is more an ongoing organizational process aimed at promoting 'mindfulness'—continuous wariness of analytic failure—than a set of tools that analysts are encouraged to employ when needed. This means that Intelligence Community analytic organizations need to institutionalize sustained, collaborative efforts by analysts to question their judgments and underlying assumptions, employing both critical and creative modes of thought.[40]

A concept of 'mindfulness' captures the spirit of being constantly aware of cognitive limitations and pitfalls and introducing challenge throughout the intelligence process, rather than removing oneself from the analytic coalface to conduct challenge in structured and formulaic ways. In effect, this is a process

---

[39] Heuer, *Psychology of Intelligence Analysis*, n 2 above, p 97.
[40] Fishbein and Treverton, *Rethinking 'Alternative Analysis'*, n 18 above, p v.

of 'a never-ending effort to challenge expectations and to consider alterna-tive possibilities',[41] and to see that process as a symbiotic part of the cycle of intelligence analysis, rather than a separate activity which needs special and dedicated treatment at certain times.

It is important to note the limitations of alternative analysis within the intelligence community, which may mean that a 'lighter touch' approach is more effective than a grander, more systematic approach. George noted a number of such limitations, beginning with the fact that policy-makers may be neither interested in, nor understanding of the potentially quite arcane analytical processes that have gone into delivering their 'intelligence product'; generally they just want the intelligence experts to tell them what they need to know.[42] In this way, while alternative analysis, competing hypotheses, and so on may be undertaken in producing a final intelligence judgement, it is not necessarily appropriate to communicate the workings of such activities to the policy-makers.

Additionally, more structured set-piece processes of alternative analysis can be resource-intensive, and are probably not appropriate in situations in which the intelligence priority is low. Major exercises of the Red Teaming variety should probably only be used sparingly, and only on those strategic topics for which resource and time are adequately available, and the policy-maker's interest in receiving a well argued and analyzed result is of paramount importance.[43]

Judgement

Awareness of cognitive heuristics in assessing information and analyzing it for intelligence should include an understanding of the process of making judge-ments, since this is the critical outcome of the intelligence analysis process. The whole process is completed by appropriately communicating the judgements made by analysts on the available information, and this is a question to which we will turn shortly. First, however, it is worth pausing on the issue of judge-ment and decision-making.

Again, the question is a subject of comprehensive academic research and analysis, not only in the field of psychology but in a number of other disciplines, including politics, economics, finance, medicine, and marketing. As Mellers, Schwartz and Cooke pointed out, 'rational choice theory' was the dominant paradigm for many years across these disciplines.[44] The theory suggests that an individual weighs up the relative costs and benefits of a course of action, and makes a decision based on a rational and objective view of which way the scales tip.

---

[41] Ibid, p 4.

[42] RZ George, 'Fixing the Problem of Analytical Mind-Sets: Alternative Analysis' (2004) 17 *International Journal of Intelligence and CounterIntelligence* 385, 399–400.   [43] Ibid, p 401.

[44] BA Mellers, A Schwartz, and ADJ Cooke, 'Judgment and Decision Making' (1998) 49 *Annual Review of Psychology* 447, 448.

This theory has been particularly central to the discipline of criminology, for example, where, in the Western world in particular, the dominant theory has been that individuals commit crime as a result of rational choices based on environmental factors, such as the availability of targets, and motivation on the part of the offender relating to lacking economic opportunity, the need to finance an addiction to narcotics, and so on.

Increasingly, however, a renewed awareness of behavioural assumptions and dynamics has eroded the dominance of rational choice theory.[45] In the context of intelligence analysis, Morgan Jones noted that there should normally be an inverse relationship between the role of facts, and the role of judgement in problem solving.[46] A simplistic and factual problem-type would only have one answer, and if the relevant facts were not available, the question could not be answered. This relates partly to a point that Lord Butler made, in his report on WMD intelligence, about 'secrets and mysteries'.[47] The former, Butler argued, is a piece of information which may not be known but is essentially 'knowable', in that it is a factual piece of information. He suggested that an enemy's order of battle was an example, as was a leader's intentions, insofar as they had been decided and communicated to others. The intelligence agency working the problem would not necessarily need to make a judgement on such a piece of information unless it was impossible to uncover.

An intelligence 'mystery', on the other hand, is something that is inherently not knowable, such as an enemy's inner thoughts or beliefs. It was not known, for example, how Saddam Hussein intended to act in 1990 after amassing troops on the Kuwaiti border, since the final decision was something he would make in isolation depending on his own inner thoughts. This is an indeterminate problem, around which judgements are inherently conjectural, and the risk of inaccuracy is greater. (In the event, the intelligence judgement was that he would back away from an invasion, but this proved to be erroneous.) This brings us to a further cognitive limitation, in that research shows that the inverse of what you might expect appears generally to happen. As Jones pointed out, you would expect that our confidence in our judgements would decrease as the probability of error increases, but there is much evidence to suggest that the reverse often happens.[48]

Research suggests that decisions made in situations of uncertainty are generally ambiguity-averse (for example, financial managers will set higher premiums on risk-heavy decisions than on less ambiguous investments), but that where people feel confident or that they have a level of expertise in a particular domain, they will tend to prefer their own ambiguous beliefs as guidance in

---

[45] Mellers et al, 'Judgment and Decision Making', in 44 above, p 449.

[46] MD Jones, *The Thinker's Toolkit: 14 Powerful Techniques for Problem Solving* (New York NY: Three Rivers Press, 1998) p 51.

[47] Cited in P Gill and M Phythian, *Intelligence in an Insecure World* (Cambridge: Polity, 2006) p 137.   [48] Jones, *The Thinker's Toolkit*, n 46 above, p 52.

making a judgement.[49] Rieber recalls a study conducted by Philip Tetlock at the University of California at Berkeley, in which the judgements of 189 experts on various areas of expertise were examined. The results were 'dismal', in that not only were the experts' judgements uniformly only slightly better than chance, but they tended to ascribe much greater confidence to their (frequently erroneous) judgements than would a normal member of the population.[50] Rieber noted that:

> These findings confirm what cognitive psychologists have been saying for decades: people tend to overestimate the accuracy of their own judgments.[51]

His response to the problem was to suggest that a degree of 'calibration' is required by the intelligence function, whereby expert judgements are moderated, either statistically or through a process of considering alternative hypotheses. There is a question mark over whether a statistical calibration of judgements is appropriate or practicable in the daily intelligence process, but again, awareness of this particular cognitive pitfall is important.

In addition to overconfidence in expert judgements, Heuer relates weaknesses in decision-making to problems of memory, whereby confidence in a judgement can be affected by recent memory of particular instances of an event or situation, and the nature of the emotions provoked by that memory. Thus, 'the more instances a person can recall of a phenomenon, the more probable that phenomenon seems to be'.[52] This can lead to collective memory or groupthink, whereby corporate memory of a particular event or chain of events can affect collective judgement and decision-making. A nuance to this problem is that identified by Cooper of an over-reliance on previously reported 'finished' intelligence.[53] Judgements formally issued (in the sense of being published in intelligence reports) by the intelligence community in the past, tend to be accepted as the 'truth' on a particular subject and standing the test of time. Such acceptance is not necessarily warranted, but retrospective reassessment of intelligence judgements rarely happens. This in turn can lead to the problem of 'layering', whereby previous assessments are taken as the starting point for new intelligence analysis on a particular subject, without testing and validating that earlier intelligence.[54]

Echoing Heuer's neurological assessment, Jones concludes that human brains are inherently poor at making and understanding probability judgements, particularly where the issue we are estimating cannot be tested or aided visually. Thus, we are quite good at estimating a height or a distance where we can see the

---

[49] Mellers et al, 'Judgment and Decision Making', n 44 above, p 463.

[50] S Rieber, 'Intelligence Analysis and Judgmental Calibration' (2004) 17 *International Journal of Intelligence and CounterIntelligence* 97, 98.   [51] Ibid, p 100.

[52] Heuer, *Psychology of Intelligence Analysis*, n 2 above, p 29.

[53] JR Cooper, *Curing Analytic Pathologies: Pathways to Improved Intelligence Analysis* (Washington DC: Center for the Study of Intelligence, 2005) p 33.   [54] Ibid.

object or environment in question, but we are much less able skilfully to apply mathematical probability to an esoteric situation. He notes that 'we must be wary of our intuitive judgements involving probability because they can drastically mislead us'.[55]

Communication

A human weakness in making probability judgements where the information is lacking or ambiguous inevitably leads to problems in accurately and reliably communicating uncertainty. Returning to the CIA school of intelligence analysis, Heuer contends that Sherman Kent was one of the first to recognize 'problems of communication caused by imprecise statements of uncertainty'.[56] The traditional way of communicating uncertainty in intelligence reporting is to use a set of words, such as 'likely', 'probably', 'possibly', and so on, each with a flexible and elastic meaning. Heuer outlines a study undertaken among twenty-three NATO military officers familiar with intelligence reporting, in which they were asked to assign a percentage probability to a range of expressions such as those above, which are known as the 'Kent Scale of Uncertainty'.[57] With only one exception, there was a wide range of estimates for many of the terms. In the case of 'probable', for example, estimates of what this meant among those reading the word in their intelligence reports ranged from 25 to 75 per cent certainty.[58]

The study indicates differing levels of understanding of what these words mean in the context of communicating uncertainty, at degrees of difference which could easily be significant in a policy-making context: such variations could mean the difference between substantive action being taken and no action being taken, on the basis of intelligence.

Once again, the problem—and analysis of it—is not confined to the intelligence profession. The medical profession faces very similar issues in accurately conveying uncertainty and probability, and advising patients of the best action to take in response to a particular diagnosis. Weather forecasters, economists, and environmental scientists face similar issues.

Weiss describes two models which are commonly used to assess and describe uncertainty. The first is frequentist statistics, which are based on empirical data, while the second is Bayesian statistics, which are based on subjective assessments of connections and probabilities based on available information.[59] The danger with frequentist statistics is that they can demonstrate correlations and trends, but these are not necessarily the same thing as 'truth', nor are they always good

---

[55] Jones, *The Thinker's Toolkit*, n 46 above, p 225.

[56] Heuer, *Psychology of Intelligence Analysis*, n 2 above, p 154.

[57] S Kent, 'Words of Estimated Probability' in DP Steury (ed), *Sherman Kent and the Board of National Estimates: Collected Essays* (Washington DC: Center for the Study of Intelligence, 1994).

[58] Ibid, pp 154–5.

[59] C Weiss, 'Communicating Uncertainty in Intelligence and Other Professions' (2008) 21 *International Journal of Intelligence and CounterIntelligence* 57, 60.

predictors of what will happen. We are reminded here of Hendrickson's analysis of critical thinking in intelligence analysis, and the third 'central problem' of inevitability (or lack of it) of human behaviour.[60] Here, a series of events or behaviours might be observed among a group of terrorists, for example, but human behaviour is almost by definition indeterministic. The pieces of information might be pieced together to suggest a trend towards a particular event or decision, but in reality there is no telling with certainty how an individual or individuals will choose to act. Perhaps what needs to be assessed and communicated is actually a set of 'alternative futures'.

Frequentist statistics can lead down a path of using statistical measures for communicating uncertainty. The Kent Scale of Uncertainty emerged in the 1960s, when Sherman Kent expressed frustration with the intelligence profession's inability to be more precise in its communication.[61] His scale uses a set of seven expressive terms, from 'impossible', through 'chances about even', up to 'certain', and sets these against a percentage range. Thus, 'probably not' equates to approximately 30 per cent probability, while 'probable' equates to between 70 and 80 per cent probability. Heuer followed Kent by suggesting that numerical identifiers for expressions of uncertainties would be an 'appropriate means of avoiding misinterpretation'. He suggested that odds were a slightly better way of expressing such identifiers as people tend to understand those better than percentages.[62]

In the final analysis, there seem to be mixed feelings about empirical methods of communication of intelligence judgements. In its favour, as George identifies, to be presented as a policy-maker with a set of alternative possibilities can be both frustrating and run the risk of undermining confidence in what the intelligence agency is saying. A set of alternative futures could also be seen as an exercise in hedging bets, such that the intelligence analysts are less open to accusations of having got it wrong if they have presented a full range of possible outcomes.[63] To a certain extent, busy and pressurized policy-makers want the intelligence agencies to tell them directly what they perceive the intelligence judgement to be, so that they can get on and decide appropriate policy actions. In some cases there is not the time and will to consider a range of different possibilities. Thus, a clear quantitative judgement of the situation can be perceived as helpful.

On the other hand, there are a number of contrary problems with presenting empirical data as intelligence judgement. First, as Weiss noted, some people are not numerically minded and are uncomfortable with interpreting empirical probabilities.[64] Second, empirical assessments of likelihood can be both

---

[60] N Hendrickson, 'Critical Thinking in Intelligence Analysis' (2008) 21 *International Journal of Intelligence and CounterIntelligence* 679, 681–2.

[61] Weiss, 'Communicating Uncertainty', n 59 above, p 61.

[62] Heuer, *Psychology of Intelligence Analysis*, n 2 above, p 156.

[63] George, 'Fixing the Problem of Analytical Mind-Sets', n 42 above, p 399.

[64] Weiss, 'Communicating Uncertainty', n 59 above, p 60.

limiting, in that they do not offer room for ambiguity or differing interpretations, and also misleading, in that a frequentist correlation implied by statistics does not necessarily add up to an accurate prediction of what will happen in reality, as we have noted above in the case of indeterministic human behaviour. Weiss observed that a number of other disciplines have noted and tackled this inherent risk in the use of statistical correlation. In epidemiology, for example, a set of rules called Henle-Koch-Evans have been developed, which specify that even if a statistical correlation is noted, a plausible biological mechanism must be presented before a firm conclusion can be drawn.[65] Returning to Saddam Hussein, events before 1990 suggested that he had a tendency to 'sabre rattle' at other countries, but that there was a trend of him backing away from confrontation at the last minute. Thus, when the threat of war was applied following his invasion of Kuwait, it was generally estimated that he would back out and return across the border, as the correlation of past events suggested. That he did not do so shows that human behaviour (and particularly that of an autocratic leader) will not always conform to statistical correlations.

Back in the intelligence context, therefore, events such as the case for going to war in Iraq in 2003 suggest that it is increasingly essential that levels of uncertainty over critical intelligence judgements, and differences of opinion over those levels of uncertainty, are clearly expressed to the policy-makers and not swept under the carpet.[66] Uncertainty is a staple diet of intelligence analysts, and they should not be afraid to make that clear to their readers. As the former US CIA chief, Robert Gates, noted in 1992:

> While we strive for sharp and focused judgments for a clear assessment of likelihood, we must not dismiss alternatives or exaggerate our certainty under the guise of making the 'tough calls.' We are analysts, not umpires, and the game does not depend on our providing a single judgment.[67]

A good example of the difficulties surrounding the communication of uncertainty is that of the National Intelligence Estimates (NIEs) issued by the CIA on the question of Iran's nuclear capability, in the period between 2005 and 2007. In the latter assessment, a somewhat hedged analysis was presented of Iran's intention and strategy to move towards an offensive nuclear capability, which took the wind out of the sails of the assessment two years earlier, which had claimed that 'left to its own devices, Iran is determined to build nuclear weapons'.[68] The controversy unleashed by this change of tone and the dilemma it presented the policy-makers in the Bush administration on the line to take with Iran, echoed a pair of

---

[65] Weiss, 'Communicating Uncertainty', n 59 above, p 60.   [66] Ibid, p 77.

[67] Cited in *Foreign Missile Threats: Analytic Soundness of Certain National Intelligence Estimates*, Report B-274120 (Washington DC: US General Accounting Office, National Security and International Affairs Division, 2006) p 4.

[68] Cited in D Linzer, 'Iran is Judged 10 years from Nuclear Bomb', *The Washington Post*, 2 August 2005, p A01.

assessments in the mid-1990s of Iran's ballistic missile capability. With uncanny similarity to the nuclear case, the 1993 NIE suggested there was a credible threat to the US in the future from an Iranian intercontinental ballistic missile capability, while a further NIE two years later dismissed the possibility of this threat.[69] A subsequent enquiry by the General Accounting Office into how and why the assessed intelligence picture had changed so significantly, noted that:

> The main judgment of NIE 95-19 was worded with clear (100 percent) certainty. We believe this level of certainty was overstated, based on the caveats and intelligence gaps noted in NIE 95-19.[70]

The problem, therefore, was not that caveats and intelligence gaps were not noted in the building of the intelligence assessment, but that these were not communicated appropriately in the main judgement of the report, which was the part on which policy-makers would act most readily. It is not enough, therefore, to deal appropriately with uncertainty in the analysis alone, but also to ensure that analysts are skilled in how to communicate the result of their findings to policy-makers, within an environment that is not pressurized by a real or perceived desire to make robust and inflexible judgements in all cases.

Conclusions

This book argues that intelligence analysis has both art and science components. Both need to be understood, as does their relationship with one another, if intelligence analysts and their managers are to improve overall performance and professionalize the discipline.

On the art side of the picture is the question of the nature of analysis itself, and particularly issues of how human beings charged with undertaking intelligence analysis are able to deal with large amounts of complex data and derive judgements. We have seen how a great deal of investigation and discussion has been undertaken around these issues in an intelligence context in the US, and particularly by the CIA and its Center for the Study of Intelligence, and Sherman Kent School. (Relatively little, at least in so far as it relates specifically to intelligence analysis, has been undertaken as yet in other parts of the world.) Much of this work has been driven by a need to understand why intelligence analysis has gone wrong and delivered either faulty assessments (eg in the case of Iraq) or allowed intelligence surprises such as Pearl Harbor, 9/11, or 7/7. As we saw in Chapter 2, intelligence failure and strategic surprise are the result of a number of overlapping factors, many of them institutional and organizational rather than anything that could be laid directly at the door of the intelligence

---

[69] SE Kreps, 'Shifting Currents: Changes in National Intelligence Estimates on the Iran Nuclear Threat' (2008) 23 *Intelligence and National Security* 606, 609.

[70] *Foreign Missile Threats*, n 67 above, p 4.

analyst. However, processes deep within the machinery of the intelligence function where analysts conduct their thinking and assessing are surely critical pieces in the jigsaw.

We have seen how an examination of the analysis process itself quickly leads into a number of other academic disciplines, from cognitive psychology to social and behavioural science. Probably the most significant commentator on the issue, Richards J Heuer of the CIA, whose background was a combination of psychology and philosophy, asserted as his central thesis that the human brain is poorly provisioned to undertake complex and comprehensive analysis, and in particular is subject to what Sherman Kent described as 'intellectual frailties'.[71] Problems of perception, memory, and inherent bias in all of our thinking processes are liable to complicate and undermine analysis, and to lead to flawed assessments and judgements, if we do not take steps to mitigate their effects.

The key conclusion that can be drawn from this analysis takes us back to organizational factors within the intelligence community. The key issue raised by this 'analysis of analysis' is that the intelligence community has to create a working environment for analysts in which critical thinking, creativity, and challenge can be freely exercised. This environment needs to be one which does not damage the frequent necessity to undertake time-critical and 'deliberative' thought, but which allows for more contemplative and reflective thinking where the situation and subject allow. The circumstances in which this is appropriate will be determined to a large extent by the nature and priority of the intelligence question in hand. More often than not, the candidate situations will be those surrounding large and 'strategic' issues of high importance, although a basic culture of challenge and critical thought also needs to be interwoven inextricably into the daily fabric of intelligence analysis, even within fast-moving, operational scenarios.

Such an environment needs to be a supportive and positive one, whereby challenge and creativity are seen as essential and rightful components of the process, designed to deliver the best and most reliable outcome rather than necessarily to overcomplicate or slow down analysis. This might mean changes in mindset at both institutional and personal levels. In the case of the former, a leaf could be taken out of the book of high-reliability organizations such as nuclear power plants or aircraft carriers, in which an obsessive attention to analyzing failure and mistakes is seen not as a destructive and undermining function, but as an essential and constructive policy that aims to increase productivity and mitigate risk to the highest degree. At the personal level, analysts need to be recruited and developed who are highly attuned to critical thinking and self-awareness, so that they can both constructively challenge others' assumptions on a regular basis, and also be open themselves to new ideas and alternative hypotheses which might enrich and develop their own understanding of a situation.

---

[71] Cited in George, 'Fixing the Problem of Analytical Mind-Sets', n 42 above, p 388.

The final part of the process is a need for heightened awareness and skill in how to communicate appropriately the uncertainty which is usually central to any intelligence judgement. Policy-makers need to receive a clear view of the process of thinking that has gone on, and the robustness of the intelligence assessment that has emerged, before they can make a sound and appropriate policy judgement. This does not necessarily mean 'showing the workings' that have led up to a judgement being made, since these will often be arcane, lengthy, and ultimately superfluous as far as policy-makers are concerned, but they must feel confident that they fully understand and appreciate the nature of the assessment with which they are being presented. This requires advanced skills in communication which must also be seen as a critical component of the analyst's 'soft skills' in delivering their capability.

The science part of the process comprises those techniques and mechanisms which aid analysts in discharging their function to best effect.

Key Points

- Academic analysis of 'thinking about thinking' in the intelligence context has been led by CIA analysts, notably Richards J Heuer and Sherman Kent. The former's work *Psychology of Intelligence Analysis* is much examined by students of intelligence analysis throughout the Western world.

- Heuer's central argument is that the human brain suffers from a number of cognitive weaknesses which affect the efficacy of intelligence analysis. Chief among these are issues of perception, memory, and bias.

- A model for understanding the key skills required for development in the art of analysis can be structured around critical thinking, creativity, powers of judgement, and communication.

- Debate around whether creativity and critical thinking are linked to 'nature or nurture' has been going on since the Second World War, and has revolved primarily around the educational psychology arena. The general consensus is that, while environment is critical to the development of creativity, it can be nurtured and 'taught'.

- Critical thinking skills and dispositions can be seen in a political context, whereby these skills are central to a liberal democracy and severely curtailed in an authoritarian society.

- Issues of judgement have revolved around 'rational choice theory' in the past, although factors of emotion and behavioural bias are increasingly seen as relevant. These bring us back to Heuer and Kent's 'intellectual frailties' which can have a significant effect on powers of judgement.

- Good intelligence analysis is nugatory if its results are not communicated properly, and particular risks are present in the area of adequately and accurately conveying uncertainty. Customers of intelligence need to understand the levels of uncertainty inherent in an intelligence judgement without necessarily seeing all the deliberations that went into that judgement. Much debate has centred around whether communicated uncertainty should be conveyed empirically or qualitatively.

- Intelligence agencies and functions need to think about the cultural and organizational environment in which their analysts work, and particularly whether these environments encourage creativity, critical thinking, and challenge.

6

Analytical Theory:
The Science of Analysis

We concentrated in the previous chapter on the mental process of analysis in terms of the cognitive heuristics involved, and the pitfalls that analysts face as a natural product of the way the human brain is 'wired'. Since the work of Kent and Heuer, among others, awareness has risen gradually of these issues within the intelligence sector—perhaps more so in the US than elsewhere—but the events of the early years of the twenty-first century have greatly increased the impera- tive to tackle such issues, and perhaps shown that general awareness of them has not been enough to avoid major strategic surprises and intelligence failures. Such events have led to calls for improved analytical techniques and 'profession- alization' of the intelligence workforce to be progressed and institutionalized.

Managers of the intelligence analysis function, therefore, need to find plans and mechanisms for enhancing the performance of their sector, in a way that goes beyond just raising awareness. Practical realities also mean that, while crea- tivity and imagination are increasingly critical attributes of the contemporary intelligence analyst, the process of intelligence analysis cannot be an 'art' alone. If we took Picasso's analysis of artistic ability as being an innate thing that can- not be defined or shared with others, the job of those charged with recruiting, training, and managing the intelligence workforce and ensuring they delivered the best product for the policy-makers would be a very difficult one.

To a certain extent, therefore, intelligence analysis can also be seen as a science, which can be analyzed, codified, and enhanced. In this chapter we look at the scientific approaches to the intelligence analysis function and process, and do so through the framework of three factors: tradecraft techniques for mitigating cognitive pitfalls and enhancing the act of analysis; organizational structures and models around the intelligence analysis function; and technical issues of data handling and information sharing, which are becoming increasingly significant within the whole intelligence sector. To begin this analysis, it is worth considering how we define a science, and how this might apply to the intelligence analysis function.

Intelligence and Science

There have been numerous debates as to where the practice of intelligence analysis—or analysis generally—sit within concepts of science. Most would equate intelligence analysis most closely with social science, since it is the study of the behavioural patterns of human beings. As Lee noted in the late 1980s, a suitable model for social science is that of natural science, which is fundamentally about testing theories and hypotheses using case studies and experiments.[1] The traditional view of the 'scientific method' in this context is that it is a process of testing hypotheses, formed initially from deductive reasoning, with new information as it comes in, either to bolster or to disprove the original hypothesis. Popper described this as the 'deductive testing of theories'.[2]

To illustrate how this works, we can use an example from the intelligence world. An initial hypothesis may be mooted that young men in their early twenties[3] who travel from Europe to certain remote and lawless parts of the federally administered tribal areas in the Pakistan/Afghanistan border region, are generally doing so in order to undertake terrorist training. A suspect might then be found who fitted the age profile and travel pattern described in the hypothesis. The deductive theory would be that this person was most likely intending to undertake terrorist training. New information would need to be compared with this theory to see if it disproved the hypothesis. The discovery that the man in question had family members in the federally administered tribal areas and regularly visited them for family events might, for example, weaken the hypothesis. Conversely, the discovery that the man had been visiting websites extolling the importance of violent jihad in the period leading up to his travel, might bolster the theory. Each new piece of information would need to be tested to see how it sat with the original hypothesis, before an intelligence judgement could be made.

Returning briefly to the Sherman Kent school of analysis, Kent spoke early on of the virtues of the analyst developing and applying a scientific method to his or her work. In particular, he advocated using impartial and forensic analysis of events in the past, to develop theories and models for predicting how security events might develop in the future.[4] As Butterfield noted, since the 1950s,

---

[1] AS Lee, 'A Scientific Methodology for MIS Case Studies' (1989) 13 *MIS Quarterly* 33, 36.

[2] K Popper, *The Logic of Scientific Discovery* (New York NY: Harper Torchbooks, 1968) pp 32–3.

[3] Taking the suggested standard age of a terrorist derived from a sample of 350 cases, cited in CA Russell and BH Miller, Captain, 'Profile of a Terrorist' (1977) 1 *Studies in Conflict and Terrorism* 17.

[4] J Davis, 'Introduction' in RJ Heuer, Jr, *Psychology of Intelligence Analysis* (Langley VA: Center for the Study of Intelligence, 1999) p xiv.

the US intelligence sector had applied 'scientific methods to eliminate bias and increase analytic objectivity'.[5] Models of strategic thinking have also taken a hypothesis-driven approach, as Liedtka observed, which mirrors the scientific method of enquiry in that it takes the forming and testing of theories as a central pillar of activity.[6]

In the law enforcement context, Innes, Fielding, and Cope noted a trend towards the 'scientification' of police work from the 1980s onwards, which was partly due to a 'refinement of the techniques of surveillance and social control, characteristic of modern and late modern societies', and partly because of a general penetration of technology into daily police work.[7] They noted that 'many of the central methods used to analyse crime data directly parallel and share components with established research methods in the social sciences'.[8] We will return to some of these techniques in more detail later, but it is interesting to note that Innes et al introduced a dual model of 'figurative reasoning' and 'tracking reasoning' to define the two principal categories of analytical work in the law enforcement intelligence analysis function, at least in the UK.[9] The former is primarily about manipulating statistics to provide a picture of the criminal environment under analysis, while the latter is about analyzing the behaviours and movements of criminal targets in space and time. In both cases there are risks of the analysis not providing 'intelligence' at all, but merely 'wallpaper': facts and figures which only serve relentlessly to gather and manipulate data rather than to provide any directed outcome.[10]

An objective and scientific view is perhaps problematic in an intelligence context, which has to contend with deception, politicization, and a number of influences that warp the picture.[11] In a standard natural science environment, data and events are generally deterministic, and can be tested and measured in a quantifiable way with appropriate experiments and data gathering. (This is not always the case, but is often so.) In an intelligence context, not only are human beings fundamentally indeterministic in their behaviour, as Hendrickson noted,[12] but security targets will often deliberately employ deception and obfuscation to muddy the waters. Furthermore, intelligence analysts are usually dealing in situations with imperfect and incomplete data, and are generally not able to run robust and bounded experiments to fill the gaps. Extra data, if

---

[5] AP Butterfield, Jr, *The Accuracy of Intelligence Assessment: Bias, Perception and Judgement in Analysis and Decision* (Newport RI: Naval War College, paper submitted for Advanced Research Project at Center for Naval Warfare Studies, 1993) p v.

[6] JM Liedtka, 'Strategic Thinking: Can it be Taught?' (1998) 31 *Long Range Planning* 120, 123.

[7] M Innes, N Fielding, and N Cope, '"The Appliance of Science?" The Theory and Practice of Crime Intelligence Analysis' (2005) 45 *British Journal of Criminology* 39.

[8] Ibid, p 40. [9] Ibid, p 45. [10] Ibid, p 49.

[11] Butterfield, *The Accuracy of Intelligence Assessment*, n 5 above.

[12] N Hendrickson, 'Critical Thinking in Intelligence Analysis' (2008) 21 *International Journal of Intelligence and CounterIntelligence* 679, 681.

it comes, will often do so fortuitously and in an unpredictable manner. As Gill and Phythian noted:

> as intelligence practitioners themselves confess … intelligence is not a science; rather it is an imprecise art. This fact is not a consequence of reliance on any particular collection method, or because of a lack of unprocessed information. More of a particular type of input will not alter the basic fact that intelligence can deal only in probabilities, and that the range of variables that can be generated by human interaction or introduced by different, subjective analyses of a given situation will always serve to limit the utility of intelligence work and to limit the predictive power to well below 100 percent.[13]

Alexander George, examining decision-making on foreign policy alternatives, identified a number of flawed analytical strategies for 'what to do in an issue that is clouded in uncertainty',[14] which are worth examining briefly. Table 6.1 summarizes the strategies, which are: 'satisficing', incrementalism, consensus, reasoning by analogy, and relying on principles that distinguish good from bad alternatives.

Many of these strategies are natural instincts when information is lacking or incomplete, and when the policy-makers are pressing for answers. They contain a number of pitfalls, principally including the dangers of politicization of the intelligence, and the risks of intelligence analysts telling the policy-makers what they think they want to hear, rather than any inconvenient truths.

We can surmise from these findings that intelligence analysis is akin to a social science, which can usefully use a hypothesis-driven approach to evaluate theories based on deductive reasoning. However, the intelligence domain is unique in that it includes within it a number of factors that militate against a truly scientific approach to evaluating data and theories, including the deceptive

Table 6.1 George's foreign policy strategies, after Heuer[15]

Satisficing	Selecting the first alternative that appears 'good enough', rather than examining all possibilities.
Incrementalism	Focusing on a set of alternatives within a narrow range either side of a hypothesis, rather than dramatically different theories.
Consensus	Focusing on the alternative on which most agree.
Reasoning by analogy	Focusing on an alternative that matches a success or avoids a previous error.
Distinguishing good from bad	Focusing on an alternative that feels like a 'good' alternative, based on a set of principles about what is good and what is bad.

[13] P Gill and M Phythian, *Intelligence in an Insecure World* (Cambridge: Polity, 2006) p 15.

[14] A George, *Presidential Decision Making in Foreign Policy: The Effective Use of Information and Advice* (Boulder CO: Westview Press, 1980) p 19.

[15] Cited in Heuer, *Psychology of Intelligence Analysis*, n 4 above, p 43.

and misleading behaviour of the targets, and the lacking and incomplete nature of the data on which theories and hypotheses can be based. In this way, intelligence analysis diverges from the standard model of natural science, and for many, is more of an art than a science. It is perhaps no wonder that the chances of intelligence failure and surprise are therefore so high.

Tradecraft Techniques

There are a very considerable number of tradecraft techniques which have been discussed in the context of intelligence analysis, both in the state security and the law enforcement contexts. To do justice to all of them would require a complete further book, but it is interesting to note that they generally fall into certain categories, which we will discuss here. Figure 6.1 shows a model framework of four key categories, which we will examine in detail. It should be noted that this is far from being a definitive list of all techniques that have ever been examined in an intelligence analysis context, but it is a useful conceptual framework nonetheless.

Hypothesis testing

We have already looked at a basic example of where a hypothesis in an intelligence context, formed from deductive reasoning flowing from an original principle, can be informally tested as new information comes in, to bolster or disprove the theory. In many ways, this can be a constant and instinctive process that many analysts can and will employ in their daily analysis, and can be particularly effective if those analysts have developed skills in critical thinking. By this we mean that they will always be open to new challenges to their original hypothesis, and will attempt to test it in the light of new information in an objective and unbiased way. We saw in the case of the Iraq War of 2003 that the original 'groupthink' hypothesis that Saddam Hussein had weapons of mass destruction (WMD) but was intent on concealing evidence of them, led to a dangerous line of deductive reasoning in which a lack of intelligence

Figure 6.1 A framework of Tradecraft Technique categories

Hypothesis testing

Challenge

Social Network Analysis

Sorting, organizing, and visualizing

to challenge the fact that he had any WMD was seen as bolstering the case that he would be determined to hide the evidence. The fact that no new information came in was seen as vindication in itself of the theory, instead of being seen as a possible new hypothesis that there really was nothing to find. In this case, a serious lack of critical thinking was at play in the intelligence community (or if such thinking was underway in certain quarters, it failed to see the light of day).

More formal and scientific models of hypothesis testing have been developed. Jack Davis claimed that Heuer's 'Analysis of Competing Hypotheses' (ACH) was 'among his most important contributions to the development of an intelligence analysis methodology'.[16] We saw in the previous chapter the eight-step model that comprises Heuer's ACH. The model flows through a number of stages, with initial brainstorming by a group of analysts to exercise their creative powers and generate a set of potential hypotheses.[17] A process of analysis of those hypotheses then takes place through discussion and debate, with the 'disproved' (but not the 'unproven') hypotheses rejected. An example of an unproven hypothesis would be the possibility that the target is practising deception, which is always a possibility other than in the rare event that direct evidence to the contrary is found (although this may vary depending on the nature of the target: a criminal gang may practise much less sophisticated deception, if any at all, than an advanced state intelligence agency, for example).

The results are then entered into a matrix, into which evidence for and against each theory is entered. Each piece of evidence is weighted against every hypothesis in the matrix in terms of its 'diagnosticity', that is, how effectively it might prove or disprove each hypothesis. Evidence that proves to have little or no diagnostic value can then be rejected. At the end of the process, a judgement is developed of the relative merits of the remaining alternatives, and an action plan drawn up to monitor these alternative futures as they unfold and adjust the weighting of the most probable outcome.

Heuer suggests that the model has three main strengths over standard 'intuitive analysis'.[18] First, it allows for a full range of possible hypotheses to be considered rather than just favoured ones, or those based on previous reporting or intelligence. Second, the model allows for evidence to be tested for diagnostic value against a range of hypotheses, rather than just against the one theory to which the evidence is considered relevant. Third, 'the most probable hypothesis is usually the one with the least evidence against it, not the one with the most evidence for it'.[19] We tend to try to prove favoured hypotheses rather than disprove other possibilities in our analysis.

We can examine how ACH might work by attempting to apply it to a contemporary intelligence example, in this case a fictitious terrorist investigation.

---

[16] Davis, 'Introduction', n 4 above, p xxiii.

[17] The following summary of the stages of ACH is drawn from Heuer, *Psychology of Intelligence Analysis*, n 4 above, pp 95–108.   [18] Ibid, p 108.   [19] Ibid.

Table 6.2 Analysis of Competing Hypotheses: example

Evidence	Hypothesis A:	Hypothesis B:	Hypothesis C:
	The new man is a regular contact of the target, but has not been seen before due to patchy data collection.	The new man is an old friend of the target who has been away for a while, but has recently returned.	The new man has come into the country from abroad and signifies a major development in the terrorists' attack plans.
1: The new man shares a surname with one of the target's uncles	C	C	A
2: Many of the main target's contacts have recently changed their mobile phones	C	A	A
3: The new man is heard to mention that he has been living just around the corner from the main target for a while	A	I	I
4: The new man seems to be very security conscious	C	A	C

Table 6.2 shows how the matrix might work in this sort of case, in this instance using the model adapted by Morgan Jones, in which evidence is weighed against each hypothesis as consistent (C), inconsistent (I), or ambiguous (A).[20] In this hypothetical case, the intelligence question concerns an instance in which a new, young man has suddenly appeared on the scene of a major terrorist investigation, in very frequent contact with the main target of the operation. The man has not been seen before in this or any related investigations. The questions for the analyst are: who is this man, and how does he fit into the terrorist cell under surveillance?

In the example above, the strongest hypothesis seems to be A, namely that patchy data collection might be the reason why this man has not been seen before, rather than any suggestion that he has not been a regular contact of the main target previously. All of the incoming evidence is consistent with this hypothesis, with the slight exception of the information that the new man has been living just around the corner from the target: this does not necessarily have any bearing on whether patchy data collection is the cause of the lacking information about the new man, and thus the evidence is ambiguous in relation

---

[20] MD Jones, *The Thinker's Toolkit: 14 Powerful Techniques for Problem Solving* (New York NY: Three Rivers Press, 1998) p 187.

to this hypothesis. In the case of the other two hypotheses, this same piece of information is not just ambiguous in its relevance, but actually inconsistent with the hypotheses. In reviewing the assessment of the evidence against the hypotheses, therefore, the analyst might decide to reject hypotheses B and C and concentrate on A.

Clearly this is a very small sample and a somewhat contrived situation—probably the first thing the analyst would do in this case is to suspend any judgement until more information had come in—but it is possible to see how the assessment of evidence against all the hypotheses allows some of them to be effectively disproved or discounted due to inconsistencies in the data.

The question for many analysts when considering the ACH model is whether it is too clunky and formulaic a model to be used in the daily cut-and-thrust of intelligence analysis, particularly in fast-moving operational situations. Often there is not the time or the will to record evidence and hypotheses painstakingly and formally in a matrix in such situations. However, the principles of the exercise can and should be adopted as an instinctive and natural part of an analyst's daily sense-making activities. Whenever a piece of incoming information is assessed within the context of a particular operation or investigation, it should be assessed in terms of its relevance to a range of alternative hypotheses, and particularly whether it disproves or is inconsistent with a key hypothesis. This should be done in a completely objective and open-minded way, such that an inconsistent piece of evidence should be weighed carefully and given the opportunity to unravel a popular theory about the current situation, rather than ignored because it causes problems. This does not necessarily mean formally recording details in a matrix, but building the appropriate way of thinking into daily deliberations.

Challenge

Another way of testing hypotheses is to adopt a straightforward 'compare and contrast' model, whereby a hypothesis is broken down into parts, and then challenged with potentially viable alternative explanations or theories. This is essentially the essence of 'devil's advocacy', which is one of the key forms of challenge tradecraft.

As Jones describes, devil's advocacy is believed to have originated in the Catholic church as a method for testing a dead person's qualifications for sainthood.[21] Essentially, the method involves placing oneself deliberately in a contrary and argumentative position with regard to a particular theory, and considering whether plausible alternative explanations can be put forward which seriously challenge that theory. If the theory in question withstands the scrutiny thrown at it, it is bolstered and strengthened as a viable theory. If, however, the challenge uncovers substantial gaps or inconsistencies, or weaknesses in the basis

---

[21] Ibid, p 217.

Table 6.3 Devil's Advocate model: the 'airline bombing plot'

Prosecution	Defence ('devil's advocate' position)
Polemic videos made by the accused were 'martyrdom' videos.	The intention was merely to shock the public with a media stunt.
Materials were assembled for explosions with an intent to murder.	The accused merely wished to set off a bomb in public to 'cause a stir', and there was no evidence that they planned to harm anyone directly.
The bombs were due to be detonated by the accused on aircraft flying across the Atlantic.	No flight tickets had been purchased at the time of the arrest, and two of the accused did not yet have valid passports.

for the theory, then alternative hypotheses may need to be considered more carefully.

The term 'advocacy' is important in this context, because the process is very similar to that undertaken by the defence in a court case, to disprove or undermine the prosecution's theory about a suspect. In this sense, a good example of where devil's advocacy could be applied to a situation is the case of the 'airline bombing plot', for which three terrorist suspects received life sentences in the UK in September 2009, but only after an earlier trial of the men had failed to reach a verdict on the main charges. Table 6.3 above shows a set of charges levied by the prosecution, and some of the contrary positions that were taken by the defence in the first trial.[22]

In this case, the second trial in 2009 led the jury to overcome any reasonable doubt and tip towards the prosecution case, but the contrary devil's advocate position had to be overcome in so doing. In routine intelligence situations, a culture of challenge in this form can be a useful technique either to bolster or disprove a hypothesis.

We have seen numerous examples in intelligence history where such challenge was not applied, and where this may have meant that a flawed hypothesis held sway. In the previous chapter, we saw the case of the Cuban missile crisis described by Moore, in which the groupthink hypothesis that all human intelligence (Humint) information from Cuba was invariably wrong, was not challenged sufficiently.[23] It would have taken a strong analyst to stand up in the CIA at the time and suggest that a new piece of incoming information about a sighting of potential medium-range ballistic missiles on the island could have been right, because of the prevailing organizational and managerial culture in

---

[22] R Pantucci, 'Transatlantic Airline Bombing Case Collapses in the United Kingdom' (2008) 5/33 *Terrorism Focus*, <http://www.jamestown.org/single/?no_cache=1&tx_ttnews%5Btt_news%5D=5161>, accessed 2 January 2010.

[23] DT Moore, *Critical Thinking and Intelligence Analysis,* Occasional Paper 14 (Washington DC: Joint Military Intelligence College, 2006) pp 20–6.

the agency. But it would have been a tough theory to disprove, given that the only thing against it was perceived historical precedent.

A very similar institutional failure to challenge the prevailing hypothesis appears to have happened across the Western world in the case of Iraq's possible possession of WMD, leading to Lord Butler explicitly recommending that devil's advocacy and similar elements of analytical tradecraft be introduced into the process.[24] He left it to the managers of the intelligence function to determine how this was instituted among the analytical workforce, and we do not know what measures have been taken to introduce it.

In practical terms, the situation is very similar to that of ACH, in that a formulaic and structured approach to the situation may not be appropriate in all cases. Much more important is that analysts instinctively and routinely challenge their own and each other's hypotheses on a constant basis—constructively and with open minds—using the basic principles of devil's advocacy.

A similar and more structured approach to devil's advocacy is that of 'Red Teaming'. This is an approach originally developed in the military and in private business, initially in the US, and latterly adopted by a wide range of public and private sector organizations. Red Teaming comprises the running of exercises, whether 'active' (involving real-time activities by players on the ground) or 'passive' (involving table-top paper exercises). The principle is that two teams (usually) are established: a 'blue' team, which is essentially the home side, and a 'red' team, which is the adversary or competition. Players in the red team try to place themselves in the adversary's shoes, and consider how the adversary might think and act in particular situations. This challenges the blue team to think on its feet and react appropriately to unfolding situations. In a military context, the teams would represent opposing sides in a conflict, while in a commercial context, the teams would represent major competitors who need to react to each other's commercial strategies in attempting to achieve market dominance.

Since 9/11, Red Teaming has been embraced by the Department of Homeland Security in the US as a 'major initiative in the intelligence and warning mission area' to help simulate how terrorist threats might develop.[25] Meehan extols the virtues of the technique, observing that:

> Analytical red teaming provides a potential adversary's view of threats, vulnerabilities and countermeasures. Without testing the physical limitations of antiterrorism measures, analytical red teaming can challenge prevailing views, prevent surprise, allocate resources, and expand the bounds of imagination. Analytical red teaming can occur as part of a discussion-based exercise or as a standalone activity.[26]

---

[24] *Review of Intelligence on Weapons of Mass Destruction*, Report of a Committee of Privy Counsellors chaired by The Rt Hon Lord Butler of Brockwell (London: TSO, 2004) p 16.

[25] MK Meehan, 'Red Teaming for Law Enforcement' (2007) 74/2 *The Police Chief*, <http://policechiefmagazine.org/magazine/index.cfm?fuseaction=display_arch&article_id=1111&issue_id=22007>, accessed 2 January 2010.   [26] Ibid.

We will examine the options for training in intelligence analysis more extensively in the next chapter, but it is worth considering Red Teaming as a mechanism not only for testing hypotheses and processes, but also for developing the skills and awareness of actors in the security environment. However, as with all of the structured techniques we have examined, the big question for Red Teaming is how much time and resource it takes to operate, and whether this is always practical in a fast-moving operational environment. As Mark Mateski, the managing editor of *Red Team Journal* noted, 'when a decision loop is measured in seconds, minutes, or hours, the pace of events will overtake all but the most streamlined red teaming events'.[27] In the right circumstances, however, it can act as a dynamic and interactive way of testing theories and hypotheses and developing alternative possibilities.

Social Network Analysis

We have established in earlier chapters that the post-Cold War security picture, and particularly that concerning the contemporary terrorist threat, is that of a highly networked set of adversaries. In many ways this is a natural outcome of the growing 'knowledge economy' in the postmodern world, underpinned by the internet, which allows for networks of individuals to reach across borders and social structures and develop alliances and associations based on common interests and skills, in a dynamic and fast-moving way.

We have also seen how many of the modern security threats are interwoven within civil society, rather than hidden in military or diplomatic channels. Organized criminal gangs, weapons proliferators, and terrorists all operate in the civilian and commercial spheres, and comprise informal networks of individuals and commercial entities in a way that was never quite the case in the first two-thirds of the twentieth century.

To analyze such networks effectively from an intelligence perspective therefore, one of the key techniques which has been used extensively is that of Social Network Analysis (SNA). As with many techniques we have examined, SNA has been borrowed and adapted from other disciplines, notably sociology and commercial business management. Its intellectual underpinnings are derived from 'structural analysis' and 'graph theory', as used in mathematics and computer science. SNA was developed initially in the 1970s as the West's economy began to modernize away from traditional industries and towards a 'knowledge economy', and has accelerated its development from the late 1980s onwards as the internet and modern globalized communications have revolutionized international commerce. As Cross, Borgatti, and Parker described it in a commercial context:

> Movement toward de-layered, flexible organizations and emphasis on supporting collaboration in knowledge intensive work has made it increasingly

---

[27] M Mateski, 'A Call for a Red Teaming Surge', *Red Team Journal*, November 11, 2008, <http://redteamjournal.com/2008/11/a-call-for-a-red-teaming-surge>, accessed 2 January 2010.

important for executives and managers to attend to informal networks within their organizations. Performance implications of effective informal networks can be significant as the rapidly growing social capital tradition has indicated at the individual, team and organizational levels.[28]

As we saw in Chapter 3, the case of Younis Tsouli and his work for Al Qaeda in Iraq shows how contemporary terrorist organizations such as Al Qaeda are well aware of the utility of the knowledge economy, and can use it to full effect. Tsouli's connection with the organization was forged quickly, easily, and across borders in cyberspace (not just within a large organization as described above), and was based entirely on his specific expertise rather than any other factor. Thus, much as commercial business will use SNA to examine commercial connections between people and entities both within their own organizations and across the modern knowledge economy for strategic purposes, intelligence analysts can usefully employ the same techniques in looking at terrorist and other security targets.

Graph theory, used in mathematics, is a method for examining networks of nodes and the degrees of relationship between them. 'Components' within a network comprise collections of nodes with relationships between them, which can be described variously in terms of their 'density', 'centrality' (further defined under 'closeness' and 'betweenness'), and 'cliques'.[29] When applied to sociology, SNA (derived from graph theory) examines relationships between groups of individuals, and the strength, direction, and nature of those relationships. In a classic cellular terrorist network, for example, to which the IRA (for one) moved after successful Humint penetrations of its hierarchy, individuals within a local 'cell' would have close relationships with one another, but only the cell leader would have any sort of relationship with other individuals higher up the terrorist organization's hierarchy. If the nature of such relationships can be examined and measured, the role and importance of individuals within the organization can be postulated.

To achieve such analysis relies heavily on quantitative data about human interactions, the primary element of which in a contemporary security environment tends to be 'communications data', sometimes described as 'communications event data' (and many other things by various agencies across the Western world). This refers to information about communications between individuals and organizations, without necessarily including the content of those communications. With ready access to large amounts of such data, the nature of relationships between individuals can be inferred by the patterns of communications between them. In a law enforcement context, the Serious Organised Crime Agency (SOCA) in the UK has stressed the importance of such data to

---

[28] R Cross, SP Borgatti, and A Parker, 'Making Invisible Work Visible: Using Social Network Analysis to Support Strategic Collaboration' in E Lesser and L Prusak (eds), *Creating Value with Knowledge* (New York NY: Oxford University Press, 2004) p 84.

[29] E Otte and R Rousseau, 'Social Network Analysis: A Powerful Strategy, also for the Information Sciences' (2002) 28 *Journal of Information Science* 482–3.

its intelligence analysis, noting that, along with telephone intercept intelligence, communications data 'played a role in all significant SOCA operations' in 2008/9.[30]

Aside from the technical challenges of such complex analysis, we saw in Chapter 4 how large-scale databasing and mining of communications data can take intelligence actors into dangerous ethical territory, and invite accusations of a growing 'Big Brother' society.[31] We will return to some of these concerns below in the context of technical aids to analysis. SNA, in an intelligence context, does suffer from the danger that inferred relationships between individuals, and particularly instances in which individuals are linked closely to major terrorist networks, can lead to miscarriages of justice with dire consequences for the individual concerned. The case of Maher Arar in Canada is indicative. Arar was awarded 10.5 million Canadian dollars in damages by the Canadian government in 2007, after erroneous intelligence from interviews and wiretaps gathered by the police had linked him to Al Qaeda. The intelligence was passed to the US, following which Arar was arrested and rendered to Syria, where he was detained for ten months and tortured into a false confession of having attended an Al Qaeda training camp.[32]

The very real consequences for Mr Arar of a flawed analytical connection being made between him and Al Qaeda emphasize the pitfalls of SNA and similar activities in a counter-terrorist intelligence context, and the importance that such techniques are deployed carefully and skilfully by highly trained analysts. Such risks aside, however, SNA and related approaches are likely to remain one of the key techniques in analysis of contemporary security threats for the foreseeable future.

Sorting, organizing, and visualizing

Sorting and organizing information might seem like a less sophisticated and momentous technique for analysts to employ than many we have examined so far, but evidence suggests that it is a critical part of the process central to much routine analytical work. The reasons for this are threefold. First, issues of memory, and particularly the fact that the human brain is poorly provisioned to retain more than a handful of details in its short-term memory, mean that large amounts of complex information can quickly become bewildering and problematic for the analyst if rigorous systems of sorting and organizing are not employed. Second, in looking for connections and significant details in a mass of information, the task is akin to the infamous needle-in-the-haystack scenario.

---

[30] *Annual Report 2008/9* (London: SOCA, 2009) p 26.

[31] See, eg R Verkaik, 'Call for safeguards over Big Brother database', *The Independent*, 10 January 2009, <http://www.independent.co.uk/news/uk/politics/call-for-safeguards-over-big-brother-database-1297563.html>, accessed 31 December 2009.

[32] D Barrett, 'US legislators apologize to Arar', *The Toronto Star*, 18 October 2007, <http://www.thestar.com/article/268252>, accessed 2 January 2010.

Without some method for breaking down and categorizing that information, the task can prove impossible. Finally, it is important to be able to make sense of complicated networks and schemata, and methods of visualization are critical both for the analyst's own understanding of an intelligence picture, and for the communication of that picture and the intelligence it reveals to others.

Heuer noted in *Psychology* that memory comprises three processes: sensory information storage (immediate perception of the environment); short-term memory (a short holding space for relatively small amounts of detail); and long-term memory, which seems to organize itself around a system of associations and schemata.[33] Basic techniques can improve the amount and complexity of information that is transferred to the long-term memory, and these primarily revolve around sorting and organizing the information. A long grocery list, for example, is better remembered if items are grouped into food categories, or given a mnemonic which aids recall of the different items. Similarly, a number of experiments in the psychology domain have shown that master chess players can remember incredibly long sequences of moves relating to differing strategies, because they have spent years memorizing these moves into strategic schemata. In other tasks, the same people perform no better than the average for the rest of the population in routine memory tasks, and can generally not keep too many details in their short-term memory at any given time.[34]

Similarly, analysts who are heavily involved in Humint, and particularly in counter-espionage, generally need to have a good understanding of the workings and frailties of human memory. The case of Yuriy Nosenko, a KGB officer who defected to the US in the mid-1960s, is an interesting one in this regard. Nosenko was initially suspected of being a KGB double agent 'planted' on the Americans. One of the reasons for suspecting this was the question of anomalies and inconsistencies in his historical account: an area of investigation which is central to much counter-espionage analysis. At various points in his interrogation, Nosenko gave three different dates for his entry to the KGB, which was initially seen as worrying evidence of inconsistency, although in retrospect it was interpreted by his American handlers as a fairly natural human failure of memory.[35] (It could also be argued that a well-briefed double agent who had carefully memorized the details of his legend would not get such details wrong.)

The implications of this for the intelligence analyst are profound, as they are often faced with very considerable quantities of complex information, which they need to sort and manipulate in trying to develop a hypothesis. To attempt this just in the head is doomed to failure, so various techniques and technical aids are crucial.

---

[33] Heuer, *Psychology of Intelligence Analysis*, n 4 above, pp 17–20.

[34] W Kintsch, VL Patel, and KA Ericsson, 'The Role of Long-Term Working Memory in Text Comprehension' (1999) 42 *Psychologia* 186, 188.

[35] RJ Heuer, Jr, 'Nosenko: Five Paths to Judgment' in H Bradford Westerfield (ed), *Inside CIA's Private World: Declassified Articles from the Agency's Internal Journal, 1955–1992* (New Haven CT: Yale University Press, 1995) 379, 396, 402.

The issue of breaking down a problem into more focused and manageable parts is again something that many other disciplines have confronted. In the 1970s, analysis of marketing techniques saw a burgeoning interest in the concept of 'segmentation' of a market, whereby consumers are grouped into categories depending on their behaviours and buying habits.[36] Marketing strategies can then be tailored and targeted to those categories, rather than taking a 'one-size-fits-all' approach. A miniaturized MP3 player, for example, would be marketed primarily to teenagers and young adults, and not particularly to retired people, while the reverse might apply to orthopaedic mattresses.

In an intelligence context, the corollary is 'profiling' of target groups or networks to consider which parts of the population are most likely to contain key targets of interest. We have already used the example of potential travellers to terrorist training camps. A segmentation or profiling approach in this instance might determine that only males within a particular age range (in their early twenties, for example), who are travelling to areas of interest, are worth examining as a population set, while others who fell outside this group on either age or gender criteria would not be considered for analysis or data gathering.

A good example of where segmentation has been employed to good effect in an intelligence context is the original work on 'intelligence-led policing' in Kent constabulary in the UK, in the mid-1990s. We saw in Chapter 4 how this work established, through initial data analysis of burglaries and vehicle thefts, that a small number of individuals with existing criminal records were responsible for the majority of crimes in these categories. Further data gathering and intelligence analysis then focused on this sector of the local population to the exclusion of others, with good results.[37]

Such an approach might also be physically employed by border security personnel in ports or airports (ie old ladies would be less likely to be pulled over to have their bags searched for drugs than would young men within a particular age bracket), with all the attendant pitfalls of being seen to be discriminatory towards particular groups or communities. We can also see analytical dangers of constraining hypotheses in certain circumstances. The analyst would need to make sure that they did not always discount individuals or situations which fell outside the segmentation criteria, since there is always room for anomalies.

One way of sorting large amounts of complex information and organizing it in ways that are both easy to remember, and easy to communicate to others, is to use effective methods of visualization. In an intelligence analysis context, there are three critical dimensions in which information usually needs to be organized and visualized: time, space, and interconnectedness. We will not say too much more about the latter at this point, as this is the essence of SNA, although it is worth noting that intelligence agencies use a variety of techniques and

---

[36] R Grover and V Srinivasan, 'A Simultaneous Approach to Market Segmentation and Market Structuring' (1987) 24 *Journal of Marketing Research* 139.

[37] J Ratcliffe, *Intelligence-Led Policing* (Cullompton: Willan, 2008) p 6.

methods for depicting network charts and relationships between elements in an investigation. Many of us will be familiar with the principles of organizing elements of information within an intelligence operation in ways that depict relationship and connections, from watching crime programmes on the television. These will almost always include scenes in which detectives and police officers affix pictures or names of key targets onto a wall or whiteboard, and draw lines between them to establish connections. This is a basic process of visualizing a network, and it aids sense-making of disparate pieces of information.

A flat network diagram can be found wanting, however, if it does not find methods for organizing facts and events chronologically, or spatially. As Innes, Fielding, and Cope observe, for years, much as every TV programme featured a board with pictures and names on it, 'a staple feature of many police offices was a map of the local jurisdiction, with coloured pins pushed into it, plotting the occurrence of different incidents'.[38] An instinct for basic spatial organization of information has been present in policing probably since its inception. Now, of course, pins on maps on the wall are increasingly being replaced by GoogleEarth and other mapping software, but the principles are the same. Such practices allow for immediate analysis to be made of the pattern of incidents or events, and the relationship of this to particular districts in the locality, or indeed to the addresses or frequent haunts of particular individuals. For planners of surveillance, whether on the issue of placing static devices such as cameras, or active assets such as surveillance teams, information about where (and indeed when) to look with limited resources can be crucial.

Temporal information is also critical in investigations, and can be of material value to an intelligence assessment. Again, a basic technique in police investigation is to ask a suspect where he or she was at a certain time (and whether this can be verified) to test a hypothesis of whether that person could have been involved in a particular incident. Substantive evidence that he or she was either elsewhere at the time of the incident, or in a place that did not allow him or her time to reach a particular locality at a particular time, would count as inconsistent evidence in the model of competing hypotheses we used above, and would thus relegate the hypothesis concerning that individual's involvement in the incident.

Returning to the case of Nosenko and counter-espionage investigations in general, Heuer noted that temporal inconsistencies in a suspect's account, and particularly whether he or she was employed in a position that would have placed him or her in a particular place at a particular time to have had access to specific information, are critical pieces of information in the puzzle. One item of particular interest in Nosenko's account was the issue of the arrest by the KGB of Oleg Penkovsky at a dead-letter box in Moscow in November 1962, and intelligence reporting Nosenko claimed to have read about the incident while

---

[38] Innes et al, 'The Appliance of Science?', n 7 above, p 41.

he was stationed in the American Embassy department at KGB headquarters. Subsequent information showed that he had already been transferred out of that department at the time of the incident to one where he would not have had a need to receive reporting on it.[39] This inconsistency added to the initial theory that Nosenko was a KGB plant, although it was later concluded that he had muddled his recollection of what he had actually seen and what he had read about subsequently.

'Timelining', therefore, has become a standard tool in the armoury of most intelligence practitioners, and particularly investigative analysts in the police.[40] Its key value is as a method of organizing large amounts of complex data and contributing towards understanding the relationship between individuals and events. Numerous IT tools are used across the intelligence sector to assist with building timelines, but the basic principle is very straightforward, and can be executed on a wall or a large piece of paper using a hand-drawn line pertaining to a particular timescale.[41] Timelining can help to make sense of a sequence of events in a way that the human brain cannot always manage alone from memory. Morgan Jones illustrates the effect with two versions of a newspaper article involving a story told over a period of time, in which, in one of the versions, the events are deliberately presented out of sequence. In this version, it is very difficult to make sense of the story and it has to be read several times with great care in order to understand it, while in the sequential version of the story, the picture is immediately understood.[42] Again, while sorting information chronologically is a basic mechanism, it can have a significant effect on helping to interpret a set of data.

A synthesis of time and space can also be very significant in attempting to understand an intelligence picture. Returning again to our example of attending terrorist training camps, information about travel, including lengths of time spent in different places, and when individuals were at home or away, can be very significant to an investigation. Again, the story of the 'airline bomb plot' case shows how a careful cross-referencing of travel patterns, to and from Pakistan in this case, with phone calls, emails, and other communications, was a central part of the painstaking analysis that built up over time and established relationships between figures of significance to the investigation.[43]

---

[39] Heuer, 'Nosenko: Five Paths to Judgment', n 35 above, pp 396–7.

[40] M Peterson, *Intelligence-Led Policing: The New Intelligence Architecture* (Washington DC: US Department of Justice, 2005) p 7.

[41] See, eg RS Stering, *Police Officer's Handbook: An Analytical and Administrative Guide* (Sudbury MA: Jones and Bartlett Publishers, 2008) p 73.

[42] Jones, *The Thinker's Toolkit*, n 20 above, pp 89–90.

[43] V Dodd and L Glendinning, 'Airline bomb plotters case threatened by US fears', *The Guardian*, 8 September 2009, <http://www.guardian.co.uk/uk/2009/sep/08/airline-bomb-plotters-us-fears>, accessed 2 January 2010.

The Technical Dimension

The importance—indeed criticality—of technical support to intelligence analysis has been realized from its earliest experiences in the modern era. We now know that the most telling example was perhaps the decryption activities by the Allies in the Second World War, and particularly the work at Bletchley Park against the German Enigma codes, which led to the creation of what was effectively the world's first operational electronic computer in the shape of the Colossus machine.[44] Colossus tackled the problem of massive data overload, in this case the process of checking decrypt possibilities against intercepted encrypted messages, at a speed and consistency which would have been impossible for any human being to achieve unaided. We have already discussed in Chapter 3 the extreme operational significance this work had on the fortunes of the Allies in the war.

Since that time, much intelligence work has involved a need to analyze large amounts of very complex data, looking for deeply concealed patterns or inconsistencies. Automation is an obvious need for many of these processes, to allow the analyst to concentrate on analyzing, rather than on data preparation and sifting.

In the contemporary world and particularly with the advent of the information revolution heralded by the internet age, all sectors of public and private society have available to them a greatly enhanced depth and range of information about people and their activities. We have seen how this has led to public anxiety about the collection and analysis of such personal data, whether it be by government authorities or by commercial organizations, manifesting a concern about the 'surveillance society' which seems to be endemic in postmodern twenty-first century society. Clearly the explosion of personal information in the public domain in recent years has led to enormous opportunities for the intelligence analyst, but also risks in the shape of inadvertent or indeed wilful misinterpretation of such data.

On the opportunities front, the relentless advances in information technology have meant that ever more ambitious techniques and processes for tackling large amounts of complex data can be considered. All intelligence sectors across the world have seen a burgeoning growth of official and commercial projects in the 'homeland security and defence' sectors, which now represent whole new sectors of the economy dealing with information security as it applies to intelligence and security issues. For intelligence actors, the trick is to ensure that the right technologies are deployed which will allow analysts the greatest freedom to practise their tradecraft.

---

[44] That this was the first electronic computer is the contention of Jack Copeland (*Colossus: The Secrets of Bletchley Park's Codebreaking Computers* (Oxford: Oxford University Press, 2006)), although its existence was kept secret for 30 years after the war, by which time arguments had arisen as to when the first computer was deployed.

One of the most notable developments in this area is the Advanced Research and Development Activity's 'Novel Intelligence from Massive Data' (NIMD) programme in the US, which has been running since approximately 2002. NIMD represents a substantial line of funding for academic and commercial enterprises involved in research and design of automated aids to the intelligence analysis process. A considerable number of scientific experiments and projects have been undertaken, including the 'Knowledge Associates for Novel Intelligence' (KANI) project, and associated 'Glass Box', which aims to capture and model the activities of typical analysts with a view to examining how elements of their activities can best be automated. KANI's role is described as:

> to help analysts identify, structure, aggregate, analyze, and visualize task-relevant information and to help them construct explicit models of alternative hypotheses (scenarios, relationships, causality etc).[45]

The project is aiming to achieve these aims by building 'an encompassing knowledge integration architecture', which comprises four main 'associates' (or systems) for the analyst to use, namely:

- Hypothesis Generation and Tracking Associate
- Background Knowledge Identification and Assembly Associate
- Massive Data Extraction and Structuring Associate
- Information Interaction Associate[46]

The principles here are sound, namely to assist analysts in spending as little time and energy as possible finding and extracting data needed for their analysis, and automating as much of their transactional data processes as possible. As Badalamente and Greitzer noted, 'research efforts seek technology-based solutions to reduce the analyst's workload and improve the throughput and quality of IA [intelligence analysis] products'.[47]

The problem, however, is that more sophisticated data-mining activities, which may attempt to apply some of the more scientific and mathematical approaches we have described earlier to large datasets in an automated way, run a number of risks. An example of such a proposal was described by Badia and Kantardzic, who examined the problem of spotting link analysis patterns in social network data of relevance to law enforcement, intelligence, and counter-terrorism analysts.[48]

---

[45] AJ Cowell et al, 'Knowledge-Worker Requirements for Next Generation Query Answering and Explanation Systems', paper presented in the proceedings of the Workshop on Intelligence User Interfaces for Intelligence Analysis, International Conference on Intelligence User Interfaces, Sydney, 2006, <http://tw.rpi.edu/proj/portal.wiki/images/1/1b/KSL-06-02.pdf>, accessed 2 January 2010.   [46] Ibid.

[47] RV Badalamente and FL Greitzer, 'Top Ten Needs for Intelligence Analysis Tool Development', paper presented at First Annual Conference on Intelligence Analysis Methods and Tools, May 2005, <https://analysis.mitre.org/proceedings/Final_Papers_Files/319_Camera_Ready_Paper.pdf>, accessed 2 January 2010.

[48] A Badia and M Kantardzic, 'Link Analysis Tools for Intelligence and Counterterrorism' (2005) 3495 *Lecture Notes in Computer Science* 49.

Badia and Kantardzic noted that analysts are often looking for subtle patterns in the data which do not have 'large support', that is, they are not replicated very often. This challenges the normal parameters for pattern matching in automated data analysis, which tend to look for patterns that are repeated frequently and thus have greater statistical degrees of significance.[49] Following experiments aimed at automating the search for such subtle patterns, Badia and Kantardzic observed that:

> Determining which patterns are random and which ones are interesting is an intuitive, unformalized process that analysts in these fields must deal with. Here we have presented some measures that are formal and therefore can be supplied to a computer for efficient processing of large datasets. We stress that, even though we have kept our presentation intuitive and used examples to introduce the main ideas, the approach presented here can be completely formalized.[50]

To navigate a path of automation through territory that has previously been the preserve of intuitive judgements on the part of the analyst is an exercise fraught with dangers. The key risk is that the methods used in such cases may be very complex and somewhat arcane, so that analysts or indeed their intelligence customers do not really understand the data results they are receiving from the process. This, in turn, can lead to a crisis of trust in the system which is producing the recommendations as to which groups and networks are significant, with the danger that the results will be unpicked and scrutinized before being passed on (thus not saving any time after all), or worse, ignored as being irrelevant or 'too dangerous'. We have already seen the severe pitfalls of making flawed connections between individuals and terrorists or criminals. While analysts may accept that their own intuition in these cases is not always reliable, they may be more inclined to trust their own intuition than that of a complex computerized process whose workings are not fully understood.

The key in such situations, therefore, is probably not for automated processes of this nature to follow all the way through to making automated intelligence judgements, but merely to assist analysts with data preparation and segmentation, so that they can then apply their tradecraft to a more focused dataset.

Many on the civil liberties front have serious concerns about programmes such as NIMD, seeing it as greatly increasing the chances of innocent civilians being wrongfully accused of having criminal or terrorist connections. They also see NIMD as a thinly-disguised resurrection of the Defense Department's 'Total Information Awareness' programme, which was suspended in 2003 in the face of pressure from the public and legal experts over apparent transgressions of the constitutional right to privacy.[51] James Dempsey of the Center for Democracy

---

[49] Badia and Kantardzic, 'Link Analysis Tools', n 48 above, p 49.   [50] Ibid, p 58.

[51] MJ Sniffen, 'Pentagon's terrorism research lives on at other agencies', *Associated Press*, 23 February 2004, <http://www.fas.org/irp/news/2004/02/ap022304.html>, accessed 2 January 2010.

and Technology in the US noted that expansions in data mining activities like those of the NIMD programme increase 'the risk of an innocent person being in the wrong place at the wrong time, of having rented the wrong apartment ... or having a name similar to the name of some bad guy'.[52] It seems clear that automation of such analytical connections and network building across personal data can only increase the anxiety, and fears of a Big Brother society. The intelligence sector needs to be very wary of developing tools that cross the boundaries of human analytical application and move into automatic generation of inferences across large datasets of personal information. Most of the public still have an inherent distrust of the machines 'taking over', and, as misguided as these perceptions and fears may be, they have to be taken into account in the planning.

Perhaps the most important area in which technical advancements in IT could help with the intelligence process is in the raison d'être of the internet itself, namely in increasing and improving knowledge sharing, information flows, and networking of analysts across boundaries. If the targets are sharing techniques and information across the internet in ever more flexible and sophisticated ways, then surely the intelligence and security sectors should be doing the same? Herman noted the experience of the 'revolution in military affairs' following the 1991 Gulf War, in which IT had been harnessed to create a 'system of systems', linking together data on intelligence, surveillance, and reconnaissance and making it quickly and readily available to those serving the front line in the war.[53] The counter-terrorism community would surely have similar opportunities for its own 'system of systems', which would 'make all the different kinds of relevant data accessible by every counter-terrorist analyst at every IT workstation'.[54]

Unfortunately, the reality appears to be somewhat disappointing on this front. Herman noted that the British intelligence sector, which has remained distinct from military and law enforcement agencies, was based around an organization established in 1919 which has remained in place and been 'unaffected by the incessant reorganisation of the rest of the public sector over the past 30 years'.[55] Within this, vertical barriers between organizations, which affect information equities and facilities for sharing data either between the intelligence agencies, or between them and the law enforcers or military, remain stubbornly in place. (Whether the financial tsunami of the 2008/9 global economic crash will finally breach the barriers, remains to be seen.) In the US, the situation is no better, with 'institutional separation ... deeply entrenched'.[56] We have already seen in the policing sector how data sharing and matching between systems within

---

[52] Cited in Sniffen, ibid.
[53] M Herman, 'Counter-Terrorism, Information Technology and Intelligence Change' (2003) 18/4 *Intelligence and National Security* 40, 45.   [54] Ibid.   [55] Ibid, p 46.   [56] Ibid.

individual police forces is still difficult in many cases, let alone between different constabularies.

It appears, therefore, that great potential exists to harness technical solutions to data sharing and mining that could pay enormous dividends for intelligence analysis, but for various institutional reasons, these opportunities are not yet being realized.

Conclusions

Sherman Kent noted back in the 1960s that he foresaw the 'intelligent man' remaining the 'intelligence device supreme' for all time.[57] By this, he meant that the intuitive and analytical power of the analyst's brain would always be paramount, in his opinion, over any machine or automated system in deriving intelligence from complex data and making recommendations to the policymaker. At the same time, however, Kent advocated analysts taking a scientific approach to their analysis, rather than completely unstructured methods for gathering and analyzing data. In particular, he observed that a careful and formulaic analysis of previous incidents and intelligence failures could lead to a better capability in preventing similar failures in the future.

Scientific approaches to intelligence analysis primarily comprise systematic methods for organizing and sorting data, and for generating and testing hypotheses, which have the dual purpose of overcoming the natural frailties and biases of the human brain, and of allowing critical and creative thinking to take place. Such methods range from generating and challenging alternative hypotheses and models, to analyzing complex networks of individuals and their degree of interrelationship using techniques derived from scientific and mathematical approaches to mining and analyzing very large datasets. In this sense, intelligence can be seen as something of a branch of scientific enquiry, floating somewhere between natural and social science, and mathematics and statistical analysis.

However, we have seen how the peculiar factors surrounding intelligence analysis—principally that human beings are not only undeterministic in their behaviour, but sometimes deliberately evasive and deceptive—mean that the natural science approach to intelligence will always have limitations and boundaries. It is on these outer borders of the scientific approach that the human being's powers of reasoning, and sometimes plain intuition, will always need to come into play, and indeed to remain the dominant factor as Kent suggested they should be almost half a century ago.

These factors, in turn, mean that the issues of probability and uncertainty are always inherent in intelligence analysis, and that these factors have to be appropriately communicated to the consumers of the intelligence, so that they

---

[57] S Kent, *Strategic Intelligence for American World Policy* (Princeton NJ: Princeton University Press, 1965) p xviii.

understand the limitations of the information and judgements they are receiving. In many ways, similar challenges are faced by those working in other professions, such as doctors delivering a diagnosis to a patient, and weather forecasters postulating what the weather is going to do at the weekend. All of these actors join the intelligence analysts in facing opprobrium when probabilities are not properly communicated and things go wrong.

On the technical front, almost exponential increases in information technology since the late 1970s have offered intelligence practitioners enormous opportunities to work more efficiently and to deliver better results. With an explosion of personal information, there are much bigger haystacks now in which to find the deeply embedded information about terrorists or criminals, but there are also much more capable tools for manipulating and interrogating massive datasets. A panel at the Human Factors and Ergonomics Society Annual Meeting in 2004 noted that 'intelligence analysis is a domain that has a particularly difficult version of the data overload problem'.[58] Used correctly, ever more capable tools to handle the burgeoning datasets can overcome this problem and assist analysts to continue doing their job.

The ideal situation, therefore, is to harness creative and capable IT tools to cover the data extraction, preparation, and sorting phases completely, so that all the analyst has to do is to analyze. This allows a maximization of the application of 'brain power' and cognitive capabilities to the intelligence problem at hand, without the need to think about how to unearth the relevant data. This would also imply an ability to search across and compare datasets held in different places, and more often than not in different agencies across the intelligence, military, and law enforcement sectors. The IT capability increasingly exists to achieve such tasks, but it appears that institutional rivalries and legacy systems that do not communicate with each other are still preventing major progress on this front even after 9/11 and the numerous major incidents that have followed.

With manipulation and sharing of personal data on a massive scale, and increasing automation of inference making across that data, a number of risks are present. Some of these are technical, in that they concern the ability of automated systems reliably and appropriately to manage tasks of network analysis and hypothesis building in an environment of incomplete and ambiguous data, which is very much the nature of the beast in intelligence analysis. Perhaps more difficult risks are those in the ethical category, which concern questions of an individual's right to privacy, and the right not to be wrongly identified as a criminal or terrorist just through being 'in the wrong place at the wrong time'. The official organs of the state are having a hard time at present balancing the need to provide sophisticated security with the need to deliver trust in their

---

[58] WC Elm et al, 'Designing Support for Intelligence Analysts', paper presented at the Human Factors and Ergonomics Society Annual Meeting, September 2004, <http://www.ingentaconnect. com/content/hfes/hfproc/2004/00000048/00000003/art00028>, accessed 2 January 2010.

competency at making the right judgements from sets of personal data and not placing innocent individuals in severe jeopardy.

Scientific approaches to intelligence analysis are, therefore, increasingly essential given the range and complexity of the analysis task at hand. Sophisticated IT tools and techniques can help, but their limitations at the frontier of data extraction and preparation have to be properly understood and applied, so that analysts can get on with applying their cognitive skills in analysis.

Key Points

- Intelligence analysts and their managers have to apply formulaic and 'scientific' approaches to their work, to ensure the most efficient and effective outcomes.

- In many ways, intelligence analysis is akin to social and natural science, in that it involves deductive reasoning and subsequent testing of hypotheses with data.

- In other ways, however, the particular aspects of the data in question, and principally the fact that Humint targets are usually indeterministic, obfuscating, and devious, coupled with the fact that available data is often patchy and ambiguous, mean that intelligence analysis is subtly different in essence from a classic natural science.

- A number of tradecraft techniques exist which can help the analyst to overcome cognitive weaknesses and biases. These can be grouped into the categories of hypothesis testing; challenge; social network analysis; and data sorting, organizing, and visualization. Such techniques can either be applied in systematic and formulaic ways (such as 'Red Teaming'), or in lighter-touch ways which capture the main principles.

- Technical aids to analysis include sophisticated systems for handling large amounts of quantitative data, and for applying complex network analysis algorithms to that data. Technical assistance can also be found in the fields of sharing and cross-referencing data.

- However, risks are present in overly-automated approaches to intelligence analysis, both in the shape of overly complex and potentially flawed automated judgements, and the ethical considerations surrounding invasions of privacy and faulty associations being made between people and organizations.

- For this reason, technical aids need to concentrate primarily on the automated extraction and sorting of data, leaving the analyst to get on with the job of analyzing.

7

Meeting the Skills and Training Challenges

We have noted how, in the UK, following the Butler enquiry into intelligence on weapons of mass destruction, one of the many recommendations was to set up a centralized effort on steering analytical careers and professionalization in the UK's intelligence community. The official report on the Butler report's recommendations, presented to Parliament in 2005, noted that:

> The Government has decided to establish a post of Professional Head of Intelligence Analysis [PHIA], to advise in the security, defence and foreign affairs fields on gaps and duplication in analyst capabilities, on recruitment of analysts, on their career structures and on interchange within and beyond Government; to advise on analytical methodology across the intelligence community; and to develop more substantial training than hitherto on a cross-Government basis for all analysts working in these fields. The post of Professional Head of Intelligence Analysis will be established in the Intelligence and Security Secretariat of the Cabinet Office, whose Head is the JIC Chairman.[1]

It is interesting that the emphasis in this recommendation was on developing analytical skill and methodology 'across the intelligence community', and we can take this to mean not just the state intelligence agencies, but law enforcement bodies also.

To place this function close to the central intelligence assessment body in the UK seems a logical and entirely sensible move. We do not know what projects the PHIA has undertaken or how successful it has been subsequently, since much of its activity inevitably takes place behind closed

---

[1] *Review of Intelligence on Weapons of Mass Destruction: Implementation of its Conclusions* (London: TSO, 2005) pp 9–10, <http://www.cabinetoffice.gov.uk/media/cabinetoffice/corp/assets/publications/reports/intelligence/wmdreview.pdf>, accessed 3 January 2010.

doors. We do know, however, that one of the first things the office of PHIA did was to establish an academic connection for the intelligence community, which manifested itself in a training programme run jointly with the University of London's King's College: the King's Intelligence Studies Programme. The architects and leaders of the programme, Michael Goodman (from King's College) and Sir David Omand (the Intelligence and Security Coordinator in the UK government at the time of Lord Butler's 2004 enquiry) observed that:

> The high level of secrecy that is inevitable within an intelligence community means that training has to be largely in-house, but that, in turn, makes it more important to provide opportunities for analysts to meet and develop a wider professional outlook . . . The label 'analyst' should be interpreted widely to include researchers who regularly use secret intelligence, for example in the Foreign Office or in the Serious and Organised Crime Agency (SOCA), and not just be confined to 'all-source analysts'.[2]

Much of the purpose of the King's programme is to forge together a network of analysts across the intelligence community, but also to ensure that 'the choice of analytic methodology is examined, drawing on the experience of other professions grappling with problems of knowledge'.[3] This approach starts to bring the UK into line with the Sherman Kent approach in the US, which recognized from as early as the 1960s the need to bring some academic rigour and analysis to the intelligence analyst community.

In the policing analysis sphere, Ratcliffe notes that organizations such as the International Association of Crime Analysts and the International Association of Law Enforcement Intelligence Analysts have increasingly developed practical short training courses in aspects of intelligence analysis, arguably making more extensive progress than efforts to educate higher management in issues such as crime analysis.[4] These organizations have been mostly centred in the US, although some connections are being made internationally with the UK and other areas.

Within the UK, the National Policing Improvement Agency and National Analysts Working Group, both of which are organs of the Association of Chief Police Officers, run courses on intelligence analysis and 'investigative skills'. The framework for such training is that of the National Intelligence Model (NIM), which was established in 2000 and forms the administrative and organizational basis for all intelligence work in police forces in England and Wales.

---

[2] MS Goodman and D Omand, 'Teaching Intelligence Analysts in the UK. What Analysts Need to Understand: The King's Intelligence Studies Program' (2008) 52/4 *Studies in Intelligence* 1, 2, <https://www.cia.gov/library/center-for-the-study-of-intelligence/csi-publications/csi-studies/studies/vol-52-no-4/index.html>, accessed 3 January 2010.

[3] Ibid, p 3.   [4] J Ratcliffe, *Intelligence-Led Policing* (Cullompton: Willan, 2008) p 230.

Criticisms of such training include suggestions that it is stuck in the foundational layer, particularly since there has been a pressing need to get waves of new recruits up and running quickly, but also that a firm connection to the NIM runs the risk that the training is formulaic and simplistic, in the sense that it focuses on data gathering and manipulation rather than deep analysis of that data: essentially producing 'information' rather than 'intelligence'. We saw in Chapter 2 that the NIM is first and foremost a management model, describing the intelligence products that should be produced and how they should flow through the administrative process rather than necessarily the analytical skills required to produce them.[5] Within the UK, a website[6] has been set up by a group of analysts disgruntled with the way in which the NIM constrains the business of providing training in intelligence analysis in the policing sector. It notes that intelligence analysis courses for police in the UK, through being inextricably linked with teaching the NIM, acknowledge no distinction between 'analysts as investigators and as statisticians'.[7]

How representative such views are of the majority of analysts in the law enforcement sector in the UK is a moot point, but they emphasize the importance of ensuring that analysts have skills not only in the first parts of the intelligence cycle (the data collection part) but also in the more important analysis part. This brings in all the aspects of cognitive heuristics, tradecraft and techniques, and creative and critical thinking, that we have examined in previous chapters.

In this part of the book, we examine some mechanisms for developing and promulgating such analytical skills in the intelligence community. These are presented at a reasonably generic and high level, as they apply to the wider community of analysts that the PHIA has identified across the 'intelligence community', from strategic analysts in the Foreign Office to tactical analysts in the law enforcement sector. All are, at various levels, intelligence analysts.

Figure 7.1 shows the framework we will use for describing the training options, within which examples of scenarios and methods will be used.

Much of my experience of dealing with such issues comes from my own efforts to teach postgraduate students Security and Intelligence Studies in the UK, which include attempting to inculcate skills in critical thinking, evaluation, and communication around complex issues of security and intelligence. I have also tried to use the same principles in short training courses delivered primarily to police officers in the UK in counter-terrorism and intelligence analysis.

I will draw on such experience as we tackle the framework of training options, but, as ever, it should be stressed that these are not the only approaches that will work for developing analytical skills in the intelligence

---

[5] Ibid, p 113.   [6] <http://www.intelligenceanalysis.net>, accessed 3 January 2010.
[7] <http://www.intelligenceanalysis.net/Training.htm>, accessed 3 January 2010.

Figure 7.1 A framework for training in intelligence analysis

Critical and creative thinking exercises

Tactical intelligence

Strategic intelligence

Simulation and 'gaming'

workforce, and it should always be the case that training mechanisms are tailored as far as possible to the particular needs and objectives of the students in question.

A Few Words about Training

Before we commence discussion of the above framework, it is worth pausing briefly on the question of developments and best practice in training design and delivery. The most significant issue here is probably the whole question of 'blended learning', which has increasingly become a buzzword and a trend across the transatlantic training sectors since the early years of the twenty-first century. As with many such trends, it quickly became apparent that different people understood blended learning to mean subtly different things, thus leading to confusion.

The most commonly held view is that blended learning refers specifically to 'particular forms of teaching with technology', as Oliver and Trigwell suggested.[8] With more capable new technologies coming on stream, training increasingly enjoys opportunities to deliver learning through computer-based packages, virtual classrooms, and other technology-based methods for accessing and promulgating learning. However, as Graham noted, blended learning can also mean more generally combining different instructional modalities (delivery media) or methods.[9] Thus, technology can be important, but as an aid and assistant to more traditional forms of stand-up-and-talk training.

However it is defined, blended learning has raised the issue of the opportunities for using technology in training and learning, and we will return to some of these opportunities in the specific context at hand, of intelligence analysis training. Generally, best practice dictates that training courses and modules

---

[8] M Oliver and K Trigwell, 'Can "Blended Learning" Be Redeemed?' (2005) 2 *E-Learning* 17.

[9] CR Graham, 'Blended Learning Systems: Definition, Current Trends, and Future Directions' in CJ Bonk and CR Graham (eds), *The Handbook of Blended Learning: Global Perspectives, Local Designs* (San Francisco CA: Pfeiffer, 2005) p 3.

should also be designed within the framework of a systematic approach to training, which determines that training responds to an analysis of training needs, and is evaluated for its effectiveness in meeting those needs after delivery.[10]

Critical and Creative Thinking Exercises

We saw in Chapter 5 that critical thinking has come to be seen in terms of a set of characteristics that critical thinkers will display, and a set of dispositions towards critical thinking. We also saw that academic enquiry has concluded that, while a person's environment during their upbringing can be a deterministic factor in how easily and readily they conduct critical and creative thinking, there is nothing inherently genetic about whether one person is any less able to think creatively than the next. The conclusion to which this leads is that critical and creative thinking *can* be nurtured in the workplace with the right mechanisms, but also that the environment in the workplace is as important for encouraging these cognitive skills as specific training exercises. Many analysts in all sorts of organizations have complained that after they go on a training course and are enthused by what it teaches them, they often find on returning to the workplace that it is difficult to take ideas forward because the environment is wrong. This can apply either to organizational processes and procedures in the workplace which militate against change or creativity ('We have to follow the process like this'); or to mindset issues in colleagues or managers ('We don't do things like that around here'). The suggestions for training presented in this chapter, therefore, cannot be taken as a panacea for organizational change unless the working environment is addressed holistically.

In practical terms, critical thinking involves critically analyzing a situation or piece of data, and creative thinking is the process whereby possible alternative hypotheses are created and proposed. The two fit closely together in such processes as Analysis of Competing Hypotheses.

At the most basic level, exercises to enhance critical thinking can be seen all around us, and include the sorts of things found on the miscellaneous page towards the back of the newspaper. They include basic logic and semantic problems (such as cryptic crosswords), all of which are about exercising thought and language to overcome a problem and unlock a riddle. Anyone who is particularly good at cryptic crosswords will usually say that it is as much about technique as 'being clever': practising thinking in a certain way can improve performance. (This is essentially how the tutors who prepare children for school entrance tests based on numerical and linguistic problems earn their money.)

One of the easiest ways to introduce critical thinking into the intelligence analysis workplace, therefore, is to make available logic problems and exercises which test the analyst's powers of reasoning. The environmental factor in this

---

[10] R Buckley and J Caple, *The Theory and Practice of Training* (London: Kogan-Page, 2004) p 25.

case would be represented by developing an organizational culture that sees occasional time spent on solving logic problems as a legitimate and useful activity to sit alongside operational intelligence production.

One of many methods is to take a newspaper article about a particular event or issue, and go through it with a critical eye, looking for alternative explanations or weaknesses in the story which could be challenged. In some research conducted at the University of Hong Kong, Joe Lau used an example of a story that had appeared on German TV about a blind woman who claimed to be able to identify colours entirely by touch. She said it was a skill she had developed over twenty years, and which she used to decide which clothes to wear in the morning.[11] A critical analysis of this skill which 'baffled scientists' would be to question how long she had been blind, and whether she once knew the colours of particular clothes and got to know them by touch before she fully lost her sight. One could also postulate that particular designs of clothes or particular materials used might usually conform to particular colours, and that the woman had learnt the probabilities of particular garments or materials being particular colours. And so on. All we are doing here is reading the story with a very critical eye, and identifying the points in it which could be opened to scrutiny, and for which alternative hypotheses could be presented (the latter process signifying the creativity aspect).

Experience shows that, particularly in an operational intelligence analysis environment, generic exercises of this nature which do not appear to have a direct relevance to security and intelligence questions at hand can be viewed with impatience by analysts. Such is the operational impetus among many analysts that they generally like to deal with exercises and problems which are much closer to the sorts of issues they are likely to face in their work situation, and for which they can see immediate benefits when they return to the workplace.

One exercise I have used recently with my university class is to conduct a critical reading of press reporting on the unfolding story of allegations of torture in counter-terrorist operations. The issue is a 'live' one at the time of writing, in that investigations are underway as to whether British intelligence officers were complicit in the use of torture by third-party agencies, or at least turned a blind eye to such practices when interviewing suspects. This makes it particularly relevant and dynamic to students or indeed practitioners of security and counter-terrorism work. We do not yet know the outcome of such investigations, so there is plenty of room for creative and critical analysis of the evidence that is emerging. Figure 7.2 shows a fictitious extract from a newspaper article which we used to conduct a critical analysis test.

---

[11] J Lau, *Critical Thinking Exercises—version 1* (Hong Kong: Department of Philosophy, University of Hong Kong, 2006), <http://philosophy.hku.hk/think/misc/ex-public-1.pdf>, accessed 3 January 2010.

Figure 7.2 Torture newspaper article[12]

The Chronicle, 11 March 2004

TORTURE POLICY WAS ESTABLISHED FOR TERRORIST SUSPECTS DETAINED OVERSEAS

During the case brought by Martin Gomez at the High Court this week, an MI5 officer who had dealt with Gomez's case during his initial incarceration in Kokastan was cross-examined. The intelligence officer, appearing behind a screen, was referred to as 'X'.

It was put to 'X' that, when he had interviewed Gomez after he had been in jail in Kokastan City for four weeks, he did not make any comments on Gomez's apparent loss of weight, or ask if he had been mistreated in any way. This was despite 'X' admitting that Kokastan was known to have a poor human rights record regarding terror detainees.

Shortly after 'X''s interview of Gomez, the latter was handed over to US authorities in Kokastan City, after which he disappeared for some weeks, to re-emerge in Guantanamo Bay at the beginning of the following month.

When asked if he had threatened Gomez with the prospect of transfer to Guantanamo or with torture by the Kokastan authorities, 'X' denied that any such threats had been issued. He further added that Gomez had appeared well enough to be interviewed.

A British student from Rochdale, who is now working for the Inland Revenue in Basingstoke, claims he was extensively tortured by the Kokastan authorities after being detained in Kokastan City in the aftermath of the 2005 London bombings. He claims he was interviewed several times by MI5 officers in the jail in Kokastan City during this period. He is thought to be still deeply traumatized by the episode.

Other detainees in Kokastan have been deported to the UK or convicted of terrorist charges, while a handful have disappeared in suspicious circumstances, including one who was apparently killed in a huge explosion at Kokastan City's central jail in the course of an attempted jail-break. The family of this man have not been given his body despite repeated appeals through the British Embassy.

Examining this article, we can consider it through the lens of the key critical thinking skills of analysis, inference, interpretation, explanation, self-regulation, and evaluation, as identified by Facione and outlined in Chapter 5.[13]

In this case, the first thing worth doing is to consider the source of the article. *The Chronicle* is not a real newspaper, but every newspaper tends to lean one way or the other politically, especially when it comes to issues such as civil liberties and intelligence. The inference in this article is that the state, in the shape of the intelligence agency MI5, has some explaining to do to account for apparent complicity in allowing torture of terrorist suspects. The evidence of

---

[12] *The Chronicle*, and this article, are fictitious, while being based loosely on real events. Any connections with real individuals, places, or events are not intentional.

[13] PA Facione, *Critical Thinking: What It is and Why It Counts: 2009 Update* (Insight Assessment, 2009) p 5.

apparent wrongdoing is presented in such a way that the sympathy lies with the suspects who allege that they were tortured with the connivance of the British government, rather than with the MI5 officers. For students of intelligence analysis—indeed for students generally—it is very important to understand these nuances of source sympathy and analyze critically source materials of this nature with such factors in mind.

In this instance, a useful method for examining the article and situation critically would be that of 'devil's advocacy', which we discussed in the previous chapter. This is apt in this case because there are two sides to the dispute (the suspects, and the government), and the newspaper has presented things with a slight leaning towards the viewpoint of the suspects. To challenge and scrutinize this view, it is useful to place oneself in the shoes of the government and think about whether alternative explanations and hypotheses can be offered in its defence.

It is important to stress at this point that taking the devil's advocacy line here is entirely objective, and for the purposes of encouraging critical thinking on all sides. Students undertaking this particular exercise might have a variety of views about the situation, and many would no doubt be sympathetic towards the suspects' case as presented by the newspaper. For these people in particular, an exercise in which they place those preferences to one side and position themselves in the mindset of the opposing view is difficult, but is the very essence of critical thinking. As Facione outlined, three of the important dispositions towards critical thinking involve being judicious, truth-seeking, and open-minded.[14] To be able to do this in a completely unbiased and objective way, particularly on issues that are controversial or emotive, is difficult, but is a skill that can be developed through practice.

For this particular example, Table 7.1 below picks out some instances in which an alternative hypothesis could be presented to counter the dominant one presented in the newspaper article: that the suspects had been tortured with the full knowledge and connivance of the MI5 officers, in contravention of the British government's stance on torture.

The purpose of this exercise would be to discuss the article and the situation as a group, and to steer conversation and challenges by asking pertinent questions. With skilful facilitation in this way, the tutor would not necessarily personally hold the contrary views, but would aim to tease them out to see if they stood up to objective scrutiny by the group, and generally encourage vibrant debate. If the exercise worked well, with good engagement from the group, the students themselves would do all the work and critically examine the article from all sides.

Exercises of this nature can be conducted in different ways, and in different contexts. They work best with reasonably small groups, and with careful facilitation. With a large group, it might be appropriate to split the participants into

---

[14] Ibid.

Table 7.1 Exercise to generate possible alternative hypotheses

Newspaper article evidence	Critical thinking challenge, and possible alternative hypothesis
Para 2: 'X' did not ask whether Gomez had been tortured or mistreated, and did not enquire why he had lost weight, despite knowing that Kokastan has a 'poor human rights record'. (Inference: 'X' wilfully turned a blind eye to likely torture having happened.)	Anyone who has been arrested and detained in violent situations is likely to be unsettled and may naturally lose weight through having an aversion to sub-standard prison food. 'X' may have had no particular cause to ask if Gomez had been tortured or mistreated based on his appearance.
Para 4: 'X' denied he had threatened Gomez and said the prisoner appeared well enough to be questioned. (Inference: an allegation has been mooted that 'X' raised the threat of mistreatment or extraordinary rendition.)	'X' may be telling the truth: he did not issue any sort of threat of mistreatment, and was genuinely satisfied from Gomez's appearance that he had not been tortured and was fit for interview.
Para 5: A British student claims he was tortured while in custody in Kokastan and then questioned extensively by British intelligence officers. He is 'thought to be still deeply traumatized'. (Inference: the British officers were fully aware that he had been tortured and turned a blind eye.)	This is an unverifiable allegation from a single source, which may be generally unsympathetic towards the British state. There is no source attribution for the evidence that the student in question remains deeply traumatized. It seems surprising that he would return to Britain and work in the public sector if he had been wilfully mistreated with the connivance of the British state.
Para 6: One of the detainees had disappeared in 'suspicious circumstances' and was said to have been killed in a large explosion, although his family have not been given the body. (Inference: the detainee was probably not really killed in this way, but unlawfully by the authorities while in detention.)	The incident is one of conjecture, from an unidentified source. It may be true that the detainee was killed in an explosion, and if so, there may not be a body to hand over.

smaller teams who could each debate the article, and then compare thoughts in a plenary wrap-up session. Alternatively the smaller groups could be given a range of different topics to tackle. One similar exercise which I have run several times on part of a counter-terrorism course where we were looking at gaining a brief understanding of the Arab-Israeli conflict, involves splitting the group into two teams, and assigning one to the Israeli position and one to the Arab position. Each team is then instructed to place itself in the mindset of the community to which it has been allotted and to come up with a resumé of its team's main political points in the conflict. This works quite well as it is something of a bipolar, adversarial situation, and it encourages each side to find compelling challenges to the other side's arguments. A testimony to the powers of creative thinking is our experience of students enthusiastically taking to the task in ways that would normally seem counter-intuitive based on the communities to which they belong.

It might also be possible to tackle such exercises remotely in virtual communities, ie by placing an article of this nature on a web forum and inviting discussion threads which examined it critically and offered alternative hypotheses. This could be a useful side activity for a learning community involved in developing its intelligence analysis and critical thinking skills. In all cases, the key is for the participants to be able to develop techniques for critiquing and analyzing a hypothesis objectively, forensically, and constructively, without becoming emotional or irrational, and by demonstrating an openness to contrary points of view.

We have seen in previous chapters how the general academic consensus on creativity has been, for some years, that it is something that can be taught and learnt by anyone, given the right environment. To establish alternative hypotheses after a critical reading of a set of information requires a certain degree of creativity. Returning briefly to the theory, Sternberg identified two key models for understanding creativity. First is the 'confluence approach', which recognizes that creativity is not just about seeing a problem in new ways (the 'synthetic' intellectual skill), but also about working out which ideas and hypotheses are worth pursuing (the 'analytic' skill) and how best to persuade others that the new idea is a good one worthy of taking on board (the 'practical-contextual' skill).[15] A really effective creative thinker will be able to deploy all three skills. Second, Sternberg suggests that effective creativity follows the 'investment theory', whereby a creative thinker 'buys low but sells high'. From this, he means that new ideas will initially be accumulated by a creative thinker at a time when there is much general scepticism about their validity and not much enthusiasm to take them on, but, following persuasive work by the creative thinker, the ideas will take hold and really pass a threshold where they can be 'sold high'.[16]

There are several techniques for stimulating creative thinking, but one of the few that has really been exercised and analyzed in any great depth is that of 'brainstorming'.[17] Mednick noted that the creative thinking process is defined by the 'forming of associative elements into new combinations'.[18] As Hender et al noted, this means achieving a 'shift in perspective' to a problem, whereby new and original associations to it can be made.[19] In classic brainstorming, a group will generate thoughts or maybe simply words or ideas around a particular question, all of which are captured on a board, initially without discrimination. As words and ideas emerge, they trigger connections with new and further

---

[15] RJ Sternberg, 'The Nature of Creativity' (2006) 18 *Creativity Research Journal* 87, 88.

[16] Ibid, p 87.

[17] JM Hender et al, 'Improving Group Creativity: Brainstorming Versus Non-Brainstorming Techniques in a GSS Environment', paper presented at the 34th Hawaii International Conference on System Sciences, 2001, p 2, <http://www.computer.org/plugins/dl/pdf/proceedings/hicss/2001/0981/01/09811067.pdf?template=1&loginState=1&userData=anonymousIP%253A%253A86.144.60.52>, accessed 29 March 2010.

[18] SA Mednick, 'The Associative Basis of the Creative Process' (1962) 69 *Psychological Review* 220, 221.   [19] Hender et al, 'Improving Group Creativity', n 17 above, p 2.

words and ideas, providing the group is feeling sufficiently relaxed and creative. Stimuli to help achieve creativity, such as objects, sounds, pictures, or analogies can be used, but research shows that the degree of 'unrelatedness' of these factors to the original question can be important in generating truly novel ideas.[20] (Thus, stimuli that are too closely related to the original question at hand may constrain ideas.)

Brainstorming was originally devised as a technique in the commercial world, and is believed to have been pioneered by Alex Osborn, who started life in a New York advertising firm before helping to establish the Creative Studies Department at Buffalo State College.[21] Osborn identified that there are two key principles to brainstorming: deferred judgement; and quantity breeds quality. These, in turn, are demonstrated by applying four rules:

• Criticism of ideas is initially prohibited—everything gets recorded.
• Unconventional ideas are welcomed as they may turn out to be significant.
• Quantity of ideas is key—the more ideas generated, the more likely you are to find some good solutions.
• Combination and grouping of ideas (linking them together) can often stimulate further ideas.[22]

In a counter-terrorism context, I have frequently used a basic group brainstorming process to open terrorism training modules (both with university students and with police practitioners) by asking the group to identify what words they would use in defining the term 'terrorism'. The process generally captures certain key words straight away, such as 'violence' and 'fear', then gradually moves into more complex areas such as 'ideology', 'media', and 'asymmetric conflict' as the students think harder about the question and range around the issue. Sometimes, when the ideas are drying up, I may nudge the group with a question such as 'what sorts of targets do terrorists attack?' This can stimulate extra avenues of thinking based around words such as 'civilians' or 'military', which usually trigger a number of other thoughts—this is the aspect of linking together ideas into themes or categories.

The purpose of the exercise is threefold: to work as an icebreaker for the group in getting them thinking and talking at the beginning of a course, to demonstrate that something as seemingly straightforward as 'terrorism' turns out to be a quite complex and multi-faceted concept, and to provide a basis for connecting ideas and concepts back to the original question as we proceed through the course. It also has the benefit of getting the students into a mode of critical and creative thinking. Usually I will record the words fairly randomly on a large whiteboard and leave it up throughout the course, so that I can periodically go back to it and pick out certain words that we identified at the beginning to make a connection with a particular issue. Because the group had thought of

---

[20] Ibid.   [21] MR Teuke, 'Applied Imagination', *Creative Living*, Autumn 2006, p 12.
[22] Hender et al, 'Improving Group Creativity', n 17 above, p 4.

these words themselves, they can generally more readily see and appreciate the connections being made.

A group, a whiteboard, and a pen are very basic tools for brainstorming which do not involve any particular stimuli other than a relaxed environment, which is usually set by spelling out on commencement the 'ground rules' for the exercise, such as 'there is no such thing as a stupid idea'. Again, some of the same process can be achieved virtually using web forums or discussion threads, where ideas can be recorded and seen by others to trigger further ideas, although these run the risk of being considerably less dynamic and stimulating if the members of the group are not together and feeding off each other in the same time and space.

Extra unconnected external stimuli, which I have sometimes experienced on personal development and management courses, such as the playing of emotive music in the background ('whale music') or use of supposedly relaxing and inspiring media such as aromas or colours, should again—in my experience—be deployed very carefully in operational environments. There are cultural factors here which will vary between groups and environments, but generally there is a risk of unusual and radical external stimuli distracting from the main purpose of the exercise by becoming talking points and distractions in themselves. A skilful deployment of such devices can work very well, but can also have negative effects if used inappropriately.

Another key factor in the use of brainstorming-type techniques in stimulating creativity is the element of teamworking to solve a problem or analyze a complex issue. In their seminal book, *The Wisdom of Teams*, Katzenbach and Smith noted that 'teams often form around … [demanding performance] challenges without any help or support from management'—this is a 'commonsense finding'.[23] If you have a complex problem, it makes sense to deploy a number of brains on the task rather than to try to solve it alone. In an intelligence analysis context, this is something that does not just apply to training mechanisms and techniques, but arguably to the way that the analysis function is organized as a whole. Clark's model of 'target-centric analysis' holds teamwork to be a critical element, whereby the team involves not just the analysts but their intelligence customers too.[24] Brainstorming as a group can be a powerful exercise in a training context, but it should not be confined just to the classroom. As a central technique for stimulating creative thinking, therefore, brainstorming should be deployed regularly as part of the day-to-day intelligence analysis process.

Tactical Intelligence

In training and exercising for how analysts deal with specific intelligence scenarios and problem types, it is necessary to consider that there are differing modes of intelligence gathering, which we can loosely delineate as tactical and strategic

---

[23] JR Katzenbach and DK Smith, *The Wisdom of Teams: Creating the High-Performance Organization* (Boston MA: Harvard Business School Press, 1993) p 3.

[24] RM Clark, *Intelligence Analysis: A Target-Centric Approach* (Washington DC: CQ Press, 2007) p 279.

intelligence. Although many of the generic skills and challenges apply to both modes of intelligence activity, there are some important differences between the two in terms of scope of enquiry, resources available for alternative hypothesis building and testing, and the requirements for judgements and decision-making.

A tactical (or operational) intelligence analysis situation generally involves a relatively fast-moving situation on the ground, and comprises analysis of specific movements of individuals, their activities, or events associated with them, within temporal and spatial dimensions. Intelligence assessment and judgement is likely to be fragmented, short, and often 'unassessed' in the sense that individual pieces of intelligence will not yet be considered for any long-term patterns or trends that they may signify. Decisions and communications of pieces of intelligence will usually drive tactical assets within the context of a specific operation. This will often happen largely at a working level, with little oversight or assessment by senior-level policy-makers, other than where important decisions need to be made about the allocation of resources, or if the risk of a tactical decision having wide-reaching consequences is large. Examples of where tactical intelligence might come into play are where intelligence gathering is supporting the day-to-day activities of a specific counter-terrorism or law enforcement operation, or a live military situation.

Some of the issues and challenges that are unique to a tactical intelligence situation include:

- Judgements and decisions will often need to be made under time pressure, usually in the face of lacking data (as is inherent with intelligence generally).
- The distinction between information and intelligence will often be thin, with resultant risks that the tactical assets receiving guidance from the intelligence analysts are flooded with potentially unhelpful or indeterministic data. Much of this data will turn out to be irrelevant, or take the investigation down blind alleys.
- Because fragments of intelligence will need to be communicated in near real-time, the connections between those pieces of intelligence, their relevance to one another, and any significant trends or patterns over a period will often be difficult to see, particularly in the early stages of an operation.

In the policing context, the NIM in England and Wales contains provision for an Operational Intelligence Assessment (OIA) as one of its 'Analytical Techniques and Products'. The NIM describes the purpose of the OIA as follows:

> The operational intelligence assessment tries to provide real time evaluation of, and research into, all incoming data connected with an operation, together with an analysis of other events and discoveries connected with the targets. The result should continually be compared with the objectives of the original collection plan. This will help identify gaps in and priorities for the operation's intelligence effort and ensure the continuing alignment of the work.[25]

---

[25] *The National Intelligence Model* (London: NCIS, 2000) p 37.

We can see from this description that the OIA is as much about retaining focus on a specific operation and avoiding 'mission creep' as about ensuring good intelligence analysis in an operational (or tactical) situation. This reflects the primarily managerial nature of the NIM, as we have discussed on a number of occasions previously.

Much work has been conducted in the military on tactical exercises and training, since this is the bread-and-butter aspect of their work, and the importance of getting it absolutely right is high. The military shares a challenge with the intelligence-gathering function (albeit on a different scale and sometimes with different consequences), namely that significant operational situations may not arise very often—and certainly not within the usual work cycle of a new or recent recruit—which means that, without exercising, when officers do face a suddenly unfolding tactical operation they are very often doing so for the first time. But a critical operation with many risks and challenges is not necessarily the right time for officers to be cutting their teeth and making mistakes. 'Learning by doing' is not always appropriate or possible in these particular cases: officers need to be equipped and confident to deal with a situation when it does happen.

Tactical training exercises therefore need to simulate real situations as far as possible, so that officers can consider how they are equipped to react. For the intelligence analyst, a good exercise will simulate the key challenges present in a tactical situation, which include all of the cognitive challenges we have discussed, with the addition of time pressure, data overload, and so on. Exercises in this area can be in a number of different formats, from paper-based table-top exercises, to intelligence support, to actual operational manoeuvres on the ground, or simulated exercises using information technology in creative ways. Any of these can be useful in different situations. Real simulated exercises involving events on the ground can add the element of surprise and uncertainty, since events will usually not unfold in exactly the way anticipated. They can also add the experience of decision-making in pressurized situations: there is nothing like being pressed for a decision on whether a tactical unit should raid a building, when people are on the ground standing ready for the decision and will get very impatient if there is hesitation or uncertainty.

Real exercises can be extraordinarily complex and resource-intensive to organize, however, and can divert precious operational resources from real priorities at crucial times. The easiest and most practical of the exercises are often, therefore, table-top paper exercises, which generally do not entail large amounts of organization or resource, but can still test an analyst's skills very effectively in a safe and benign environment. This allows analysts to consider how they need to supplement their skills, and can give them confidence to act appropriately in a real situation when it comes around.

I have used a basic half-day tactical paper-based scenario exercise with university students studying intelligence analysis, and with practitioners such as the police. The operation is run in the morning with minimal preparation or discussion, then the results are analyzed and discussed afterwards in a more relaxed and reflective mood. Any number of scenarios can be used, but I generally use a fast-moving counter-terrorism operation which looks at a fictitious group of individuals believed to be an attack cell nearing readiness for an operation. I structure the exercise around flooding the students with a considerable amount of data, which contains a number of analytical pitfalls and challenges, and apply a strict time constraint. This entails simulating a call (robustly made) from a senior operational commander for a situation report after one hour, and a call for a final 'go/no-go' decision after two hours from an armed police unit supporting the operation. I have seen many similar exercises in a number of other scenarios, including those based on a murder enquiry, a hostage scenario, and so on. It is very intriguing to see whether or not planes have been stormed, or major urban areas evacuated based on an analysis of the information available.

Table 7.2 below shows how I structure one particular exercise that I have run recently in this area. This involves an operation which has been brought to the group, who are told they are members of the fictitious Counter Terrorism Tactical Coordination Centre. They are briefed on the fact that they have to coordinate the intelligence and tactical decision-making on a fictitious operation called SEARCHLIGHT, and that they will be asked for an intelligence update after one hour by the 'Gold' Commander's office,[26] and a final decision on tactical steps to take after two hours. A debrief follows thereafter. All of the information comes completely cold to the group, and they are told that they have to meet the above deadlines to the minute. Time-checks are provided as the group progresses, to ensure an environment of time pressure.

It is very interesting how, in this particular operation, the ultimate question is one of a balance of probabilities, and includes specific considerations such as balancing public safety with accurate intelligence. These are very real challenges faced by the likes of the police and military in tactical situations. In this particular scenario, one hypothesis suggests that the group is preparing a home-made explosive device in a garden shed, within a built-up residential area. For the local police in this situation, they would need to understand whether and when intelligence had passed a certain tipping-point of probability whereby the residential area needed to be evacuated and the property entered with appropriately trained and equipped explosives and chemicals experts. The intelligence analysts would be under extreme pressure to come up with this decision by the end of the task, which exercises their assessment of probabilities and how to communicate those appropriately to the customer.

---

[26] In the UK, when a large incident unfolds which requires coordination of several different agencies on the ground, a command and control structure is put in place with three levels: Bronze (operational control on the ground), Silver (overall tactical control near the scene), and Gold (strategic control of the whole incident, usually slightly removed from the actual scene). The regional police commander supplies the latter. For a good explanation of this structure, see Cheshire Police's website at <http://www.cheshire.police.uk/showcontent.php?pageid=638>, accessed 3 January 2010.

Table 7.2 Tactical intelligence scenario—analysis

Incoming information	Analysis required	Analytical thinking skills being tested
Initial tasking: SEARCHLIGHT involves a spin-off from another operation which involves possible local links to a radical Islamist organization based in Pakistan. The key link is a student at the local university who is emerging as a spokesperson for the organization.	First stage: critically examine the available information on the Pakistan-based organization and debate how significant membership of, or connections with this organization would necessarily be an indicator of impending terrorist activity.	Critical analysis of the **Requirement** stage of the intelligence cycle: how useful and deterministic is this original piece of tasking? Do we need to keep an open mind at this stage? How significant an indicator of terrorist intentions is religious zeal? Should we challenge some of the inferences made by the intelligence customer?
Background information on each of the key target's associates, most of whom share student accommodation with him, but one of whom is a local car dealer with a criminal record.	Forensic analysis of all of the information, noting key details. Initial basic network analysis of how the individuals fit together, in terms of their relationship with one another.	Overcoming bias in filtering out which information is perceived to be irrelevant, and which might turn out to be significant later. Overcoming bias about a criminal record—this does not mean the man is inherently 'bad' at this stage. Data organizing and sorting skills, including basic social network analysis skills.
A set of surveillance logs and witness statements on many of the key target individuals undertaking various activities, with location and time/date information. Includes details of a meeting some distance away between a known terrorist linchpin and two individuals fitting the description and behaviour of two of our targets.	As above, a forensic analysis of all of the information, noting details which may or may not turn out to be significant later. Space/time analysis, noting how the various incidents relate to one another in terms of locations and timings. Updating the network analysis as appropriate.	Challenging relevancy and determinacy of incidents and events to the central hypothesis that this group is preparing a terrorist act. Overcoming bias and over-interpretation, in which innocent activities (like buying a car from the local dealer) could be interpreted as suspicious in some way. Critically evaluating potential bias in some of the witness statements. Overcoming perception shifts—could the two individuals at the distant meeting really be our targets? Sorting and organizing skills, and particularly timelining: could our targets have got to the distant meeting and back again in time?

Incoming information	Analysis required	Analytical thinking skills being tested
A large set of communications data relating to the student accommodation in which the main targets live.	Interpreting, sorting, and organizing the data, and relating it to the other pieces of information received, both in terms of location and time details. Updating the network analysis with new information on connections between individuals.	Critical analysis of how significant the communications data is, and how much certainty there is of who is communicating. Overcoming the data-overload problem by organizing and collating the information effectively and ensuring significant details are extracted from the mass of routine data. Ensuring tests of time and location are accurately cross-referenced with the other received information. Challenging inference and hypothesis building: is it significant that two individuals are communicating with one another, and how much or how little does this communication event tell us about what is happening?
Open source information on a range of issues, including details of the extremist group in Pakistan; news reports on other terrorist groups who have behaved in similar ways; scientific information about a dual-purpose chemical that one of the group purchases.	As above, assimilating this information and testing its utility to the other information received.	Further tests of relevancy, and critical thinking. Challenging hypotheses and perception shifts: because this chemical has been used by other terrorist groups elsewhere for building home-made explosives, is that necessarily the case here? Is there any other information in this case that supports the alternative hypothesis that it could be used for legitimate purposes? If the extremist group has sponsored attacks overseas, how likely is it to do so in the UK, and how reliable are the allegations of its direct involvement with terrorism? Evaluation of sources—where is the open source coming from and how much do we trust those sources?

This particular aspect of the exercise is modelled on various real-world examples. The infamous 'Operation Crevice' in the UK involved a situation where the key suspects were found to be storing a quantity of ammonium nitrate (a fertilizer-based explosive material) in a lock-up garage in a residential area in West London. In this particular case, the police chose to tamper covertly with the material to make it safe,[27] but there were very delicate public safety considerations to be made under time pressure. In other cases, as we have seen, raids of properties turn out not to uncover the material or information sought, and unsightly acquittals can follow.

It may well be understood by everyone involved in these cases that the intelligence might be wrong, and a high-profile and dramatic evacuation of neighbouring properties or a police raid turns out to be a false alarm. This, in turn, attracts further adverse publicity about a 'police state' and victimization of certain groups in society, but this may be a calculation that the police have to take into account in the interests of public safety. We saw in Chapter 2 that, up until September 2005, less than 3 per cent of arrests made under the Terrorism Act 2000 in the UK resulted in convictions.[28] This might seem like a low rate with plenty of room for improvement, but what would an acceptable rate be in balancing false alarms with the protection of public safety? Somewhere between 3 and 100 per cent is probably the answer, but that is not necessarily helpful and could usefully be the subject of further research.

For our exercise, the main point is that the intelligence analyst, in a tactical situation, faces a number of pressures and issues that bear down heavily on his or her ability to undertake accurate, efficient, and reliable intelligence judgements, in ways that do not always apply in other situations. Overcoming these pitfalls are skills that the intelligence analyst needs to develop, but doing so in a suitably designed exercise environment allows for mistakes to be made and subsequently analyzed objectively without any real-world consequences. It is arguably the case that an environment of frequent exercising and practising of these skills, and an analysis of mistakes, should be inherent components of the intelligence function.

We can see from Table 7.2 above that the analytic skills being tested are very generic, and relate to any number of intelligence scenarios beyond counter-terrorism. Overcoming data overload and information source evaluation, for example, are skills that can be developed in a range of situations, providing the right materials are assembled. The above model can therefore be taken as a basic template for a number of different intelligence scenarios.

---

[27] I Cobain and R Norton-Taylor, 'The phone call that asked: how do you make a bomb?', *The Guardian*, 1 May 2007, <http://www.guardian.co.uk/uk/2007/may/01/terrorism.politics1>, accessed 3 January 2010.

[28] A Gillan, R Norton-Taylor, and V Dodd, 'Raided, arrested, released: the price of wrong intelligence', *The Guardian*, 12 June 2006, <http://www.guardian.co.uk/uk/2006/jun/12/terrorism.politics>, accessed 3 January 2010.

Strategic Intelligence

In many ways, a strategic intelligence problem comprises many of the same generic issues as the tactical intelligence challenge examined above, in terms of critically analyzing available information, evaluating source materials, overcoming bias and perception resistance, and so on. The differences are principally:

- More time is available, usually, to explore and extract further information which may help with the case. There might also be a larger archive of previous information on which to draw.
- Greater amounts of available information, and more time in which to analyze it, allow opportunities for applying structured and 'scientific' methods of hypothesis building and challenge such as Analysis of Competing Hypotheses.
- In a strategic situation, the main task is to develop a judgement, expressed in probability terms, of trends and patterns based on an analysis of previous information relating to a long time period, including potential analogies with historical outcomes in other similar situations. This, in turn, may lead to a number of different strategy recommendations beyond merely tactical activity.

Again, a table-top paper exercise in this particular situation allows for a problem to be analyzed and discussed as an exercise in its own right, without necessarily having a direct bearing on a pressurized real-world situation. If there is an element of 'movement' in the exercise, aspects of computer simulation or other new learning technologies can be introduced. For example, at the time of writing, the question of Iran's possible offensive nuclear capability is a key strategic question in the West. While this is being debated, a sudden event such as the test firing of a long-range ballistic missile (as Iran undertook in late September 2009) can add a sudden twist to the assessment and pose new questions about Iran's intentions and capabilities. In an exercise scenario, for example, this sort of event could be introduced as a video-clip interrupting the group's deliberations.

It is important to pause briefly at this stage and consider what we mean by a 'strategic' intelligence assessment. In a state security context, this would relate to an assessment of a major national security issue, such as the subject of a CIA National Intelligence Assessment or the deliberations of the Joint Intelligence Committee (JIC) in the UK. In a law enforcement or counter-terrorism context, a strategic assessment could involve a collation of a number of tactical or operational assessments into a statement that analyzed trends or patterns over time. An example might include the *Strategic Assessment Report on Child Trafficking* produced by a SOCA-affiliated agency, which analyzed a number of case histories and statistical information about the origin and circumstances of child trafficking cases in the UK to deliver a strategic assessment of the nature and scale of the activity, and the likely involvement of organized crime in it.[29]

---

[29] *Strategic Threat Assessment: Child Trafficking in the UK* (London: Child Exploitation and Online Protection Centre, 2009).

Returning to the NIM, the strategic assessment is identified as a key analytical product, and is described as follows:

> The main purpose of the strategic assessment is to give the tasking and co-ordination group an accurate picture of the situation in its area of responsibility, how that picture is changing now and how it may change in the future. It is by definition a longer term, high level look at the law enforcement issues and it will, therefore, not only consider current activities but also try to provide a forecast of likely developments.[30]

This identifies the skill of predicting the future, which, as we saw in Chapter 1, equates to the 'foreknowledge' of which the great military strategist Sun Tzu spoke some centuries ago.[31] From a practical, policy point of view, this also reflects how the policy-makers need intelligence to tell them how to frame their strategic policies on particular issues in the future, in terms of identifying and prioritizing the key issues and considering how best to allocate resources.

In my university class we undertake an exercise which simulates a strategic intelligence task, by asking the class to co-produce an in-depth assessment on a security issue of current importance within a term's time period. The idea is loosely based on a simulation of how the JIC in the UK might approach a strategic intelligence question, by holding a number of committee discussions to collate and assess available intelligence, and then jointly producing a drafted statement on the issue which will be passed up to the Prime Minister to assist in policy formation. While we do not really know exactly what a JIC paper looks like or how it is formatted, since all of this activity happens behind closed doors, we know enough to recognize that the process involves producing a paper with a condensed and focused assessment of available intelligence on the question in hand, leading to a set of policy recommendations. Critically, the task is not just to regurgitate a set of information, but to draw judgements and policy recommendations from it.

This process involves a number of analytical challenges, such as assessing and interpreting information from a number of sources of varying reliability, to making reliable judgements and recommendations with the appropriately communicated level of probability and caveat. Importantly, the process also involves some particularly challenging organizational issues, such as agreeing and co-drafting a robust statement across a team of individuals who do not sit together all of the time, and who might have different opinions about how to interpret various pieces of information. This, in itself, is a useful part of the exercise in terms of assessing how well the students can work as a team, and how they manage to conduct objective critical thinking which is open to the views of others, but ends up at a negotiated and agreed position.

---

[30] *The National Intelligence Model*, n 25 above, p 16.
[31] Sun Tzu, *The Art of War*, trans by Samuel Griffith (Oxford: Clarendon Press, 1963) xiii(3), p 144.

In our particular exercise we run the operation over eight weeks, although a much shorter exercise could be designed for one or two days, in which the students receive a controlled set of inputs and have to discuss and negotiate an agreed assessment of the information. This is a technique used in recruitment processes for organizations such as the civil service, where skills of teamworking, communicating, assessing, and evaluating are under the spotlight. This is a particularly pertinent mechanism for simulating the sort of law enforcement strategic assessment described above, which is as much about identifying trends and patterns from a set of information as about generating a wholly new assessment of a situation from scratch.

In my university class, I particularly like to include a fairly current topic which is in the news, and which might twist and turn during the course of the students' work, in such a way that they have to evaluate and reassess the situation in the light of newly emerging information. This tests hypothesis building, considering alternative hypotheses, and overcoming perception resistance in interesting ways. This also means that the question in hand is not chosen until close to the time that the exercise is undertaken, and thus students cannot come to the exercise with fully-formed research and ideas.

We also try to allocate particular sources of information to particular members of the group, such as academic research, media reports, official government publications, online blogs, think-tanks, and so on, to simulate the importance of critically evaluating different information sources, and the process of information equities that exists around the JIC table and the negotiating activities that take place in establishing an agreed assessment. A blog or think-tank report on a particular issue, for example, needs to be examined within the context of any political alignment of the organization in question (and whether this might lead to bias), and how widely read and respected it is. This, in turn, may mean that students have to explore secondary sources for particular pieces of information in certain cases to bolster their utility.

In a policing context, evaluation of source material is a central part of the intelligence-gathering process, and is generally assessed and recorded in the UK using the '5x5x5' mechanism for each piece of recorded information. As John and Maguire describe, this entails using a 1-5 scoring of the information in the three dimensions of source, quality of information, and 'handling code', which specifies how the information can be distributed to others.[32] Sheptycki describes this as a 'risk assessment for dissemination'.[33] The embedded understanding and practice of information evaluation in this context is somewhat too formulaic to be suitable to every intelligence situation, but it does reflect how routinely important it is in the intelligence function to know, understand, and

---

[32] T John and M Maguire, 'Criminal Intelligence and the National Intelligence Model' in T Newburn, T Williamson, and A Wright (eds), *Handbook of Criminal Investigation* (Cullompton: Willan, 2007) p 206.

[33] J Sheptycki, *Review of the Influence of Strategic Intelligence on Organised Crime Policy Practice.* Special Interest Paper 14 (London: Home Office, 2004) p 12.

communicate the reliability or otherwise of pieces of information when delivering an intelligence assessment.

Again, all of these are very useful generic skills that any intelligence analyst will require to develop to differing degrees, and are becoming more important in an age of exploding information availability from a great variety of sources.

Simulation and Gaming

We have mentioned on a couple of occasions the opportunities afforded by modern information technology for introducing sophisticated simulation into training and exercises. This can:

- enhance the number, range and nature of participants in an exercise (by allowing remote access to a particular activity or class);
- increase the number of possibilities in an unfolding scenario (by introducing automated generation of data or events, or introducing a randomness to the nature and timing of developments in an exercise);
- make exercises more interesting and stimulating (by virtually simulating environments and scenarios, or by using simulating media such as videoclips and audio files).

IT can also allow pre-deployment training and exercise in high-risk activities while closely simulating real environments, with the classic example being the flight simulators used by pilot training schools. Similarly, the military are increasingly making use of sophisticated virtual reality mechanisms for training in battle situations. The more realistic the scenario, the more stimulating and stressful (in a positive way) the training can be for the student. The requirement for such training mechanisms is enhanced by the fact mentioned earlier, that scenarios of this nature may happen infrequently for trainees, so they may have little opportunity to acquire experience before they are eventually deployed into a live situation. The advent of such software as Second Life, which is rapidly becoming increasingly sophisticated and workable, introduces a whole new range of simulation-based training possibilities for those working in a range of fields, including intelligence.

One of the interesting avenues of research in this area involves the use of 'game theory', with particular reference to terrorism. Sandler and Arce note that, since 9/11, a number of analysts and researchers have suggested that classic game theory is a useful mechanism for approaching the problem of transnational terrorism and understanding how terrorist groups might act.[34] They observe that

> game theory captures the strategic interactions between terrorists and a targeted government, where actions are interdependent and, thus, cannot be analyzed as though one side is passive.[35]

---

[34] T Sandler and DG Arce, 'Terrorism and Game Theory' (2003) 34 *Simulation and Gaming* 319.
[35] Ibid.

In an unfolding terrorist situation, whether an extended incident or a campaign developing over many years, each side in the conflict (the terrorists and the government) will learn from each other and deploy a range of different strategies in a dynamic and evolving manner. The trick for each side is to try to anticipate how the other side will react to a move, and how to outflank or surprise them, rather like a pair of chess players. This requires a number of analytical skills, such as creativity, imagination, and overcoming perception resistance, on both sides of the fence. Game theory offers a mechanism for structuring an approach to such a dynamic environment.

The problem with the tactical and strategic exercises described above is that they can be somewhat 'static', in that students will often want to request and extract new sources of information as they pursue particular analytical avenues, but such sources may not be available if they have not been prepared beforehand. The tutors can usually explain this away by mentioning that intelligence is always a process of incomplete information and analysts have to live with that, but it can constrain an exercise. A more dynamic exercise that allows for the development and production of materials and events as the exercise unfolds can be more effective, and more instructive of life in a real intelligence situation. Red Teaming is an example of where this can be deployed in a training scenario, where each side in the exercise is a team of individuals charged with acting and reacting in accordance with a general understanding of their position, rather than in compliance with a pre-prepared set of instructions and materials.

Game theory provides a method of understanding and analyzing terrorist situations, and can be a tool 'to enlighten policy makers on the effectiveness of antiterrorist policies'.[36] As such, it could also act as a useful basis for designing and operating training exercises in a counter-terrorist context, especially in conjunction with creative use of IT simulation mechanisms.

Conclusions

While there are several different levels of intelligence analysis, and intelligence analyst, from strategic to tactical and from single to all-source assessment, Lord Butler recognized in his enquiry report in 2004 that a certain set of generic intelligence analysis tradecraft skills is required across the community. Consequently, a cross-community mechanism for evolving and developing these skills makes good sense, particularly in an age of constrained budgets.

Training and exercise can address these skills requirements in a range of dynamic and practical ways, if the central mantra of a systematic approach to training is recognized and understood. At its heart, the key requirement of this approach is to think about the organizational culture and needs of the particular set of intelligence analysts in question, and deliver to them a training programme which satisfies these needs in the most appropriate way.

---

[36] Ibid, p 335.

In this chapter we have examined a number of mechanisms for tackling the various component parts of analytical skill and exercising, and presented them in a suitably high-level and generic way, such that they can be adapted and deployed to a range of situations in a range of different organizations. We have also stressed, however, that training courses alone will not solve the upskilling challenge for any organization, if a holistic view is not taken of the environment in which the analysts work. This includes the system of organizational hierarchy and bureaucracy, the promotion of creative and critical thinking, and the flexibility of operations such that analysts can easily develop and adapt their methodology to the twists and turns of their intelligence targets. As we saw in the context of game theory, dealing with terrorists is not a static and transactional process, but a symbiotic relationship between terrorist and government which learns, develops, and morphs all the time. Without these issues also being addressed, the training courses will prove to be a nugatory waste of money, as the analysts will not be able to maximize their operational activity back in the workplace.

We have alluded a few times to the importance of conducting training exercises in teams, an aspect which Clark suggested was absolutely central to the model of target-centric analysis.[37] The significance of this lies particularly in the analytical need to overcome perception resistance, which, we have seen, is central to both tactical and strategic intelligence analysis operations. By working with analysts from different organizations, cultures, and positions within the hierarchy, a wide range of differing perspectives and biases can be experienced. This can be challenging, particularly in situations where consensus needs to be achieved on a course of action to take or a recommendation to make to the policy-makers, but it can also be very illuminating and instructive. Being open to new ideas and perspectives is one of the key attributes of critical thinking, and this can be introduced into the learning environment very easily just by ensuring a good mix of students on any given training course or exercise. In all of the above exercises, therefore, conducting them with a mixed group of analysts is a given to ensure the maximum effectiveness of the exercise.

Key Points

- The Butler enquiry in the UK, which followed the Iraq War, established a Professional Head of Intelligence Analysis in government. This office is charged with developing methods across the intelligence community for collectively enhancing skills in intelligence analysis.

- A framework for training can be presented under the categories of critical and creative thinking, tactical intelligence exercises, strategic intelligence exercises, and simulation and 'gaming'.

---

[37] Clark, *Intelligence Analysis*, n 24 above.

- Analysis training has to be treated holistically, including attention dedicated to the organizational and managerial environment in the workplace, otherwise training initiatives run the risk of falling on stony ground and having no lasting impact.

- When considering exercises, both in tactical and strategic contexts, it is often important to frame them in the context of current and relevant intelligence challenges rather than overly esoteric or obscure situations.

- In many of the exercises and in the intelligence analysis function generally, the element of successful teamwork is critical. This can be tested and developed during exercises.

- Tactical exercises should include the additional element of time pressure, creating stress around the analyst's need to provide the policy-maker with timely judgements.

- Simulation and gaming can bring an element of movement and dynamism to an exercise, where traditional table-top exercises can be somewhat static and predictable.

8

Conclusions: Art or Science?

The great military strategist, Karl von Clausewitz, once noted in the context of intelligence generated during the fog of war that it was fraught with imperfections. The officer receiving the intelligence has to employ extensive powers of judgement. Clausewitz noted that:

> Much of the intelligence that we receive in war is contradictory, even more of it is plain wrong, and most of it is fairly dubious. What one can require of an officer, under these circumstances, is a certain degree of discrimination, which can only be gained from knowledge of men and affairs and from good judgement. The law of probability must be his guide.[1]

These words were used to open the Butler enquiry report in the UK into the use of intelligence on weapons of mass destruction following the Iraq War, and, as Rolington observed, set the tone for the report in the sense that it emphasized the 'art' rather than 'science' nature of the intelligence business.[2] Intelligence, it was argued in the Butler report, is inherently imprecise and flawed, and requires a degree of judgement if not guesswork in its interpretation, so it is hardly surprising that the intelligence machinery—and the policy-makers it informs—make frequent mistakes.

We have seen how Sherman Kent, on the other hand, advocated a rigorous and structured set of techniques for approaching the task of intelligence analysis, which he explicitly referred to as a 'scientific' approach[3] in an effort to mitigate the imperfections. He observed that intelligence needed an approach

---

[1] K von Clausewitz, *On War* (London: Penguin, 1982, original edn 1832) Book 1, pp 162–4.

[2] A Rolington, 'Objective Intelligence of Plausible Denial: An Open Source Review of Intelligence Method and Process since 9/11' (2006) 21 *Intelligence and National Security* 738, 746.

[3] J Davis, 'Introduction' in RJ Heuer, Jr, *Psychology of Intelligence Analysis* (Langley VA: Center for the Study of Intelligence, 1999) p xiv.

'much like the method of the physical sciences'[4] in order to ensure its efficacy. Empirical data, where available, and analysis of the data using structured techniques, were essential in the eyes of Kent. Rolington argues that these differing perspectives, from Clausewitz to Kent, 'get to the very heart of ... what should frame the agenda for the current issues surrounding intelligence, and they range from an empiricist interpretation to a postmodernist perspective'.[5]

So, in our postmodern world of asymmetric and de-centred security threats, is intelligence an art or a science? The answer, perhaps inevitably, is both, and neither. Scientific and structured methods of analysis and data handling are essential, and there is much that can be learnt and copied from the natural and social sciences, particularly the latter since intelligence is, after all, a question of analyzing and predicting human behaviour. At the same time, not only are human beings more often than not frustratingly indeterministic in their behaviour, but intelligence targets are frequently—by their very nature—elusive, evasive, and keen on employing deception and obfuscation. A terrorist or an underground weapons trader does not want the authorities to see what he is doing, and will make the job of intelligence gathering as difficult as he possibly can. Add to this the frequent problem of incomplete coverage of a target's activities, and it is clear that intelligence analysis can never be a precise science. The analyst will always have to employ a fair degree of judgement, prediction, and sometimes a good dose of gut feeling, to be able to interpret the data and patterns that he or she is seeing.

Intelligence Failures

We opened this book with a discussion of how we should define intelligence. In 2006, Wheaton and Beerbower claimed that this was a fundamental and serious problem for the US intelligence sector:

> The words used to define intelligence—what it is, who does it, what its purpose is, and why it is necessary—are unclear and, in many cases, contradictory. The US intelligence community employs hundreds of thousands of people and spends approximately forty billion dollars per year on collecting, analyzing, and disseminating intelligence. Both law enforcement agencies and businesses employ tens of thousands more people and spend billions on intelligence as well. Yet nowhere is there a single agreed-upon definition of intelligence.
>
> The intelligence community, quite literally, does not know what it is doing.[6]

They go on to note in this somewhat harsh assessment that 'even seasoned intelligence professionals' see their business as 'something vague and nebulous, which is constantly re-imagined in a never-ending search for purpose'.[7]

---

[4] S Kent, *Strategic Intelligence for American World Policy* (Princeton NJ: Princeton University Press, 1949) p 2.

[5] Rolington, 'Objective Intelligence of Plausible Denial', n 2 above, p 747.

[6] KJ Wheaton and MT Beerbower, 'Towards a New Definition of Intelligence' (2006) 17 *Stanford Law and Policy Review* 319.   [7] Ibid, p 320.

It could be argued that this does not necessarily matter, and that semantics are not important in an operational and practical business which does not need to explain—indeed positively should not if it is planning to protect secret and sensitive sources—how it obtains the information and assessments that it passes through to the policy-makers. On the other hand, as Wheaton and Beerbower note, 'the people responsible for spending the nearly forty billion dollar intelligence budget' appear not to have a 'clear idea of what it is they are supposed to do'.[8]

The sentiment expressed here is one of an understandable frustration with the question of why major intelligence failures seem to continue to occur with stubborn regularity, despite billions being spent on the intelligence capability and countless enquiries and reviews suggesting reform. We have seen that, right from the time of the Japanese aerial bombardment of Pearl Harbor in 1941, the West has continually asked probing questions of itself about its intelligence infrastructure and capability in the light of a succession of intelligence failures. The Cuban missile crisis, resolved at the eleventh hour with some very telling imagery intelligence, was a much-analyzed situation in which it appeared that earlier failures of intelligence interpretation and imagination had allowed the situation to run almost disastrously out of control. There have been numerous other examples that have been subjected to considerable scrutiny over the years, such as the Yom Kippur war in the Middle East in 1973, and the Argentine invasion of the Falkland Islands in 1982, to name only two.

In the modern age, the Hizbollah bombings of the US and French military barracks in Beirut in 1983 marked, in retrospect, the transition to a new form of security threat, which a failure of imagination in the intelligence community perhaps failed to recognize. A few years later, the horrific 9/11 attacks in the US seemed to set a new high-water mark in the history of intelligence failures, which, for some, took us straight back to Pearl Harbor and suggested that little progress had been made in 60 years of experience and investment.[9] Again, with the benefit of hindsight, we have seen that 9/11 was just the beginning of a string of similar attacks, from Bali to Madrid to Istanbul and to London, which the intelligence agencies and law enforcement partners were struggling to anticipate in their intelligence-gathering activities, even if they were able to interdict some of the protagonists after the event.

The Threat Picture

Part of the reason for the continued difficulties despite enhanced investment and improved technologies is, as we have seen, the fact that the nature of the security threat has metamorphosed at an increasing rate and degree of

---

[8] Ibid, p 324.

[9] J Sims, 'Intelligence to Counter Terror: The Importance of All-Source Fusion' (2007) 22 *Intelligence and National Security* 38, 41.

complexity; particularly since the Berlin Wall came down in 1989 and the Soviet Union collapsed. The Western intelligence sector in the 1990s was faced with a rapidly-changing threat picture, in which traditional state- and military-centred preoccupations were becoming eclipsed by a range of international and non-hierarchical threats such as organized crime, weapons proliferation, and terrorism, which were inextricably embedded in civil society. The intelligence targets had therefore changed very radically, and the key question was whether the intelligence actors could—or should—change accordingly in ways that mirrored the unfolding nature of the threat. In practical terms this involves a number of factors such as knowledge and information sharing across organizational and national boundaries to a degree where those boundaries become increasingly irrelevant; flatter, de-centred, and non-hierarchical organizational models; and extensive and creative use of new information technologies connected with the internet.

Byman asked in 2003 whether we understood our new adversary, Al Qaeda,[10] which seemed to epitomize the current threat picture. Part of the problem initially was a widely differing set of opinions on whether Al Qaeda was 'a small fringe movement or a cohesive network'.[11] Gunaratna noted of Al Qaeda that:

> It is neither a single group nor a coalition of groups: it comprised a core base or bases in Afghanistan, satellite terrorist cells worldwide, a conglomerate of Islamist political parties, and other largely independent terrorist groups that it draws on for offensive actions and other responsibilities.[12]

In these terms, it is not just a traditional terrorist group with a clear hierarchical organization and geographical concentration, but more of a borderless ideological movement.

Others have taken a more scientific approach to analyzing Al Qaeda as an organization akin to a successful twenty-first century business. Marion and Uhl-Bien argued that Al Qaeda is 'a complex organisation catalyzed by Complex Leadership (or Complex Adaptive Agents)'.[13] Expanding on the definition, they noted that 'Complex Leaders foster network construction, build interdependence that enables tension, stimulate bottom-up behavior, spark creativity, and foster distributed intelligence'.[14] We saw in Chapter 3 how Younis Tsouli was able to begin working for Al Qaeda in Iraq by presenting his internet expertise to them virtually, and showing what he could do across cyberspace.[15] This

---

[10] DL Byman, 'Al Qaeda as an Adversary: Do We Understand Our Enemy?' (2003) 56 *World Politics* 139.   [11] Ibid, p 140.

[12] R Gunaratna, *Inside Al Qaeda* (New York NY: Columbia University Press, 2002) p 54.

[13] R Marion and M Uhl-Bien, 'Complexity Theory and Al Qaeda: Examining Complex Leadership', paper presented at Managing the Complex IV: A Conference on Complex Systems and the Management of Organizations, December 2002, <http://isce.edu/ISCE_Group_Site/web-content/ISCE_Events/Naples_2002/Naples_2002_Papers/Marion_Uhl-Bien.pdf>, accessed 3 January 2010.

[14] Ibid.

[15] R Pantucci, 'Operation Praline: The Realization of Al-Suri's Nizam, la Tanzim?' (2008) 2/12 *Perspectives on Terrorism* 11, 12.

is excellent practice for a modern, flexible, and knowledge-based organization, and would be the envy of many commercial entities.

Many observers have pondered the implications for security and intelligence agencies of the manner in which Al Qaeda and similar terrorist groups are mobilizing in cyberspace. O'Rourke notes that:

> Recent advances in information and communications technology (ICT) are providing a medium for individuals or groups who subscribe to extremist worldviews to form networks, access training and obtain information, whilst remaining virtually undetected in the online world.[16]

This activity is not confined just to Al Qaeda and the Islamist terrorist networks, but applies also to a number of modern, extremist networks across political and ideological spectrums.[17] The mode of organization leads to a fear that traditionally organized terror groups with a clear structure of command and leadership can increasingly become a thing of the past, giving way to 'self taught' radicalization and terrorism, which makes use of knowledge sharing and flat, globalized structures to identify and mobilize foot soldiers across the world in a highly flexible and unpredictable way.[18]

Countering the Threat

The question for the intelligence agencies is how well or otherwise they are structured, organized, and skilled to be able to counter such a threat effectively. Herman examined the clamour for change that followed the 9/11 attacks in the US, noting that much of it 'had a strain of managerial radicalism in it, linked with the IT revolution'.[19] He noted that:

> Information and information-handling were being transformed, and intelligence must follow suit. There was a consensus about the need for change, though less agreement on the direction.[20]

The stated options were varied, from rethinking the entire nature of the intelligence sector and opening it up to competition from non-governmental sources of information (such as news agencies), to a rethink of the way in which the

---

[16] S O'Rourke, *Virtual Radicalisation: Challenges for Police*, Proceedings of the 8th Australian Information Warfare and Security Conference, December 2007, p 29, <http://scissec.scis.ecu.edu.au/conference_proceedings/2007/iwar/2007_IWAR_proceedings_final.pdf#page=33>, accessed 3 January 2010.

[17] See, eg the case of the recently-emerging English Defence League in the UK, which one report has described as a 'child of the internet': N Tweedie, 'The English Defence League: will the flames of hatred spread?', *Daily Telegraph*, 10 October 2009, <http://www.telegraph.co.uk/news/6284184/The-English-Defence-League-will-the-flames-of-hatred-spread.html>, accessed 3 January 2010.

[18] G Weimann, cited in J Forrest (ed), *Teaching Terror: Strategic and Tactical Learning in the Terrorist World* (Lanham MD: Rowan and Littlefield, 2006) p 110.

[19] M Herman, 'Counter-Terrorism, Information Technology and Intelligence Change' (2003) 18/4 *Intelligence and National Security* 40.   [20] Ibid.

existing intelligence structure was organized internally.[21] On the nature of the target itself, Herman noted that 'counterintelligence is particularly all-source and holistic',[22] comprising a mixture of secret and non-secret sources and the need to make connections across an increasingly diverse and complex range of datasets. He noted that this makes it 'a natural for advanced IT', and, importantly, that the beneficial intervention of IT applies to all stages of the intelligence cycle, from collection, through processing and analysis, to delivery of intelligence to the customers.[23] He also noted that:

> There is the obvious parallel with police methods; no murder investigation in Britain would now take place without an IT system to handle the evidence.[24]

This brings us to the organizational point that the nature of modern security threats such as terrorism has increasingly brought together the intelligence-gathering and analysis activities of the state security agencies and the law enforcement bodies, such as the police. This applies not only in an operational sense (in that intelligence on specific targets and groups needs to be shared across these organizational boundaries) but also in a basic sense of the tradecraft being used. As Lord Butler noted in his enquiry report, the analytical skills of the state security and law enforcement intelligence analysts have much in common, and, at a certain level, can be taught and developed collectively.[25]

We saw in earlier chapters how the issue, posed notably by 9/11, of how far state intelligence should be combined with law enforcement has caused a number of severe organizational difficulties, not least in the US, where some have said that the likes of the CIA and FBI are fundamentally incompatible in their thinking.[26] The US intelligence community is characterized by a large number of separate agencies (eighteen under the official definition, to which the Department of Homeland Security was added after 9/11), within which there have traditionally been deliberate delineations between law enforcement and state intelligence, and between domestic and foreign. This is for good reasons of avoiding politicization and undue influence between intelligence gatherers and policy-makers, but Turner notes that the nature of the contemporary terrorist threat is turning these norms on their head, and generating a debate about whether a new entity is needed that straddles the divides.[27]

Aside from the creation of the new Department of Homeland Security, the 9/11 Commission called for the creation of a new cross-agency chief in the shape of the Office of the Director of National Intelligence (ODNI) in the US, whose

---

[21] Herman, 'Counter-Terrorism', n 19 above, pp 40–1.   [22] Ibid, p 44.

[23] Ibid.   [24] Ibid.

[25] MS Goodman and D Omand, 'Teaching Intelligence Analysts in the UK. What Analysts Need to Understand: The King's Intelligence Studies Program' (2008) 52/4 *Studies in Intelligence* 1, 2, <https://www.cia.gov/library/center-for-the-study-of-intelligence/csi-publications/csi-studies/studies/vol-52-no-4/index.html>, accessed 3 January 2010.

[26] Senator Shelby, cited in M Gladwell, 'Connecting the Dots: The paradoxes of intelligence reform', *The New Yorker*, 10 March 2003, p 88.

[27] M Turner, *Why Secret Intelligence Fails* (Dulles VA: Potomac Books, 2006) pp 59–60.

remit would be separated, for the first time, from management of the CIA as was previously the case with the Director of Central Intelligence position. The subsequent Intelligence Reform and Terrorism Prevention Act of 2004 gave the ODNI primary responsibility for coordinating intelligence assessments for the President, and enabled it to be staffed with some 600 personnel,[28] within the US and abroad, which is a not insignificant new addition to the intelligence community. The changes were substantial, and many shared Fessenden's view that they were 'a set of proposals for overhauling not just the spy agencies but congressional oversight as well', and 'a political feat of the highest order'.[29]

The purpose of the new role and department was to ensure that the intelligence community's immediate channel into the policy-makers (and particularly the President) would be less affiliated with any one particular agency, and thus avoid any problems of bias or politicization of intelligence. With a large community to coordinate, this makes good sense, and mirrors developments in other intelligence communities such as the UK, for example, where the Joint Intelligence Committee is detached from the primary intelligence agencies and is designed to offer a coordinated and unbiased assessment of intelligence on any given topic. The questions, however, are whether the new office has real budgetary and decision-making power across the myriad of agencies, and whether it is able to tackle the sheer size and complexity of the community in any meaningful way that makes a difference. The jury is still out on how successful the ODNI will be in these endeavours, but the risk, as Fessenden describes it, is that the ODNI 'is simply another layer of bureaucracy over all agencies rather than a force that can push through necessary structural changes'.[30]

There is no doubt that successful prosecution of the likes of Al Qaeda, intelligence on which would probably touch all of the eighteen agencies in the US intelligence community in some shape or form, is an extraordinarily challenging activity to coordinate under this structure. However, care perhaps needs to be taken about the imperative of reorganization in the face of pressure. The issue is a common one in the commercial world, where Schweber has noted the tendency for 'when in doubt, reorganise'.[31] As Betts observed, major intelligence failures in history seem to have been met frequently with examination of the organizational structure of the intelligence community, and with recommendations for changes to be made to it.[32] This is not necessarily always the only, or the best issue to tackle in the aftermath of a major intelligence failure, not least given the degree of disruption and

---

[28] K Lieberthal, *The US Intelligence Community and Foreign Policy: Getting Analysis Right*, John L Thornton China Center Monograph Series No 2 (Washington DC: Brookings Institution, 2009) p 7.

[29] H Fessenden, 'The Limits of Intelligence Reform' (2005) 84/6 *Foreign Affairs* 106, 106–7.

[30] Ibid, p 119.

[31] B Schweber, 'When in doubt, reorganise', *EDN Europe*, 1 February 2002, <http://www.accessmylibrary.com/coms2/summary_0286-25381632_ITM>, accessed 3 January 2010.

[32] RK Betts, 'Analysis, War and Decision: Why Intelligence Failures are Inevitable' (1978) 1 *World Politics* 61, 63.

anxiety that it can cause within the intelligence community, and subsequent temporary drop-off in capability.

Departmental organization and oversight is one issue, but one of the main problems within the intelligence community that many enquiries have highlighted is the question of the ability physically to share data across organizational boundaries. As we have seen, this is a problem not only of secrecy and equities within the community itself, but also of basic questions of IT. Describing the US intelligence community on the challenge of counter-terrorism, Fessenden noted that:

> thanks to the years of entrenched independence of the individual agencies and a long tradition of information hoarding, major shortcomings remain. Although the NCTC [National Counter Terrorism Center] is generally regarded as an improvement over the status quo, the status quo is a poor benchmark for comparison. NCTC analysts have access to 26 information networks across the intelligence agencies (housed in three computers on each analyst's desk), but there is no one database that unites these networks, nor is it possible to conduct a search across all 26.[33]

We can be certain that the US is not the only community to be facing these problems of linking up datasets across the different organizations working on intelligence, and it has to be asked whether the targets are facing the same problems. In the case of Al Qaeda, probably not, as the internet is its international network.

Opportunities and Pitfalls

Where information technology poses difficulties and obstacles in the intelligence community's organization, however, many have observed that it also offers opportunities for working differently. Lieberthal noted a number of excellent developments within the US intelligence community, sponsored by the ODNI, which begin to show what may be possible.[34] These include:

- A Library of National Intelligence which aims to hold all disseminated intelligence products on any subject. By September 2008, it held 750,000 documents.
- A-Space: a virtual collaborative workspace where analysts across the community can work on a common problem, and share emerging insights and pieces of analysis in an interactive way.
- Intellipedia: a classified version of Wikipedia for analysts to access across the community.
- Analytic Resources Catalogue and Analyst Yellow Pages: a detailed directory of all analysts across the community, including their skills and experience.

The interesting aspect of all of these initiatives is that they offer the potential of superseding and overcoming the traditional, interdepartmental, and

---

[33] Fessenden, 'The Limits of Intelligence Reform', n 29 above, p 118.
[34] Lieberthal, *The US Intelligence Community*, n 28 above, p 4.

hierarchical nature of the intelligence community, much as the internet has offered to commercial and public life generally. With these tools, any analyst anywhere in the community (at any level) can reach out and work across boundaries on a particular issue. From an intelligence theory point of view, it also further challenges the linear Intelligence Cycle model, in that interactions and processes through the cycle become much more networked, collaborative, and multidirectional, than transactional. This potentially includes interactions between policy-makers and intelligence analysts, for example, whereby the former could ponder emerging analysis—and contribute to it—before it was 'finished' as such.

Administratively, these tools also pose very challenging questions of traditional practices and structures: how, for example, are issues of varying levels of secrecy and limited access around particular sets of data handled, and how are 'audit trails' of sensitive data controlled when such data is swilling around a large, collaborative pot? From the point of view of the interface between secret intelligence and the evidential chain, the fully collaborative and open model is a problematic one. As Brodeur and Dupont explain, many of the enquiries and reports which have chastised the intelligence community for failing to share intelligence across boundaries more effectively, have tended to underplay the very real legal impediments built into the system that complicate sharing of different levels of classified information very considerably.[35] These apply both between and within agencies. In the policing context, for example, classified information cannot easily be shared between central and local agencies, for basic security clearance reasons.[36]

In many ways, these issues echo, in microcosm, the challenges of the modern, globalized world at large for the intelligence community. We have seen how, for the police, the juxtaposition of modern societal threats and the function of intelligence gathering can cause all manner of problems. As Gill described, globalization has expanded the territory that policing must occupy in three different dimensions: a 'deepening' of levels of society means that there is an increasing interaction between local and international developments; a 'broadening' of the security sector means that more actors are involved in delivering security beyond just the police; and a 'stretching' of spatial interactions means that events in one part of the globe can increasingly have an impact in another part, far away.[37] Brodeur noted that the difference is essentially between what he described as the two poles of policing: 'high' and 'low' policing.[38]

The latter has grown in importance politically in recent years, in the shape of a resurgent interest in 'community' and 'reassurance' policing. A growing interest in such local and community-oriented policing may be a natural development

---

[35] J-P Brodeur and B Dupont, 'Knowledge Workers or "Knowledge" Workers?' (2006) 16 *Policing and Society* 7, 18.   [36] Ibid.

[37] P Gill, 'Not Just Joining the Dots but Crossing the Borders and Bridging the Voids: Constructing Security Networks after 11 September 2001' (2006) 16 *Policing and Society* 27, 30.

[38] J-P Brodeur, 'High and Low Policing in Post 9/11 Times' (2007) 1 *Policing* 25, 27.

born of the general anxiety of life in a postmodern society, where traditional family and community structures are increasingly blurred and broken down by urbanization and globalization. We saw in Chapter 4 that, because policing is a deeply political issue of significance for political parties in the West, models of policing and intelligence have waxed and waned, and moved in a number of different directions in response to perceived public anxieties and needs. A growth of 'intelligence-led policing' from the mid-1990s onwards, encouraged in large part by the widening opportunities for more creative and ambitious data handling delivered by advances in information technology, has been met since the turn of the century with a gathering anxiety about surveillance and the 'Big Brother' society.

Current debates in the UK about how best to go about preventing violent extremism illustrate the complexity of the situation for the police very well. As part of the Counter Terrorism Strategy (CONTEST), the UK government has recognized that an effective strategy involves the simultaneous prosecution of a number of strands of activity, whereby the obvious need to pursue terrorists and disrupt current attack plans is supplemented with plans to prepare for terrorist attacks when they occur; to protect public spaces and critical infrastructure as far as possible from the effects of terrorist attack; and to consider what pulls young people into terrorism in the first place, with a view to determining how such pathways of radicalization can be interrupted or eroded.[39]

The problem with the prevention strand of activity is that it places the police in a very complicated dual role of both engaging communities and building bridges with them (so that those communities will feel they can naturally turn to the police when they have a problem or a concern), while simultaneously gathering intelligence on where the risks may lie within those same communities. Civil liberties pressure groups such as Liberty have criticized the Preventing Violent Extremism programme, claiming that it targets the Muslim community as a whole as potential 'subversives' rather than just specific terrorist suspects.[40] The Liberal Democrat Home Affairs spokesman, Chris Huhne, noted that 'combating radical Islamist ideas is one thing; gathering and keeping intelligence on the innocent is another'.[41]

The importance of intelligence gathering by the police in the modern threat scenario is a complex issue therefore, both because the span of responsibility from low to high policing is very wide (and resources are generally not growing but diminishing), and because the dual function of reassuring and engaging the community while gathering intelligence from deep within it is a highly complicated and sometimes very controversial issue. This has a number of implications for the intelligence function in a modern state.

---

[39] <http://security.homeoffice.gov.uk/counter-terrorism-strategy>, accessed 3 January 2010.
[40] V Dodd, 'MPs investigate anti-extremism programme after spying claims', *The Guardian*, 18 October 2009, <http://www.guardian.co.uk/uk/2009/oct/18/prevent-extremism-muslims-information-allegations>, accessed 3 January 2010.   [41] Ibid.

First, the role and justification for intelligence gathering and surveillance in a modern, liberal state is far from clear and not universally accepted. One of the most successful stories in the history of intelligence is that of how encrypted military communications in the Second World War were intercepted and decrypted using sophisticated techniques, to the huge tactical advantage of the Western Allies. It would probably be fair to say that most citizens of the West would understand the need for and the function of this episode of intelligence-gathering, and would heartily support it as an appropriate and morally justifiable thing to do, in that particular context. Wind the clock forward sixty years, and intelligence gathering in the modern nation-state is not necessarily seen in quite the same way, and causes anxiety among many sections of the population, despite the fact that incidents such as 9/11 and 7/7 have clearly posed very serious security questions.

As a result of this, the contemporary intelligence community, whether it is in the tactical policing part of the forest or in the strategic state security arena, needs to be keenly and increasingly aware of the ethical, moral, and legal justifications and mandates for what it does. Sometimes it may even feel the need to state the case explicitly and address inaccuracies in reporting of its activities, as we saw GCHQ do recently in the case of alleged plans for large-scale gathering and mining of communications data, stressing firmly that it 'does not spy at will'.[42]

Second, the intelligence community needs to demonstrate that it is taking its responsibilities very seriously, and to counter anxiety over intelligence failures by some celebration of success on occasion. It is notable how, in the modern information age, all the major intelligence agencies have taken the bold steps of launching their own websites and public communications channels, with a growing amount of information made available on their activities and structure. Some of this information stresses the successes that have been achieved. MI5, for example, note on their website that:

> The Security Service, police and other UK agencies work together to identify terrorist plots and bring their authors to justice. Our combined efforts have achieved a number of notable successes . . . Between 11 September 2001 and 31 March 2007, 41 individuals have been convicted under the Terrorism Act and another 183 have been convicted of terrorist-related offences, including murder, illegal possession of firearms and explosives offences. 1,165 people have been arrested under the Terrorism Act and 114 were awaiting trial as of the end of March 2007.[43]

The information offensive, in this case, goes towards calming anxieties about the ills of surveillance and intelligence gathering in a modern, liberal democracy, and stresses the important real-world outcomes of such activities that bolster

---

[42] GCHQ press release, 3 May 2009, <http://www.gchq.gov.uk/press/prelease.html>, accessed 3 January 2010.

[43] MI5 website: <http://www.mi5.gov.uk/output/terrorist-plots-in-the-uk.html>, accessed 3 January 2010.

the public's security. It is clear that the intelligence agencies see the importance of circulating these messages in the public domain in a way that they would not have done previously.

The Analyst's Trade

We saw in Chapter 7 that, despite ever more ambitious automated and scientific ways of collating and mining large datasets (some of which start to move into the territory of automated reasoning), Sherman Kent's original exhortation that the human analyst will never be replaced as the 'intelligence device supreme' is still a very valid and important belief.[44] We have examined in some detail in this book the question of the skills that analysts need to be able to develop to take their intelligence tradecraft to a higher plane. In the previous chapter we noted that the workforce development issues around the analyst's trade were among the key recommendations that came out of the Butler enquiry report in the UK, follow-ing the Iraq War. These included recruitment and deployment of analysts, devel-opment of their career pathway, and development of the analytical methodology they were to use. All of this was to be conducted collaboratively and in a unified way across the UK intelligence community, and it is interesting that Butler and the government chose to label the analyst's job as a 'profession', by forming the office of Professional Head of Intelligence Analysis in the Cabinet Office.[45]

The model used in this book identifies the key skills required by the analyst as:

- Critical thinking
- Creativity
- Judgement and decision-making
- Communication

Clearly, at a level below this, these skills can be broken down into a number of sub-activities and attributes in various circumstances. We have seen that the dominant academic and scientific judgement is that these skills, and particularly creativity, are not 'genetic' as such, and can be learnt and developed by anyone given the right conditions. Those conditions are critically important. In an intelligence analysis context, this means that analysts need to be working in an environment where creativity and critical thinking are fostered and encouraged, and where there is time and space to step aside on occasion and undertake activities such as 'brainstorming'. In many ways, the concept should be similar to that of research and development in a corporation, where there is a broad remit for flexible and creative working, and a tolerance of failure and blind alleys as long as a percentage of the work comes up with useful new products and strategies.

---

[44] Kent, *Strategic Intelligence for American World Policy*, n 4 above, p xviii.

[45] *Review of Intelligence on Weapons of Mass Destruction: Implementation of its Conclusions* (London: TSO, 2005) pp 9–10, <http://www.cabinetoffice.gov.uk/media/cabinetoffice/corp/assets/publica-tions/reports/intelligence/wmdreview.pdf>, accessed 3 January 2010.

The question of the managerial culture is also very important, in the sense that senior managers and policy-makers need to understand and endorse the setting of this environment in the analytical workplace. Undue pressure always to get it right, to tell policy-makers what they want to hear (and to do so quickly and repeatedly), or even to fit in with a political or ideological 'groupthink', are all managerial environments that can militate against the development of the above skills and make intelligence failure considerably more likely.

In a US context, Lieberthal noted a further skills issue in the area of 'country knowledge', and specifically a worrying lack of it among sections of the analytical community.[46] This is partly a consequence of Area Studies declining as a popular subject at university, and also a reflection of the manner in which the key intelligence targets have changed and diversified rapidly since the end of the Cold War in a number of different directions. For many years in the state intelligence sector in the West, a knowledge of Russia and Russian was the key requirement. From the early 1990s onwards, suddenly the areas of interest were everything from Yugoslavia to the Middle East to Central Asia. Coupled with a lack of country knowledge is a decline in students taking languages as a subject, which has been noted in the UK[47] and many other countries. We saw how Berkowitz suggested that the traditional 'case officer' model in the CIA (and doubtless in many other Humint agencies) found itself to be ill-equipped to deal with the new threat of terrorism, and particularly in the area of appropriate language capability.[48]

Lieberthal's suggested remedy for the situation is to establish a physical National Intelligence University in the US (to supplement the virtual one established by the ODNI in 2007).[49] This would mirror institutions in the military such as the National Defense University and National War College (and Defence Academy in the UK). Lieberthal notes that 'there is no institution that houses a distinguished faculty of professors ready to teach and conduct research on the history, culture, ethics, management and analytic tradecraft of the profession'.[50] The suggestion is a sound one, although budgetary pressures across the public sector in the West at the time of writing are likely to mean that any university in this space will remain a virtual one for the foreseeable future. In the meantime, it may be appropriate for training and professionalization among the intelligence community along the lines of those mechanisms supported by the Professional Head of Intelligence Analysis in the UK, for example, to include considerations of language and country studies as well as analytical tradecraft and techniques.

---

[46] Lieberthal, *The US Intelligence Community*, n 28 above, p 42.

[47] Higher Education Academy, 'British Academy raises new concerns over decline in language learning', 3 June 2009, <http://llasnews.blogspot.com/2009/06/british-academy-raises-new-concerns.html>, accessed 3 January 2010.

[48] B Berkowitz, 'Intelligence and the War on Terrorism', *Orbis*, Spring 2002, p 296.

[49] Lieberthal, *The US Intelligence Community*, n 28 above, p 47.   [50] Ibid.

Recommendations

Bringing all of these factors together leads to the suggestion of a set of key recommendations for the intelligence community in the West, which will offer the opportunity of adapting more effectively to the contemporary security challenges, and enhance overall performance. This is not an exhaustive list, nor should these factors be taken with any degree of authority by intelligence practitioners, who will have their own understanding of their business and awareness of the key measures that need to be taken in the future.

Think about the environment in which analysts work, and particularly how supportive that environment is of creative and critical thinking. The first recommendation stresses that training courses and familiarization mechanisms to do with cognitive techniques and analytical tradecraft will not be effective in the workplace if the right cultural conditions are not in place. This is largely a management issue, although it can also be an issue of appropriate accommodation and facilities in some cases. What this means is that intelligence analysts need to work in an environment where creative thinking and brainstorming are normal and readily accepted aspects of the day's work, and are able to flourish despite pressing operational deadlines and requirements. Within this environment, the essential elements of critical thinking, which include openness to new ideas and a willingness to accept alternative views, also need to be embedded in the operational and managerial culture. A facility to make mistakes, and to be able to analyze them objectively afterwards, are also important parts of this working environment.

Continue to break down barriers and share data across boundaries. A globalized world and globalized security threats mean that it no longer makes sense for the intelligence community to work in a diametrically different way from the rest of society, with incompatible legacy systems, inter-agency equities and rivalries, and multiple barriers to information attempting to move across the community. Legal requirements of source protection, levels of classification, and issues of where the evidential chain starts and finishes clearly remain present and important, but every effort should be expended to work within these limitations in enhancing cross-community data and knowledge sharing.

Harness the power of internet-age applications and processes. Intellipedia, A-Space, and numerous similar applications which individuals and corporations use freely 'outside the wire' of the intelligence agencies, should be made to work within the intelligence community in the same ways. If these applications cause the Intelligence Cycle to be ripped up, and hierarchical and bureaucratic strictures to become increasingly obsolete, so be it. The benefits of such new ways of working have been proved comprehensively, and perhaps more importantly, the key intelligence targets are using them very much to their advantage. It makes no sense for the intelligence community not to do so also.

Further develop structures and processes for professionalizing Intelligence Analysis. Initial forays into cross-community shared training and tradecraft exchange, which bring together analysts from different parts of the intelligence community, are important and critical. This should arguably include such issues as country and language studies as well as analytical techniques. The criticality of developments in these areas relates not only to the fact that many of the core, generic, analytical skills and techniques are universally applicable, whether an analyst is in tactical law enforcement or in strategic state policy analysis, but also because the building of knowledge networks across the community is a further enabler to breaking down institutional and bureaucratic barriers. In this way, change 'comes from below' as a new generation of analysts are schooled in a mindset of cross-community collaboration and networking.

Continue to be acutely aware of legal and ethical issues surrounding intelligence. The nature of postmodern, Western society, is very different from that which pertained when the intelligence agencies were first appearing in organized form at the beginning of the twentieth century. Not only are security threats embedded in a complex way within civil society, but public anxiety about disproportionate surveillance and an erosion of the fundamental values of a modern, liberal state are very real and not something around which compromises should be made. Continued public support for the work of the agencies is essential, and issues such as perceived complicity in torture and rendition can be extremely damaging to future operations. With new capabilities come tremendous new opportunities to undertake intelligence analysis in ever more sophisticated, and—hopefully—effective ways, but these opportunities must always be viewed through the lens of the ethical issues surrounding security and intelligence in contemporary society, and the proportionality of response. Today's intelligence analysts need to be highly attuned to these issues and to understand them in depth.

During 2009, the EU launched a collaborative research project called INDECT, which aims to deliver an '[i]ntelligent information system supporting observation, searching and detection for security of citizens in urban environment [sic]'.[51] The project's objectives can be summarized as:

- developing systems for capturing (through sophisticated surveillance mechanisms), storing, searching, and sharing multimedia data on individuals between police forces in the EU.
- developing and sharing methods for 'automatic detection of threats and recognition of abnormal behaviour or violence'.[52]

The pilot project is supported by seventeen organizations across Europe, including a number of universities, multimedia companies, and the Police Service of Northern Ireland.

---

[51] INDECT Project, <http://www.indect-project.eu>, accessed 3 January 2010.   [52] Ibid.

185

In many ways, the INDECT project typifies both the opportunities and the challenges facing the intelligence analysis profession across the sector in the twenty-first century. The project recognizes that the targets on which data needs to be gathered and analyzed for intelligence purposes are very much in the civic sphere, and involve tracking the behaviour and movements of private individuals in their public and private lives. Under 'expected results', INDECT lists the following as some of the planned outcomes:[53]

- To realize a trial installation of the monitoring and surveillance system in various points of the city agglomeration and demonstration of the prototype of the system with fifteen node stations.
- Construction of a search engine for fast detection of persons and documents based on watermarking technology.
- Construction of agents assigned to continuous automatic monitoring of public resources such as websites, discussion forums, UseNet groups, file servers, p2p networks, and individual computer systems.

INDECT is well aware of the ethical issues inherent in the project, noting that 'all of the activities within INDECT are carried out so as to ensure the appropriate balance between the protection of the rights of the individual and the protection of society'.[54] It further specifies that:

> The value that will be added by INDECT is that existing systems would operate with less human intervention, which will lower the level of subjective assessment and the number of human mistakes. The main objective of INDECT is to make the monitoring and search process (and procedures) more automatic. This will allow for more informed decision-making.[55]

In this way, INDECT is aiming to act in the best traditions of technical and scientific support to intelligence analysis, in that it seeks to develop systems not to automate intelligence analysis itself, but to assist the analyst with processing data so that he or she can get on with the job of analysis.[56] In theory, this is the right and proper way for scientific methods and technical aids to plug into the business of intelligence analysis: essentially, the 'science part' of the piece.

This approach is not necessarily understood or appreciated, however, in modern society. INDECT has been described in some sections of the media as an 'Orwellian artificial intelligence plan' which would involve a 'huge invasion of

---

[53] INDECT Project, n 51 above.

[54] INDECT, *Ethical Issues*, <http://209.85.229.132/search?q=cache:RvVG74NW9FoJ:www.indect-project.eu/aggregator/ethical-issues+all+of+the+activities+within+indect+are+carried+out+so+as+to+ensure&cd=1&hl=en&ct=clnk&gl=uk>, accessed 29 March 2010.   [55] Ibid.

[56] RV Badalamente and FL Greitzer, 'Top Ten Needs for Intelligence Analysis Tool Development', paper presented at First Annual Conference on Intelligence Analysis Methods and Tools, May 2005, <https://analysis.mitre.org/proceedings/Final_Papers_Files/319_Camera_Ready_Paper.pdf>, accessed 3 January 2010.

privacy'.[57] The director of Liberty in the UK, Shami Chakrabarti, was quoted as saying:

> Profiling whole populations instead of monitoring individual suspects is a sinister step in any society. It's dangerous enough at national level, but on a Europe-wide scale the idea becomes positively chilling.[58]

The problem for contemporary intelligence analysis is how to find those specific individuals who will need to be kept under surveillance, and who are embedded deeply in our own societies, without trawling through public communications and activities in a disproportionate manner, or without seeding society with multiple human agents in a manner reminiscent of 1930s Russia, or East Germany under the Stasi. Modern information technology allows ever-increasing opportunities to collect, trawl, and interrogate large amounts of data in ever more directed and sophisticated ways, so that analysts can more quickly and efficiently home in on the specific individuals perceived to be a security threat. How this is to be achieved in modern society is clearly a matter of conjecture.

All that the science part of analysis can deliver, therefore, are tools and techniques to allow an analyst to bring his or her cognitive skills to bear in the most effective fashion. What the analyst is then able to achieve is more of an art, in that it involves judgements, probabilities, and assessments based on imperfect, incomplete, and sometimes simply inaccurate data. A skilful combination of these two processes is the essence of modern intelligence analysis.

---

[57] I Johnston, 'EU funding "Orwellian" artificial intelligence plan to monitor public for "abnormal behaviour"', *Daily Telegraph*, 19 September 2009, <http://www.telegraph.co.uk/news/uknews/6210255/EU-funding-Orwellian-artificial-intelligence-plan-to-monitor-public-for-abnormal-behaviour.html>, accessed 3 January 2010.   [58] Ibid.

187

Index